J B Hannay

Sex Symbolism

in

Religion

by

J. B. HANNAY

With an Appreciation by

SIR GEORGE BIRDWOOD

K.C.I.E., C.S.I., M.D., LL.D.

Fredonia Books
Amsterdam, The Netherlands

Sex Symbolism in Religion
(Volume One)

by
James Ballantyne Hannay

ISBN: 1-58963-879-4

Reprinted from the 1922 edition

Fredonia Books
Amsterdam, The Netherlands
http://www.fredoniabooks.com

SEX SYMBOLISM

APPRECIATION
by
SIR GEORGE BIRDWOOD,
K.C.I.E., C.S.I., M.D., LL.D.

My interest was keenly aroused in 1914, when reading the Author's earlier volume on religious origins, by the fact that a new writer imbued with the modern spirit of research had arisen and caused me to look forward with lively interest to the series of short studies on which he was then engaged and which form his Bible Folk Lore Series.

The Author has attempted what the scholars of the Church of England in 1905 vainly asked their Bishop to allow, that is to apply the same methods of criticism to the New Testament as had been applied to the older Scriptures—in the *Encyclopedia Biblica* for instance.

I have carefully read these, to me, intensely interesting works, for copies of which I have had occasion to gratefully thank the Author, and I feel that he has illuminated the way to rational and interesting paths for future explorers.

It is only by the study of the customs of primitive peoples who are in the early stages of civilisation portrayed in the Hebrew Scriptures, that such literature can be understood. Having read the Author's first book, I was keenly interested to learn how he would treat the later Christian literature and symbolism.

I have read his studies through eagerly and with zest, for I delight in the subject—the humanising studies of the deep pit out of which we were all digged, from microscopic cells to man. I have read every book in English and some in French (none in German) on the subject, and therefore am well up in the literature of religious customs and symbolism, and I have found that the Author's books are learned and scholarly, his arguments sanely pursued, and the conclusions moderately expressed, and that the illustrations are authentic and carefully and truthfully draughted.

I have observed many astonishing things during my sojourn in India, some of which I have detailed to the Author; but those—while corroborating, in fact, intensifying all he has to say about phallic practices—are difficult to treat in an open publication.

Anyone, however, may find a great storehouse of facts as to extreme phallic practices still extant in India in Sir Joseph Arnold's judgment and Chisholm Anstey's pleadings in a famous Hindu libel case dealing with the promiscuous phallic practices which are parallel with the Hebrew "Hags," wrongly translated "Solemn Sacrifices" in the English Bible.

I think the Author, while guarding against any too literal descriptions of phallic practices and symbols in use in religion, has given us original and scholarly treatises on the parallelism of these practices and symbols in all great religions, and thrown much light on the construction of Biblical literature.

But I am inclined to go further than the Author, and, seeing that the generative organ is the most considerable thing about us, and to primitive man must, from the moment he began to think, have been a perpetual miracle, I hold that early races identified the thing with Deity—not a symbol of Deity, but the actual Deity.

The Author's idea of the Roman influence in the construction of the Christian story, and the true origin of its symbolic names and material and its imposition on Europe by Rome, seems to be quite a natural conclusion from the somewhat scanty evidence in our possession. These books should have a keen interest to all open-minded students of religion.

George Birdwood

PREFACE

These short studies need no further preface than that in my book on *Christianity* reprinted here, and their own special titles which explain their purport, but the ecclesiastical mind is rapidly broadening and nearing a more rational view of the true origin of our Scriptures, and this deserves a moment's attention.

The following quotations will serve to show the great advance which has been made since the eighties and nineties of last century, when I had practically completed the study for the works I am now issuing. In my first preface I said :—" The Bible is the history of the " evolution of a spiritual religion from a material " paganism "; and now the *Times* " Literary " Supplement," in reviewing Frazer's completed *Golden Bough*, says :—" *The Golden Bough* " has demonstrated ' that the great religions of " the world were born in hot-beds of savage " sorcery, and that mummeries of the primitive " medicine-man still sway mankind,' " and the task I have set myself to accomplish is to trace the sources and lay bare the nature of some savage ideas which still sway even the most intelligent of our race.

Huxley once made an eloquent appeal to the young man to follow knowledge wherever it may lead " in singleness and honesty of purpose," trusting " in the sure faith that a hell of honest " men will, to him, be more endurable than a " paradise full of angelic shams " ; and we find the learned Dr. Davidson, Archbishop of Canterbury, saying in the Convocation of May, 1914, as reported in the *Times* :—" They did not say to " honest students and seekers after truth, ' Stop, " that path is barred; that conclusion is for- " bidden; you must not go there.' He would " say to every honest student ' Follow the truth; " do your utmost to find it; let it be your guide " wherever it may lead you.' Such study, fear- " less and free, was the strength of the Church's " progress. Such study must not be hindered by " a single thought of the consequences of what " the conclusions might be to others."

When the Archbishop of the Church of England echoes Huxley's words, we students of knowledge may well rejoice; the dawn has not only arrived, but we can feel the warming beams of the sun of freedom.

One last quotation :—Dean Inge, our beloved lively " gloomy Dean," preaching at St. Paul's Cathedral on Ascension Day, 1914, said :—" I " do not believe that there ever was a time when " Christians thought less about Heaven than they " do now. Those who are most in earnest about " improving the condition of human society in " this world look upon this heaven as a fairy " story, and many of them think that the clergy " are trying to keep them quiet by giving them " promissory notes to be paid in another world " which does not exist. They even look upon " the doctrine of a future life as a profitable " fraud, which, after many centuries, has at last " been exposed, and so they say, ' We prefer " payment in cash ; your bank up in the sky has " stopped payment.' Eternal life is not some- " thing in the future ; it is now. Working-men " would rather hear us say, ' I do not know,' " than have crude symbols given them as literal " facts."

Here we have three theses enunciated from high places of Church and the press for which I have always earnestly pleaded.

(1) The development of religion from natural origins not suddenly given by divine reve- lation.

(2) Truth is the only god worth serving, even if it destroys dogma.

(3) Be honest in religion as in science, even if you have to plead Huxley's humble " don't " know," or declare yourself what he termed an Agnostic.

These triumphs for Huxleyism in the Church have been gained by the fearless work of Bishop Colenso sixty years ago. All the enormous volume of Higher Criticism has but served to widen and confirm his conclusions, for which he was persecuted by the Church.

But this great result has been obtained by study of only one side of Christianity, and that not the most important nor the most vital.

All the *ideas* in the Bible, the nature of the gods, the stories of creation, miracles, life and death, the manner of sacrificing, worshipping, vowing, building altars, arks, tabernacles, and temples, the sacrifices or feasts in these temples, their dress, altar furniture, and symbolism—in fact, the entire religion as taught us in the Bible —are absolutely and totally founded upon and saturated with Phallism; and the Phallic cult is that on which Christianity has been founded. Phallism is sex symbolism, and all creative power in a god is symbolised by the actual facts of creation of life in nature by means of the organs

of sex. In my preface to Christianity I wrote :—
" Any work on the symbolism of religion, with-
" out treating its phallic basis, would be like
" Hamlet without the Prince of Denmark."

A great modern biologist, Julian S. Huxley
—worthy descendant of Thomas Henry Huxley
the incomparable leader, in my youth, in the
defence of Knowledge against Dogma, tells us (in
a paper on the theory of Sex read before the Royal
Society of Arts, 18th January, 1922) that " the
" latter-day psychologists have shown us how
" primitive instincts such as those of Fear and Sex
" wind themselves round the roots of all mental
" life, become sublimated by the acquisition of
" new objects and are parts of the indispensable
" subterranean driving force of legend and doc-
" trine." " Once the attention of the human mind
" has become entangled with the problem, un-
" satisfied wonder and curiosity are begotten, and
" in their turn beget a varied progeny of myth and
" taboo, legend and doctrine."

This might epitomise my studies for more than
half a century embodied in my books of the last
ten years.

These little studies are intended to show the
real roots of the Christian religion and its symbolism, and the author hopes it will lead to
Christians leaving the old gods and dogmas with

the dead past, and evolving a Religion of Kindness which will consider the existence of an ignorant, hungry, or naked child—or man or woman either—in their midst, as the greatest crime any community can commit.

COVE CASTLE,
LOCH LONG. N.B.

LIST OF ILLUSTRATIONS.

OLD TESTAMENT GODS.

LIST OF ILLUSTRATIONS.

THE GODS OF THE HEBREW BIBLE

INTRODUCTION

As man is, so are his gods. George Eliot imagined Cain with his love of fruits and flowers, the children of sunshine, and haunted by the terrible memory of his dead brother, into whose murder he was trapped by the favouritism displayed by the blood-shedding Hebrew god,—seeking joyous gods " who lived on fragrance for their food and wine," gods
" Who winked at faults and folly,
And could be pitiful and melancholy;
He never had a doubt that such gods were
He looked within and saw them mirrored
 there."
The most terrible gods were those evolved by tribes whose life is hard, harassed by enemies both man and beast, or who draw a scanty livelihood from a barren soil, or who live in gloomy forests or malaria-infected swamps. The Romans, who, by their wonderful organising power, drew wealth from all the world, and had at headquarters a very easy existence, drew jolly gods for us. Their god-names were

not originally of their own manufacture; they got their Jupiter from Babylon, their Bacchus and Mercury from Greece, and even their Venus existed long before in the Benoth (or Venus, for they are the same) of the Babylonians, which we find the Hebrews ardently worshipping, as commanded by their tribal god Iové.

But the Romans gave more joyous characters to their gods, as they themselves were joyous, and, like the Hebrews under their Queen of Heaven, they " had plenty of victuals, and were well, and saw no evil " (Jer. xliv., 17). So we have a god which has given us the adjective " jovial," with his wife Juno, a fine stalwart, good-living Roman matron, and their Venus, with her love-begotten Cupid, a pair overflowing with life and ravishing beauty without an evil thought towards man.

As we go eastward we find Greece, a country always harassed by attacks of enemies and poor in soil, evolving gods of a more stern character, jealous malevolent gods, who could rend poor Niobe's heart by making her see all her children, clean limbed sons and beautiful daughters, die one after the other, simply because, without thanking the gods, she in the warmth of her love, poured out her heart in praise of her beautiful children. This land also produced these dread tragedies where inevitable doom is rung out in the very first lines, and where the implacable gods pursue the poor mortal to his awful destiny, or deride all his puny efforts to evade his miserable end—an end generally prepared for him, and due to no conscious fault on his part. Still the Greek conceptions were grand. No petty ideas entered into their heavenly tragedies, but they themselves in their mental evolution saw that their gods were mere creations of their poets and they ceased to believe in them as realities.

It was reserved for the priests of a tiny clan in a barren land, whose inhabitants were perpetually in slavery, to draw a picture of a terrible god and to impose that picture, not only on their clan, but, by one of those strange happenings of which history records so many, on the peoples of lands utterly unlike their own, whose inhabitants were quite capable of evolving their own gods.

But as all religion is founded on fear, so the most fear-inspiring god evolved by the imagination of man won the day, and it is to the evolution of the cult of this god from many practised by the Hebrews and its imposition by the sun-worshipping Romans on Western civilisation that my present study is devoted.

The further development of religion in the Western nations, being fettered to the sacred book dealing with this Palestinian god, is one of the most curious mixtures of savagery, spiritualism, and gross sensualism the world has yet produced. The savagery has been commented on by innumerable writers, from such different men as Voltaire, Tom Paine, to our Huxleys, Allens, and Bradlaughs, or Robertsons, and the host of able writers, such as Ingersoll or Blatchford, who almost daily protested against the imposition of such a god upon the civilisation of modern Europe.

The spiritual side is dwelt upon by our clergy, and they extract the best parts of the curious documents at their disposal, and they have now, with a few miserable exceptions, dropped the savage god and his torture and hell, and are preaching a real message of peace and goodwill of man to man, exactly the opposite of the Hebrew message of the Old Testament. But even those two sides of the Bible are only a small fragment of the real teaching, and the true central core of the Hebrew religion is conveyed to us by their practices, and told in their god-names and symbolic tales (pp. 156, 178), their accounts of creation, conversations with their gods, miracles, floods, arks, tabernacles, feasts, dances, modes of worship, temple practices with their Kadeshoth and Kadeshim, worship of pillars, and other customs of the Old or Hebraic Testament (pp. 165 and 188; see p. 225, my *Christianity*), with a later edition of the same practices only modified in name and more efficiently concealed by symbolism, which equally characterises the New or Greek Testament. This side of the Bible teaching has been tacitly ignored by all but a very few writers, and these few were so astonished at what they found and so certain that its exposure would prove a terrible shock to all believers in the Hebrew religion that they timidly expressed their opinions and discoveries in privately printed books, which, of course, only reached the hands of those who were already slightly cognisant of this side of prophetic literature, and who were wealthy and eager for further enlightenment. Besides, as all religion, and especially the Christian religion, is founded on the idea of the creation of life by the two sexes and symbolised by the actual organs involved in reproduction, writers have found great difficulty in selecting language in which to tell the truth about the all but unreadable Hebrew scriptures—the natural shyness of Northern nations about any public reference to sexual matters being a ban to a clear open exposition of the true contents of the Hebraic Scriptures and their later " revelations."

Thanks to our knowledge of such practices from the records of travellers in Southern nations, Africa and Asia especially, and the uncovering of like practices by the reading of Cuneiform and Hieroglyphic writings of Babylon and Egypt contemporaneous with the Old Hebrew Bible, and the unearthing of sculptures, monuments, seals, and engravings, illustrating the customs referred to in the Hebrew scriptures, I think the time is now ripe for a true account of the gods, the meaning of their names, their characters, and the modes of their worship, which are detailed with such a wealth of imagery and symbolism in our Bible.

CHAPTER I

SYMBOLISM

Many intelligent people express surprise when they are told that much of the Bible is written in symbolical language, which can be understood only by deep study, and which conveys a meaning quite different from that expressed in the English version.

They consider it to be almost blasphemy to state that the inspired writer could ever be directed to veil God's meaning from honest readers, or to write anything but plain straightforward statements.

On the contrary, the one characteristic of the Hebrew scriptures is symbolism. The *Encyclopædia Biblica*, to which I will have very often to refer, tells us, in column 3271, that every name in the Bible—and there are thousands of them—" has a special meaning," a purely symbolical signification, and to discover this meaning is of great importance, since much light may thereby be thrown " upon the manners and thought both of the ancient Hebrews and of neighbouring peoples." So every page of the Scriptures is saturated with symbolism in this respect alone, and we must not forget that Christianity is founded on the Cross, the most ancient phallic symbol known.

But we meet with other symbolical writings very early in the Bible. In the first chapter of Genesis, verse 27, we read :—" So God created man in his own image, in the image of God created he him, male and female created he them." This is repeated at Genesis v., 2, but its English rendering does not quite convey the meaning of the original. The Hebrew says :—" Sword and sheath created he them ;" or to follow the original more clearly, " Piercer and womb created he them "—a purely symbolical statement. Not only is it a symbolic statement, but it is a statement relating to only one of the functions of the human beings, the most important function in all animals, that of reproduction, and one which we shall see is the core and centre of all the symbolism and imagery of the sacred writings. This is indicated by the first commandment given to man (and before that to the beasts), which follows immediately on the above statement of the creation of the pair— " Be fruitful and multiply "—not only the first commandment given, but that most frequently

and pointedly repeated of all commandments
in the Bible.

It is not only a personal injunction as to the
relations of the two sexes just created, but,
by the use of the symbolical terms " sword and
sheath," it describes the organs through which
the increase and multiplication was to be
effected. We shall find that this kind of symbolism is constantly employed throughout the
Bible, and forms the priestly basis of all sacred
feasts, god-names, tales and parables, sacer-
dotal vestments, vessels, and structures, arks
and tabernacles, rods of God, trees, pillars,
stones, and serpents, bowls, pommels, pulpits,
and pitchers throughout Holy Writ, and which
I deal with in this and other volumes.

We find a varied symbolism of trees in the
Bible, especially a tree of " life " and one of
" knowledge," always associated in all countries with a serpent twined round the tree stem,
and the tree of life is always found " in the
midst " of a " garden." The garden is always
symbolical of the human body, as when Mary
is called by the Romish Church a " Beautiful
Garden," as was also Venus or Aphrodite.
We find rods and stems of trees being the cause
of wondrous miracles. Moses found a rod of
God in " Midian " (Exodus ii., 4), " the midst

of the Garden," and this stem or rod was so closely associated with serpents that whenever it was thrown down it turned into a serpent; and a brazen serpent was worshipped for many generations by the Hebrews. (Exodus iv., 3; vii., 10; Numbers, xxi., 8-9). Then we find this wonderful rod of God, when placed in an ark, blossomed and brought forth "almonds" (Numbers xvii., 8), and we shall find almonds and almond-shaped openings constantly used in Biblical symbolism to indicate the female reproductive organ, just as rods, pillars, and tree stems, always associated with the serpent, indicate the reproductive organ of man—rods and almond-shaped openings being identical with Zakar and Nekebah, Sword and Sheath, Piercer and belly, of Genesis i., 27. Not only were the sexual organs of man constantly employed in symbolical phraseology, but so open was the use of direct names for the reproductive organs of gods and men in the original text that the Rabbis issued a rule that where the private parts of the God were too rudely mentioned, or the words of the law written obscenely, the passage must be " changed to more civil words," as told us by Milton in his " Apology for Smectymnus Works," p. 84.

We have therefore only a bowdlerised version of the original Hebrew writings.

But, further, most of the god-names of the Hebrews and surrounding nations were founded on the reproductive organs of man and woman, or on that of man alone, as man was always the maker of things. In the symbolism of the early Hebrew scriptures the only "making" considered is the making of life (see the decision of the Chinese censors, p. 320, as in Genesis v., the begetting of children, or the exercise by man of the God-like faculty of making new life; and, as the succession of generations pointed to life without end, the combination of the male and female organs was, and is now, the emblem used all over the world as the sign of a god, or of life eternal,— living for ever being the one advantage the gods had over man. So true is it that " man always has made his gods after his own image," as Dr. Budge says, that, although he endows his gods with eternal life, yet they nearly all had fathers, and so, after all, were reduced to the level of common human clay. Not only so, but seeing that creation was a bi-sexual operation, they ultimately gave their gods wives and offspring, as Sir W. Budge so well says. Even their earliest creator of life, Ma, the great mother of all—for the earliest gods were mothers, not fathers—seemed to them to be lonely, and they finally gave her a husband. As she was the " Ark " out of which comes all life, her husband was the Ark-el, the ark's husband or god, then Arkels, Arkles, Herakles, Hercules, in French Hercule or Arkule in miracle plays, Arquelin, the little Arkel, and so on to the Harlequin in our Christmas pantomimes—the oldest god the world can show—with his rod of God or " lath," or sword, serpent, or phallus—a stone phallus is a lath in Hindu—doing miracles or conjuring like Moses. His love, Columbine, Columba, dove, was the same as Hercules' love Iolé, the dove, who always evades him in the ancient myth and in the modern dance. (See my *Seven Stories of Creation.*)

The ancient Hebrews worshipped at one time or another a great many different gods. In fact the learned *Encyclopædia Biblica* and Bishop Colenso tell us that the Hebrews " worshipped precisely the gods of the people among whom they dwelt." Yet their scriptures have been edited so as to make it appear that from Genesis on they worshipped only two forms of deity, one called the Elohim—a band of gods like those of the

Greeks and Romans, and a special tribal god or Ba Al called IhOh or IhVh, whose name was too holy to permit of its being pronounced aloud; in fact, it was death to do so. The Scripture reader said Adonai instead.

In the first chapter of Genesis, which, how-ever, was written at a very late date, the Hebrews were under the Elohim, or Eli-im, or Alé-im, a band of gods who consulted together as to what they should do, as in the Babel story. In the second chapter of Genesis, which is an older document, or at least drawn from older sources, the Hebrews are still under their god band, but headed by this IhOh (popularly Jehovah), and later on we hear of this Jehovah alone. Apparently throughout the Bible we are given to understand that they were always under this god, and the cause of the quarrel which Moses picked with the Pharoah was the refusal of a demand by the children of Israel to go three days' journey into the desert in order to sacrifice to Jehovah of the Elo-im. Yet generations afterwards Joshua tells them to serve Jehovah, " and put away the gods which your fathers served on the other side of the flood and in Egypt." So they did *not* serve Jehovah in Egypt; in fact, when Moses spoke with him in " Midian." in

the burning bush, he had to ask his name, and
got the enigmatical reply, " I am that I am "
(Exodus iii.), but later he gives his name as
Jehovah (Exodus vi.), and says he was *not*
known to Abraham, Isaac, and Jacob by that
name. Yet he is mentioned and tacitly presented as the Hebrew god from the time of the
Garden of Eden, and all through the stories
of Abraham, Isaac, and Jacob. This is like
most of the declarations in the Hebrew Bible :
what is asserted in one place is directly contradicted or stated quite differently in another.
So to place the Hebrew gods historically is an
exceedingly risky task, but we may take it as
pretty certain that their earliest god was Al
Shadai of Job, unless we take Abram as Bram
of India with the prosthetic A, when we would
have a still older god.

I will therefore deal with the gods in the
order in which they occur in the Bible. But
before going into the intimate characters of
the Hebrew gods, as explained by the priests'
esoteric, hidden, or symbolical method, we
must get a clear idea of the methods and scope
of this symbolism, and apply our knowledge to
unravelling some characteristic stories from
Holy Writ, stories which have hitherto
baffled most Biblical students. but which we

will see are quite clear when we unravel them
by the code used by the scribe.

In this preliminary study we will lay bare
new gods hitherto unrecognised in the hierarchy of the Hebrews.

Before dealing with an actual story in the
Bible I must, however, make clear to my
readers the material used by the scribe to build
up his ghostly parable, and so we will review
the symbols or tools employed by the scribes
of Holy Writ.

As I have said, all religions are founded on
the creation of life, and, as we saw by the
" sword and sheath " parallel, all creation of
life is dependent on two sexes. Even where a
single god creates, his creative agent is sexual
as we shall see, is narrated in Job. (Fully
treated in my *Seven Stories of Creation*.)
Now, all this symbolism is classified under two
different descriptive names. The first is
Phallism, a word derived through Greek and
Latin from the Hindu Pala or Phala, becoming
in other countries Pal, Pel, Pil, Phil, Poll,
Paul, Pul, Phallus, and Phulus, and as L and
R, and U and Y replace one another, Pul becomes Pur, Pyr, Phara, etc., all meaning a
Pole, Pillar, Rod, or Stem, the erect or strong
thing, with a rising, extending, or expanding

tendency, in short, the male creative organ.
We therefore talk of Phallic symbols, which
word applies to feminine Phallism as well as
masculine.

Another phrase which puzzles many writers
is " the Worship of Priapus," as used by Payne
Knight.   That a wide knowledge of early Gods
is necessary to the understanding of many of
the Roman Gods is illustrated by the name
of this popular God, Priapus.   A King-god,
illustrated by three Phalli at the top of the
middle column of the list of Egyptian Kings in
Fig. 1, was called Ka Kau, Phallus of Phalli.
But Ka was a very old Hindoo God called
latterly Priapa-Ti, so we have a Phara-oh
named after a Hindoo God.   Ka is Hindee for
" Who," a widespread method of covering up
phallic Gods, like Paul's Unknown God or
Moses' I am that I am.   Ka was the God of
the Puranas—poems founded on Phallic worship, as Pur is Pul, which the Greeks rendered
Phallos.   Places of extremely erotic Phallic
worship, illustrated by unpublishable sculpture, are called in India Puri, and Latona's isle
was called Pur pollis, male, by some, and
Kunthos, the female organ, by others, so she
was double sexed.   Lat means the phallus, and
Om or On, the womb, so Lat-ona was double
sexed, like Minerva.

Fig. 1.

This Priapati was at one time the great creative god of India, and he was the god of sexual fire or passion, or the creating father—a highly phallic god—so there can be no doubt that Priapus is the Latin form of Priapa-ti, as the name should be written. The particle Ti is used all over the East, as far as China, as indicative of god-ship,—Greek The(os) or Di(o), Latin De(us); and " Priapa-Ti " is the equivalent of " Priapus god." The name is often spelt Prajapati, but this replacement of " i " by " a " and " j " is common to such names as those in which " j " could not be pronounced alone like " i." We have it in the name of a part of Seville called Triana, after Trajan, also emphasised in a Mexican town, Tiajuana, pronounced Twana.

All Hindoo scholars state that Ka of the Egyptians was identical with Priapati, and the Hieroglyphics show that Ka was the phallus, as shown in Fig. 1, the phallic name of a King of Egypt with the phallus three times repeated. Most King-gods were like Ka Kau (top of middle column, Fig. 1), named the Phallus, or " Phallus, son of the Phallus," like Assurbanipal or Sardanapalus. The erroneous use of the English " J " instead of " I " or " Y " has served to disguise many gods, and caused great confusion in the understanding of many Hebrew names.

The term Phallic for sexual symbolism is very convenient, and I shall retain it in these short studies.

The symbolism in which the phallic cult is expressed is extremely simple, and was at one time simply realistic models of the organs involved, as in Fig. 1, and these models are found in every part of the world and go back to the time of the Cave Bear and other extinct animals, as has been shown in a cave near Venice, where the carvings were overlaid with stalagmite limestone covering the phallic engravings, along with the bones of post-tertiary animals. In more modern, though still prehistoric, times Schliemann found large numbers of carved phalli forty feet below the foundations of ancient Troy covered over by the debris of many pre-historic towns.

Wherever these phalli are found there is also found the symbol of the Cross. The Cross, ages before Christianity, was simply the conventional phallus, and remained a " secret " sign until adopted by the Christians under Constantine in the 4th century. Paul well knew that the cross was the symbol of the phallus (pp. 272. 294-296, Part II.).

Phalli of gold, silver, copper, lead, tin, lapis lazuli, agate, diorite, magnesite, porcelain, and baked clay, and even in all sorts of woods, and ivory, have been found all over the world in thousands—4000 were dug up at the temple of Isis at Pestum—so the cult was universal, and at the present day more than half the population of the world are phallic worshippers, or, say, eight hundred millions, including three hundred millions of British subjects in the East. In India it is a living religion actively taught and practised everywhere.

But we are all passive or unconscious phallic worshippers, as the Cross was the most widely used phallic symbol, and our church architecture, altars, and their furniture, and the vestments of the clergy, are entirely of phallic origin, as will appear as we proceed in this study, or in my other volumes, as it would be impossible to go over the ground in one volume.

So this cult is the fundamental basis of every religion in the world, as is shown by the serpent taking a leading part in all religions, being the cause of numerous Fall and redemption schemes, as in Christianity, yet it is absolutely ignored by all religious writers.

There were two great systems of worship, that of the Phallus as the giver of joy and life, always held fast by the common people, and the worship of the Sun, held by the enlightened priests, as the true upholder of life, and as the Saviour of mankind in the Northern hemisphere, from the fierce cold of winter, by his return every spring, and " passing over " or " crossing " the Equator to bring warmth and food to mankind. (See my *Christianity* or *Passover and Crucifixion.*)

But the slow motion of the Sun northward and the complicated motions of the Sun and its planets, with its zodiac, equinoxes, solstices, and " houses " in which the Sun dwelt, were much too difficult to be understood by the masses, and, as the sexual facts of life were more interesting to them than the motions of the heavenly bodies, they preferred to adore that which was near and dear to them, and they invariably reduced the most lofty conceptions of the astronomers as to the life and governance of the Universe to symbolical terms derived from their own bodies, as did God with his great Covenant (Genesis xvii., 10-14). They also people the heavens with purely phallic signs, which they called the

Zodiac, or zone of life, probably the heavenly Zion of the Hebrews.

Let us take a case in point. India has always been highly solar in its conception of religion, but highly phallic in its practical worship. The Indians have the Sun as a god in many forms in their pantheon, and there are several names used to-day for Sunday, such as Ravi, Yak-Shamba, Aditya, Ithar, and so on—all names of the Sun—besides Siva, Vishnu, Krishna, Sun gods. But they have a special name for the Sun as fertiliser, Surya, and that name came West, and gave their names to Assyria and Syria; as " u " and " y " are the same letters, and Easterns very often add the prosthetic "a" before (and after) terminal consonants. Now, the Assyrians called their land Surya or Assyria, no doubt at first from the Indian Sun, but it soon became identified with the Phallus, and so their god Asher or Assur was the god of the Phallus. [Note that Sur, the " rock that begat thee " of our Bible, is common to all these names.] But they also used Pala, and we find their King Asshur-Bani-Pal of the Cuneiform tablets, with a name meaning " The Phallus, son of the Phallus," or " The Sun, son of the Phallus," and his name in Greek—Sar-dana-phalus—is the same thing; as Sar is Tsur or Assur, the " Rock that begat thee," and " ana," " arising from," and " palus," the Phallus, or again, the Phallus, son of the Phallus. The altar of the highly solar Hindus is simply the two creative organs combined, and is called Maha Deva, the great God, so their actual worship is purely phallic. It is also called the Lingam-Yoni altar, Ling, Linga, or Lingam being the Hindu word for the male organ, and Yoni for the female.

The Hebrews got a great deal of their religion from Babylon, as we find the Babylonian and Persian kings sending priests several times to instruct them (2nd Kings, xvii., 27; and Ezra and Nehemiah). They had a great system of Phallic worship called the worship of Asher, and we know that the Asherim to which they prayed were upright posts or stones carved in the form of the erect phallus, worshipped by the Hebrews.

Here we see the migration of names and the degradation of the all-conquering sun to a phallic symbol. This worship of the Asher or Assur, or Assyr, or simply Sur—in our Bible the plural is used, Asherim—was that constantly condemned by the Nabis or Yogis of Palestine as the worship of the " Groves," a term employed in the English Bible to hide its true meaning. These Nabis were wandering ascetic preachers, of whom Isaiah, Jeremiah, and Ezekiel were examples. Isaiah walked three years naked, like the Hindu Yogis (see Isaiah, xx., 3, or Micah, i., 8). Even the names Palestine and Philistine are simply the land of the Pala or Palastan. They are made into two names in the English Bible, but in Hebrew they are identical, Palestina, Philistia, Philistine, and Palestine are Palast, Phalest, Pelesht, etc., used quite indifferently. On attentively reading the Bible we find the Patriarchs living peacefully and gaining wealth in the land of the Philistines (Palestine). (Genesis xxi., 34; xxvi., 1 and 14).

One point about symbolism as expressed in letters is most important. Had the Old Testament been written in Roman or Greek characters the literary symbolic method would have been quite apparent. For instance, IO, the sacred name of Jehovah, in Latin characters is clearly the rod or pillar and the circle, or, as the Persians said, "dagger and ring with which Yima created all life," or the zakar and nekebah, piercer and womb of Genesis i., 27, or rod and almond of Jeremiah. But rendered into the "invented" Hebrew letters, the I becomes a comma and the O becomes a

staff or crook, so that the two no longer form
a directly visible phallic symbol; it no longer
leaps to the eye. We must never forget that,
although the Christian religion was supposed
to have a Hebrew origin, of which, however,
we have no direct proof, it was forced on
Europe by the Romans, and their god Jupiter
or Iové was identical with the Hebrew
Jehovah, pronounced Iové (or Yovey in
English phonetic orthography), whose symbol
was IhOh, the " h's " being silent, and so the
creative symbolism of IO is quite clear. It is
generally IO when used in names. We do not
know in what characters the old Hebrew scriptures were written, as they were said to have
been sent to Rome at the request of Josephus,
and, if so, they were forgotten and destroyed,
as they were never again heard of. They may
have been secretly preserved to form the basis
of a universal religion. Minute search has
been made in Palestine for Hebrew inscriptions, but only Phœnician inscriptions have
been found, and those nearly all after the
Roman occupation. That found at the Pool
of Siloam is in Phœnician, and it mentions
Baal, the universal Palestinian god at the time
of " Kings." There is no instance of the
Hebrew square character older than the second

or third century A.D., although the Samaritan Hebrew is said to belong to the third century B.C. The pointed Hebrew alphabet cannot be stated to be older than 500 A.D., and it is Cuneiform or Phœnician, not Hebrew, of which we find traces in Syria and Palestine.

The Hebrew language of the Bible is really a dialectic variety of Canaanitish or Phœnician expressed in modified Chaldean characters. The *Encyclopædia Biblica* says, col. 2218, that the Canaanites and Israelites spoke the same language with only small dialectic differences. When Biblical Hebrew was invented, and who directed its construction, are matters of profound mystery. All the accounts of its miraculous translation giving rise to the " Septuagint " traditions may be laid aside. We have no copies earlier than 916 A.D., and even that date may be centuries wrong.

But there is a well-founded tradition that a college or confraternity of monks called Masoretes—that is, upholders or expositors of the " true tradition "—worked out the text in a monastery near the Lake of Tiberias (Galilee). They seem to have worked *under the Romans* for 300 or 400 years, and evolved the " pointed " Hebrew; that is, with the vowel sounds indicated by points and other marks. Now the complete system of symbolic names and the absorption of the names of the principal gods of the great nations as the names of Hebrew men, and the use of foreign god-names like Amen in their prayers, show that there was a purpose in the construction of the final text of the Hebrew scriptures, and that the text is as artificial as its root construction. The old stories and traditions were utilised as a framework, and were elaborated with false genealogies and allegorical stories and fictitious history (see *Encyclopœdia Biblica*, cols. 2217-2223), in order, I think, to suit the purposes of the Masoretes' masters, the Romans. There were hosts of other " harmonisers," " collators," and " adapters," such as Origen, Eusebius, Symnachus, Jerome, Theodotian, all working under Roman influence (see my *Christianity*, pp. 141-151). One of these purposes was to incorporate the names of all the principal gods from the Indus to the Atlantic into the text, so as to create a " Bible " which would serve as a combining or cementing basis of the heterogeneous religions of the scattered and shaky Roman Empire. Of course this is a mere conjecture, and the reader must form his own opinion after perusal of the proofs I offer. Ezra tells us that when he came to re-establish the Hebrew religion after their long exile, he was seated under an Oak or Alé when the Ale-im or Iové spoke to him out of a bush (as they did to Moses), and told him that he [they, for Elohim is plural] had formerly made a statement to Moses, but Iové says :—" I will reveal again all that has been lost, the secrets of the times and the end." And Ezra tells Iové that it will be quite safe to make a new Genesis or Bible (Esdras xiv., 20), " For thy law is burnt, therefore no man knoweth the things that are done of thee," . . . " and I shall write all that hath been done in the world since the beginning," and so he wrote down the whole Old Testament. Of course no one believes that these long familiar chats between all the prophets and the Elohim or Iové actually took place; they are merely putting the thoughts of the priests who were evolving the religion into this form, to impress the people with the idea of its divine origin, while it is no more divine than the lucubrations of a novel writer—Gulliver's Travels, or Bunyan's " Pilgrim's Progress."

We know how every monk of literary turn tried his hand at producing new and improved exhortations, disquisitions, and discussions of

imaginary Christian " fathers," and no doubt
the same evolution attended the production of
the Old and New Testaments, especially such
writings as the Epistles, where no shred of
history was required which might cabin, crib,
or confine the free play of the writer's imagination (see under Paul, Part II., pp. 260-262).

As the Romans forced this religion on
Europe at the point of the sword, and they
considered religion only in its political aspect,
they must have had a great interest in its
presentment; and as all the symbolism is based
on the Greek or Roman alphabet, and not on
the Hebrew, I think it quite possible that symbolism in some of its phases was engrafted
upon the original compositions. For instance,
as I have already said, the great creative symbol of dagger and ring, piercer and womb, rod
and almond, so much used in the Bible narratives and names, is represented perfectly in the
Latin IO, but in Hebrew the I becomes a small
comma and the O a staff, and all visible
symbolism is lost. Thus by putting the secret
reading into Hebrew or Chaldean characters
its true meaning was known only to the priest,
but its pronunciation—which told nothing to
the unitiated—was the same as in Latin. But
everything in religion is done by the priests to

hide direct meanings and origins, and they delight in, and demand, an " incomprehensible mystery " as the greatest desideratum of their texts and creeds.

Hyppolytus says that all " mysteries " were the Pudendum or sexual organ, and it was to prevent the common people from discovering this that the death penalty was always attached to touching or looking into all Arks, Monstrances, or Holies of Holies.

The period of Hebrew history up to Joseph is held to be entirely mythical, and the *Encyclopædia Biblica* says, col. 787 :—" It is to Egypt that the narrative of the origin of Israel points."

After the personal histories of Abraham, Isaac, and Jacob, the fathers of the Hebrew race, have been narrated, and finally ending with the migration of apparently all the Hebrews to Egypt (reduced to 70 persons), they are driven out of Egypt to find a home in Palestine by murdering all the natives there and stealing their land, cattle, houses, and goods, a system of murder and theft commanded by their god IO, and familiarised to us in modern times by German lust for power and wealth as approved of by the Kaiser's " good old German god "—a pagan god closely modelled on the so-called Jehovah of the Hebrews. During their passage to Palestine they have a highly miraculous interlude during which their religion is founded.

The use of symbolism I am about to illustrate is that detailing how Moses created the Hebrew religion and its emblems or symbolism —without which no nation or tribe could be ruled in these savage times. The symbolism was, as we shall see, largely derived from Egypt, where Moses was educated.

The story goes that the Israelites were enslaved and ground down with over-work and cruelty, and Moses had been brought up in the Kings' or Chief Priests' house, as he had been adopted by Pharoah's daughter who " drew him out of the water." He became enraged at seeing one of his poorer enslaved countrymen abused, and he slew the Egyptian who had smitten the Hebrew. Then he fled to the land of " Midian," and there met the man who explained to him how he must create a religion by which to rule his tribe. But this man Jethro, or properly Ithra—a prince or priest of Midian—was really a god as symbolically explained. Jethro should be Ytro.

First of all we are told when his name is first mentioned that he had seven daughters.

Seven is the Hebrew holy number—God rested on the seventh day—and seven is invariably mentioned in the Bible when anything holy is being described, such as a feast— seven bullocks, seven rams, in 2nd Chronicles, xxix., 21, repeated in Job and Ezekiel; seven priests bear seven trumpets, Joshua, vi., 6; seven loaves and seven baskets full; seven days of creation; the virgin is crowned with seven stars and the Magdalene with seven devils; wherever a miracle or something symbolical or holy is mentioned. So Ithra was divine.

Jethro is at first called Reuel, then Jethro, then Raguel in Exodus ii, 18, iii., 1; and Numbers x., 29. There must be some cause for the change to Raguel, as we have a similar change in the name Reu of Genesis xi., 18, rendered Ragau in Luke iii., 35. Ra was the sun god of Egypt, and Gu is Hebrew for midst or Midian, while El is, as Jacob tells us, the god of Israel, so the name Raguel means " Ra of Midian is El."   Moses had come from Egypt, where Ra is the sun, and El is the word for god all over Western Asia, and, as vowels were unwritten in these early times, the consoants are the only guide, the word was probably Raël, so Reuel is Sun god, or " Ra is El."

Jethro is identical with Ithar, an old Hindu sun god, whose name is still used for Sunday in India (see p. 21 or 108, my *Christianity*), and Ra-El is a statement that the Egyptian sun god Ra is the Hebrew El; so we have the declaration twice made that the new god Moses found in Midian was the same as the sun god of two great nations; and we are told in Exodus xxiv., 17, that " the sight of the glory of the Lord Iové was like devouring fire on the top of the mount *in the eyes* of the children of Israel," and at verse 10, " and they saw the God of Israel, and there was under his feet as it were a paved work of sapphire stone, and as it were the body of heaven in its clearness," an exact description of the Arabian sun in a blue sky, and Ra and Ithra were both the sun.

And here Moses in the " Mountain of the Ale-im " talks with Iové in a burning bush (flame represents the sun) (Exodus iii., 1), and although the writer calls him Iové, Moses does not know who he is, but Iové promptly tells him that the children of Israel are to commit theft by stealing the Egyptians' jewellery. This order to steal the Egyptian women's gold and silver ornaments —an order again repeated in Egypt—clearly shows that the whole story is artificial. The writer was preparing to describe the great tabernacle of the wilderness, and required the gold and silver for the great solid silver shoes for the half-ton beams which were plated with pure gold, called " boards " in the Bible, and to cover the ark with solid gold and to provide a gold plate for Ihoh and the Cherubim to stand upon, and for golden vessels.

Such gold could not be furnished by a poor set of slaves in a desert, and so the Egyptian women's jewellery was to pave the way to render possible the lavish use of precious metals. Then this new god suddenly bethinks him that, although he has told Moses that he is to go to Pharaoh to bring forth the children of Israel out of Egypt, it is quite possible they will not believe him, so he suddenly says :—" What is that in thine hand?" And Moses answers, "A rod." He told Moses to cast it down, and it became a serpent, which, of course, makes it a phallus, as the serpent is the symbol of the phallus or phallic passion all over the world in every religion, from Japan right through Asia to Europe round to Mexico and Peru (see my *Christianity*). He was then told to lift it by the tail, and it immediately became a rod again. Now, the Hebrew word used is Matteh, which comes from Natah, which means to stretch out or extend, to spread out or expand, or swell up, and we see that the rod was such a one as could stretch itself out into a living serpent, and therefore it was an " extensible rod," or a rod which swells up, which is a very good definition of the phallus. We are then told that this was the " Rod of God " or of Eli, to whom Jesus cried on the Cross, and Moses carried it constantly in his hand and did all his miracles with it. (See *Harlequin*, p. 12.)

So Moses went into the " Middle," made the acquaintance of a prince or priest, whose name was Sun God, and there a new god presented him with his rod. Now, we must remember that in Eden there was a Tree of Life or Rod of God in the " middle " of the garden, which was also in the " midst " of the rivers—Mesopotamia; and the word for " tree " means anything " hard or firm," any upright pole, pale, or pala. The Midian of Moses seems to have been situated on the Sinai peninsula between two waters, the Gulf of Suez and the Gulf of Akab. Akab means " heel," a euphuism for the phallus, so this sea was the gulf of the Rod of God or the phallus. Midian is Latin—not Hebrew—but,

Fig. 2.

considering the entire remodelling of the Hebrew text by Origen, Symnachus, Jerome, Eusebius, and the Masoretes, all under the Romans, the introduction of Latin or Greek words is only to be expected (see my *Christianity*, pp. 141-151). Any land lying between two waters is very holy, and holy spots were always used for phallic worship by the erection of a phallus or pillar. We have such a holy land in Britain in Dorsetshire, between High-Stoy and the Bub-down hills, from whence two waters are visible, the English and Bristol Channels, and here our phallic worshipping ancestors erected a Rod of God in the land of " Midian," as described in Exodus (see Fig. 2). Such rods of god (hundreds in Cornwall) were, and still are, worshipped all over the world. They were the true god of the ancient Hebrews, as Jacob calls the " Matzebah " or stone column he erected, " El, god of Israel " (Genesis xxxiii., 20; see also *Encyclopædia Biblica*, 3325). So the first thing Moses did on being appointed to deliver the Israelites was to obtain a rod of god, with which to work miracles. Now, in Egypt the first symbol of the native Egyptian religion was this rod of god or phallus of god.

The legend is that there were two brothers,

like Cain and Abel, called Typhon and Osiris
(or rather Osar, as Osiris is a Greek corruption), and Typhon killed Osiris, cut up his
body, and scattered it all over Egypt.   Isis,
Queen of Heaven, gathered all the pieces and
gave them sepulture, each part making a pro-
vince or country.   But she could not find the
phallus, so she had a model made, put it in an
ark, and made it the core and centre of Egyptian worship and religion.   So Moses began to
form his clan religion exactly as he had been
taught in the King's household (which is always
priestly) in Egypt.

The Hieroglyphics so well preserved to us

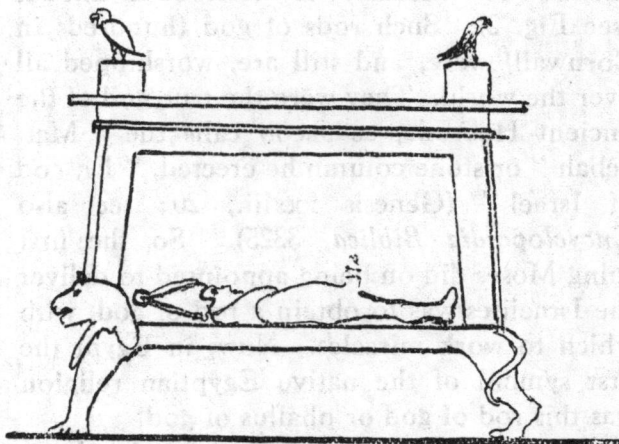

Fig. 3.

by the fine climate and hard stone of Egypt
show us that Egypt was the land of arks.
Everywhere Osiris, or his phallus, is in an
ark. When it is the god he is always ithyphallic, which I have disguised in the figure
here shown, and here we have two arks—one
with the whole body of Osiris, and the other
with his rod or phallus only, sometimes conventionalised as in Fig. 4. These arks were

Fig. 4.

in every temple, and constantly carried in all
processions, and lavishly sculptured on all
temples and public buildings, so they were a
familiar sight to Moses and his people. The
Ark itself is the oldest god, or rather goddess
or deity, worshipped by man (see pp. 11 and
12).

In Genesis i., 2, we are told—" And the
spirit of God moved upon the face of the
waters."

This spirit of God is feminine : it is Rk, our

word Ark; but in Hebrew Ruak, or Ruach, and is not the spirit, but the wife or mother of the gods. She is only "spirit" in so far as she was allocated the sovereignty of the air, breath, soul, spirit, or heaven, and was the heavenly mother who created the souls of infants as their earthly mothers created their bodies. (See Vols. I. or II., Index Numbers.) The phrase in Genesis i., 2, should be translated " the Mother of All (or of the gods) brooded on the waters " (and brought forth life). (See my *Seven Stories of Creation.*)

As the creator idea in religion was founded on the ideas of reproduction, the highest symbol of the god-like creative power, and hence the power to continue life to eternity, was the male and female organs combined; so here we see that the Egyptians by enclosing the male Osiris, or his phallus, in the female Ark created the most sacred symbol, which is also the " incomprehensible mystery " of the Christians, the Trinity in Unity, the rod and two stones of God in the Ark.

The next step Moses took after finding the Rod of God in " Midian " and freeing the children of Israel was to make an Ark, as the female member of the God-head. So he made an Ark (Exodus xxv., 10), and the Lord says (verse 16), " And thou shalt put into the ark the Testimony which I shall give thee."

The scribe seems to have forgotten that before this, in chapter xvi., verse 34, Moses had already obtained a Testimony from somewhere, and we see from the context that the Testimony was the equivalent of the Lord himself.

Moses told Aaron to " lay a pot of manna up before the Lord " (Jehovah, Yahweh, or Iové) as the Lord (Iové) had commanded him in verse 32. And " as the Lord had commanded Moses, so Aaron laid it up before the Testimony " [not before the Lord] " to be kept." The Testimony here is given a capital T to give it a holiness equivalent with the Lord, so the two were the same thing. The Lord (Iové) was terribly jealous about keeping his commandments to the letter, so they would not have dared to lay it up before the Testimony if the Testimony had not been Iové, as he commanded.

The Ark which had been made for this something called the Testimony would have been quite suitable for making the eternal life combination with the Rod of God, but we must remember that Moses always carried the

Rod of God in his hand to do his miracles with (Exodus iv., 17; vii., 15), and something else was wanted to complete the Ark symbol. This Rod of God made Moses a God, as the Lord (Iové) says in Exodus vii., 1 (English version)—" I have made thee a god unto Pharaoh, and Aaron thy brother shall be thy prophet."

But this is not a true translation. The Hebrew says—" I have made thee an Ale-im unto Pharoah, and Aaron shall be thy Jehovah " (IhVh or Iové) (Exodus vii., 1). The Elohim were the gods of the first chapter of Genesis, and Jehovah (or Iové) was apparently their leader, but the Elohim were at first supreme; so the possession of the rod of God and its occasional loan to Aaron made Moses the superior, and Aaron the equal of Iové. Hence Moses and Aaron were gods We shall find this a common practice with the Hebrews, making gods out of Hebrews, and debasing other peoples' gods to mere Hebrew men, a practice applauded by German kultur, as Dr. Falke, their theological spokesman, says, September, 1916 :—" German Christianity would humanise the divine," and he declares that this " is the secret of the marvellous picture in the Church of St. Theodoric at

Ravenna, where Christ is shown, not as the 'Crucified,' but as a German man—the Duke of our Salvation."

As Moses required his rod of God in his hand to produce lice and flies and other plagues, strike water out of rocks, and win his people's battles (see the fight with Amelek, Exodus xvii.), he had to get some other god symbol to make up a complete Holy of Holies symbol with the ark, the terribly sacred bisexual combination, so we find him going up Mount Sinai (other accounts Horeb, the mountain of God in Midian, Exodus iii., 2), and Iové, amidst thunder, lightning, earthquakes, and all sorts of fear-creating puerilities, gives him two stones, which turn out to be the " testimony," which Iové said he would give him to put in the Ark. Jove had evidently forgotten that Moses already had a Testimony before which he put the manna. These stones were afterwards called tables of the law, but the *Encyclopœdia Biblica* tells us " that fundamental laws were put where they could not be seen is in the highest degree improbable; on the other hand, the chest was certainly made to hold some sacred object, and nothing is more likely than that this object was a stone from the Mount of God "—or stones

rather, as Eduth is plural (col. 2155). See p. 44.
Now, this curious word testimony was used for
a very good reason. It is afterwards called
witness, and we shall see that these are two
very phallic words. We must remember that
it is not the man who swears who is the witness, although that meaning has crept in in
modern times. It is the thing upon which
men swear which remains the witness of their
promise, as when Joshua sets up a stone, Tzur,
to swear on he says—" Behold this stone shall
be a witness unto us; for it hath heard all the
words," etc. It was a living " hearing stone."
The method of swearing in these times, and in
some parts of Arabia the custom still exists,
was as Abraham commanded his servant,
" Put, I pray thee, thy hand under my thigh,"
and the servant swore on his testes (Genesis
xxiv., 1-9); repeated again by Israel (Genesis
xlvii., 29) and in other passages. So the Testes
were more sacred as a witness than the phallus.
As the God-like power was that of creating life,
and the Hebrews knew by the existence of
eunuchs that injury to the testes destroyed
such power, they would not allow such a man
to become a priest, " for whosoever . . .
hath his stones broken . . shall not come
nigh to offer the bread of his god " (Leviticus

xxi., 20), and this is repeated in Deuteronomy xxiii., 1.

No Hindu could swear a more solemn oath than by swearing with his hand on the testes of Nanda, the temple bull, shown here kneeling at the entrance of the door of life, the Yoni, of this Lingam-Yoni altar, the Maha Deva, Great God or sacred altar of the Hindus representing the two organs producing life.

Fig. 5.

The original is in the British Museum.

So Iové gave Moses two stones untouched by man (Exodus xxxii., 16), and told him to put them in the Ark as a Testimony. This word testimony shows that the English translators knew it was the Stones or Testes of God, like the Rod of God, which were put in the Ark, as they chose the word Testimony, founded on Testes, to indicate it, and later they use the more correct plural word witnesses, which is the real meaning of Eduth, the word in the Hebrew. Witness is, in German, the same thing, as zeugniss (witness) is derived from " zeugen," to witness or to beget or engender; " zeugung " is procreation; and " zeugungs organe " is genital organs; so either testimony or witnesses represents very well the two stones in the Ark. Even the *Encyclopœdia Biblica*, col. 2155, says :—" Two stones in the Ark were not tables of the law, but holy stones." The Rod of God finally found its way there also, and then the complete organ of the god was in the female Ark, and we have the three-in-One, the " incomprehensible mystery " of our Prayer Book. It was so called because the priests did not wish it known that their God consisted of the male and female organs in the act of creating life.

We have seen that the Rod of God was universally worshipped, and lest readers might think it very rare for the stones also to form a sacred combination, I give here several examples from coins, medals, and churches, showing the two stones prominently portrayed as the creative agent.

In one, Fig. 6, we see Hercules with his club (the phallus) and his lion's skin (emblem of phallic energy) actually holding two stones over a " fire of passion," and causing the fructification of woman, indicated by a conch shell, into which the soma or fertilising fluid falls.

Fig. 6.

Fig. 7.

Another (Fig. 7) shows the two stones in the centre as the principal object of worship, man being indicated by a tree and the woman by the usual conch shell, while passion or fire balances the picture. Stones were generally erected in Trinities, as shown in Figs. 8, 9, 10, and 11, in Alsace, Ireland, Sardinia, and Brittany. A large upright stone, such as Jacob anointed, and the two smaller rounded stones, such as no doubt Iové gave Moses to put in

the Ark. In Fig. 11 we see a Rod of God or
phallic stone with the Eduth or two Testes or
Testimony carved on it. In graves, also in

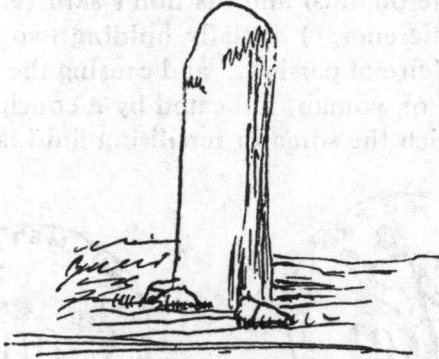

Fig. 8—Alsace.

Fig. 9—Ireland.

Fig. 10—Sardinia.

Fig. 11.—Kerloaz, Brittany.

prehistoric times, there was a niche on which were laid two egg-shaped white quartz stones, such as are to be picked up on any pebbly beach. I was present many years ago when Dr. Angus Smith opened a grave in the West of Scotland, in which were these two egg-shaped stones of white quartz, representing no doubt eternal life.

Fig. 12.

Fig. 13.

Again, we have many medals, as in Figs. 6, 7, 12, and 13, with the phallus as the Tree of Life embraced by the serpent of passion with the two stones, and one medal has the conch shell to represent woman, while the other has a rude ark (Fig. 13) showing the equivalence of these two symbols. In the church called the Hermitage of St. Michael in Spain we see the two great stones are the principal object of adoration; in fact, the church was built round them; while St. Michael, as the phallus, and quite small, is inclosed in a lingaic shrine and holds the trident, the male trinity, in his hand, showing the meaning of the combination (Fig. 14). The church itself is the ark, the whole forming the extremely holy Three in One, incomprehensible mystery. So we see again that the Hebrews were not at all singular in their symbolical worship.

Fig. 14.

This combination of ark and stones was so terribly holy that anyone going near it, except a Levite, was punished with death, and we see

Uzzah in 2nd Samuel, vi., 6, struck dead for touching it, even to steady it. "And when they came to Nachon's threshing floor, Uzzah put forth his hand to the Ark of God to hold it, for the oxen shook it. And the anger of the Lord was kindled against Uzzah, and God smote him there for his error, and there he died by the Ark of God." Uzzah was the name of an Arabian goddess worshipped of old by the Hebrews, but like Pallas or Minerva, of either sex. The name remained feminine, and this little tale is told to wipe out this troublesome relic of the past. Uzzah is a phallic god-name, meaning to "wax strong," "shameless," "goat," "strong one," from the same root as Boaz, the phallic pillar of Solomon's temple (see p. 49, Part II.). Perez-Uzzah, in 2nd Samuel vi., 7, means the "debasement of Uzzah," not his death as in the story. It would require a volume to fully demonstrate this process used by Old Testament writers of debasing and killing their abandoned gods and those of other nations. We have here an illustration of a practice used by the Hebrews, of which I have as yet found no clear explanation. While it was the wrath of Iové which was kindled, it was the Gods (Elohim) who struck Uzzah dead. This sudden change of god from a double-sexed god to a band of masculine or pillar gods in the same verse cannot be due to two different writers, and must have a reason hitherto undiscovered by Biblical scholars. For merely looking into the Ark the men of Bethshemesh were smitten to the number of " fifty thousand, three score, and ten," truly a " great slaughter," as is said in 1st Samuel, vi., 19. This may be a purely mythical slaughter, or it may be that " looking into the female Ark " is the same as " transgressing in the matter of Peor," the cleft or membrum feminum whose plague killed 24,000 (Numbers xxv., 9-18), and the disease was ophalim or syphilis, which might well slay fifty thousand. (See my *Queen of Heaven and Her Debasement*.)

The Christian Church has also an Ark of God in the Monstrance and Pyx, a lingam-yoni combination, as we shall see, to touch which was punished by a special law, inflicting death by being hanged, drawn, and quartered, and the offender's head smitten off. A soldier was actually executed before the enemy in France at the Battle of Agincourt in the fifteenth century for this offence. Death was also the penalty for looking into or touching the sacred Ark of Osiris in Egypt. So in

religion " there is no new thing, the same
ideas are worked up over and over again," as
Mr. King tells us in his *Gnostics and their
Remains*.

The further history of this Ark and Eduth,
or Testimony, introduces us to another realm
of symbolism, which has helped to keep the
Jewish race apart from the rest of mankind and
preserved their racial features unchanged for
three thousand years.   Jové declares clearly
(Gen. xvii., 10)—" This is my covenant which
ye shall keep between me and you and thy seed
after thee.   Every man-child among you shall
be circumcised. . .   It shall be a token of
the covenant betwixt me and you. . . .
And my covenant shall be *in your flesh* for an
everlasting covenant.   And the uncircumcised
man-child whose flesh of his foreskin is not
circumcised, that soul shall be cut off from his
people : he hath broken my covenant."

The Testimony and Witnesses were identical
with the Covenant, and the covenant was " that
which was cut."   But there were two cuttings
known in most religions, that of the Phallus,
or the circumcision, and that of the testes to
make a Eunuch or Kadesh.   The two stones
are certainly the Testes, Eduth, or Witnesses,
but the word Covenant is equally applied to
the cutting of the phallus.

Jové made many other " covenants," most of them never fulfilled, but this was *the* covenant with its token indelibly carved on the living body of every Hebrew.

To return to the Midian rod of Moses. To prove that this rod was a creative god there is a trial of wonder-working power; and the Rod of God, now called Aaron's rod, was put in the Ark or Tabernacle along with the rods of the other tribes, but Aaron's rod alone performed a miracle. It brought forth buds, flowers, and " almonds." This is symbolical language for saying that the rod created females (almonds), and was fruitful with them, producing children—male buds and female flowers (Numbers xvii., 8). The Rod of God was laid up before Iové (Numbers xx., 9), beside the two stones, and the Ark is then called the Ark of the Berith or B'rith of Iové, translated covenant; and covenant, we have seen, is circumcision.

The Berith is the circumcision or the circumcised thing, so the combination was the " Ark of the circumcised thing of Jové." But, further, there was a god Baal B'rith in the Ark called the " idol of the Covenant " in Judges xviii., 33, and we know that Iové was originally Baal—the *Encyclopaedia Biblica* says,

column 403 : " The Israelites had no scruple
in calling Yahoveh their Baal ;" and in column
3327 : " Baal was used without hesitation as a
designation for the god of Israel." So the
Ark, which is called in Joshua iii., 3, the "Ark
of the Covenant of Iové," is the Ark of the
circumcised thing of Iové. Iové is a Baal, and
one of David's heroes is called Baaljah,—" Baal
is Yahoveh or Iové." Now Basar and Bosheth
are words meaning "the flesh of his nakedness,"
the " shameful thing," the " phallus," and we
have Jerub-Baal in Judges vi., 32, called Jerub-
Bosheth in 2nd Samuel xi., 21; also Esh Baal
becomes Esh Bosheth. Baal is also the Elohim (gods), as we find Baal-jada becomes El-
jada, and so both " Elohim " and " Jehovah,"
the " God " and " Lord " of the Bible, are
phallic, as both are equivalent to Bosheth,
" the flesh of his nakedness," " the shameful
thing," " that which was circumcised," or the
phallus. We see the identity of Jehovah with
the phallus in joint names, for instance,
Pelaiah, the " Phallus is Iah," or Jehovah,
as all such names are tacit statements of
equivalence. Pelaliah, " that which brings
forth is Jehovah," is a similar phrase. These
names should be pronounced Pela-yah and
Pelal-yah.

Jacob says that the stone phallus he erected and anointed was " El, God of Israel " (Genesis xxxiii., 20). See p. 33.

Now that the female ark holds the Rod of God and his two stones, the triple emblem is complete, and it is now called the " Ark of God " (1st Samuel, xxxiii.), or the Ark of the Lord (Joshua vii., 6), or the ark of both Jehovah and Elohim, called in the Bible the " Ark of the Lord your God," but really the ark of " Iové of the Ale-im " or Band of Gods. We have now the three male god emblems or the complete trident, or Triune god, or Male Trinity, in the Ark; or four in all, forming the complete combination necessary for the divine act of creating new life, and of upholding the continuance of life on earth. The Ark is Una or Unity, whom we see riding on her Lion on p. 77, so we have the complete secret god symbol of all countries, the Three-in-One, Trinity in Unity, the " incomprehensible mystery " of our Prayer Book, the most sacred symbol of all religions, the creator or origin of all life. We must not forget that sacred and secret are closely allied, and all arks and their contents, rods or serpents, were secret, and it was wicked or criminal to inquire or look into such " mysteries," just as it was with our monstrance and pyx in the middle ages, or still is with the " Three in One " to-day.

The statue of Una on her Lion (p. 77) is the same thing, as the Lion was in symbolism the most salacious of all animals to the ancients, and represented the Trinity or Male force most completely; and, coupled with unity, whose very name is Una, or one-ness, we have the symbol of creative fertility, the " Three in One." Una is probably identical with Yoni, the membrum feminum of the Lingam-yoni altar.

The Hebrew language, as written, depends on Chaldee roots, and the root for IhOh is HOH or HVH, as the letter Vav may be either O, V, or U. The H's can, as in Greek, be treated as E's, so the root, HVH, of the great tetragrammaton or double-sexed god is the female Eve.

Eve is placed under the root ChVH, but Ch and H are almost identical, and freely replace one another. Vav and yod, or V and I, are also nearly identical, so we have HVH, ChVH, and HIH, ChIH and ChII, all meaning " to be," " to exist," " life," " living," to " breathe," also " calamity," " fall," " desire," " lust," and finally " Eve." The name is thus made to tell Eve's story. She was the mother of all life or living, she caused desire or lust in Adam and so brought about the calamity of the " Fall." This clearly shows the artificial construction of ecclesiastical Hebrew, just as in the case of the root ANS for woman, which has attributed to it the interpretations, " incurable," " mortal," " female," " wife," " widow," " concubine," and " one-another," thus blaming woman in every capacity as the cause of " ophalim," the incurable disease syphilis, which the sexes communicate to " one another."

Life, or the giver of life, is always represented as Breath (see Ruach as the mother, or spirit, or breath of the Gods), and H is always the " breathing " letter, neither consonant nor vowel, so Eve, the fertile one, is made up of O, the female, between two " breath-of-life "-giving symbols (see Hercules, Fig. 6, p. 45), exactly as the most sacred possession of the Hebrews was the female ark with the two life-giving stones or testes (Testimony), equal to IhOh, p. 41. Afterwards the rod of god was added, and the terribly potent life-creating or death-dealing combination, the Ark of the Berith of Iové was produced.

So by adding the rod or pillar I to the O, with two H symbols of the breath of life, or

Eve, we have the creative god, the most sacred symbol of all religions and the tetragrammaton of the Hebrews, the IhOh which we thus see is double sexed. The female element is tripled in the English rendering of the name as Jehovah,—the O, V, and the feminine termination " ah." The latter is coupled up with the first letter, I or J, giving again a double-sexed word, Iah or Jah, which forms the termination of hundreds of names in Holy Writ, such as Jeremiah or Elijah. It is identical with IO (Bible JO), which forms the beginning of so many names, such as Joseph, Joel, etc.

The famous ark with its contents was therefore the uniting or unifying female organ, mother of all, holding the complete male organ, always represented as a trinity or trident, and this joining of the three and one is always represented in all great religions as a, tetrad or four-sided god, as is shown by the four heads round the Linga on the Lingam-yoni altar, which is still worshipped everywhere in India (see Fig 5, p. 43).

The four heads represent Truth, Religion, Matter, and Passion; in fact, the whole range of divine or human activity, the two emblems being in the act of creation of life.

The Hindus have also a triune or triple male

god exactly as the Christians have, represented by a three-headed god called a Trimoortee and a triple branched column or Trisul, like the Trident, Fleur-de-lys, broad arrow, Prince of Wales' feathers—all king-god signs of Europe.

The Hebrews adopted the IO of Persia (or perhaps of Rome) as their god, but to make the name agree with the four-some or tetradic constitution of the god, they added the two H's, representing the two sacred, life-giving stones (Eduth, testes) in the Ark, producing the sacred Tetragrammaton representing the Ark with the rod of god and his two stones creating life. That the Ark with its contents was identical with IhOh is shown by the identical punishment of death being meted out to anyone pronouncing the name or touching the Ark.

That Jehovah or Iové was originally IO is shown by the use of these two letters alone in the formation of important names in the Old Testament, as in Io-nah, Io-nathan, Io-seph, Io-ab, Io-ash, Io-ed, Io-shua, etc., disguised in the English Bible by the use of the German I, which of course is written J. But as the Christians held woman to be the source of all evil, they cut her out of much of their symbolism, and although they adopted the Queen of Heaven from the Hindus and Egyptians as their virgin Mary, they took care to give her an earthly husband and several children, like Hannah (1st Samuel, ii., 21). So the Hebrews did not adopt the great Egyptian Tetrad, the four-sided pyramid, as their symbol of eternal life or continuous succession of life, yet they adopted the Ruach or spirit or breath in their most sacred Tetragrammaton. Their religion being entirely masculine, yet largely derived from Egypt, they adopted the pyramid form as a triangle, symbolical of the triune masculine deity, as one of their secret signs with which we still decorate our churches. The symbol I am about to describe is quite common, and I recall one in London at the Church of the Holy Trinity in Gray's Inn Road repeated four times on the walls of the sacred edifice, probably to indicate that it represents the Tetragrammaton or sacred four letters IhOh, which is carved in its midst.

As shown in Fig. 15, the sacred name is carved inside a triangle representing the complete male organ required for the creation of life, the Trinity, as carved on ancient grave-stones, Fig 16, which is a sort of triangle (and sometimes a rough triangle was substituted).

Fig. 15.

Fig. 16.

This again is inclosed in a ring or wreath of myrtle leaves, the whole representing the Ring and Piercer of Persia, with which all life was created. Sometimes the outer ring is a serpent, to indicate that the symbol represents the action which caused the Fall in Eden. As a matter of fact, the serpent and Eve were originally the same, as is shown by the Egyptian carving, Fig. 17, where the serpent " goes erect " and offers the apple to the man. Cleopatra is called the Serpent of Old Nile, and Forlong says that ChVH means both Eve and serpent (*Rivers of Life*, I., 126).

Of course, modern explanations represent the triangle and circle as the " three aspects of god in eternity," but the symbol is older

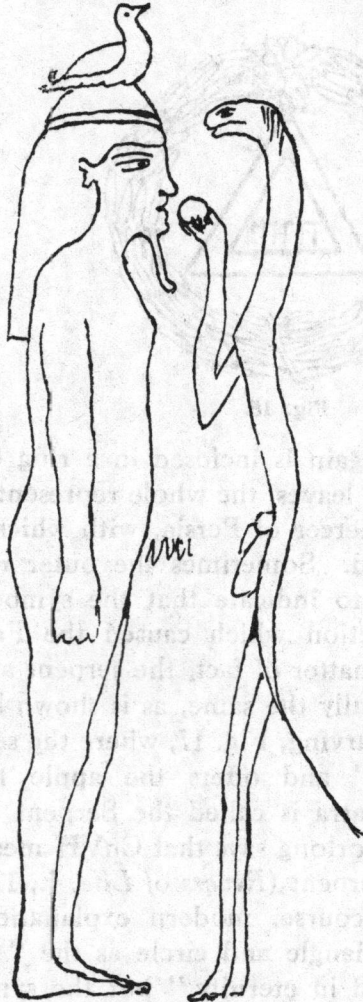

Fig 17.
Lanzoni CLXXII.

and more earthly than these highly sublimated modern ideas, which do not require to be disguised by symbolism.

The myrtle is symbolical, like the pomegranate, of fruitful woman (consult my *Queen of Heaven*), and was carried at "hags" or feasts by the female participants. It is stated by ecclesiastical commentators as having a significance which made it impossible for any virgin to carry it. It was sacred to Venus, as its leaves resemble the Vesica Piscis. In the symbol on the Church of the Holy Trinity it has this significance, as it is in the act of creating life, shown by the lotus flower at the top of the wreath (again fruitful woman, see my *Christianity*, pp. 18 and 55) and a bunch of fruit hangs below—the result of the sexual combination. Myrtle was the special symbol of fruitful goddesses, such as Cubele, Venus, and especially of Myrrha, from whom it probably derives its name. Cubele is Arabic for the Yoni, the Cupola of Churches.

Hyppolytus has told us that all the most sacred mysteries of the old religions were the sexual organs, and we know that the most sacred name of the Hebrew god was IhOh, a purely sexual combination made famous under the peculiarly distinctive name of the most

holy Tetragrammaton.   Pythagoras declared
the Square number 4 or Tetracht to be the one
ineffably perfect figure, as it represented the
God in the act of creating life (p. 318).

Iah is not called the sacred Trigrammaton,
nor is the English " god " called the " great
three letters," nor " Lord " the " most holy
four letters," although, as a matter of fact,
" god " and its Hebrew equivalent " Eli,"
both masculine, have three letters, and Lord
and IhOh, double-sexed, have four.   This
may not be entirely accidental, but the " four
letter " word was certainly used in Hebrew
to emphasise the fact that IhOh was a true
creative symbol containing both male and
female,   forming   our   incomprehensible
mystery.

That such combinations were common is
clear from the following list, which might be
indefinitely extended did we follow Sir James
Frazer's example and search the languages of
the thousands of savage tribes, ancient and
modern :—Pyx and Monstrance, Pessel in
Massekah, Pestle in Mortar, the name
Pharaoh, Phala·O (R and L indentical in
Egyptian), and his tomb, the Pyramid—pyr,
male; Am or Om, female; Greek Pyramis;
plural, Pyramides; Ophalim, female and male

diseases; Baal-peor, Phallus, and Cleft, Spire or Pillar and Dome (Pala and Om), Alpha and Omega, Lingam-yoni altar (Pala and Om), the Greek letter Phi Φ, Zaakar and Nekebah (Piercer and Womb), Rod and Almond, Rod and Stones in Ark, Triangle in Circle, IhOh, Dagger and Ring, Osiris (O Sar), Cross and Crescent, Tortoise, Bell and its Tongue, Pillar and Bowl, Pulpit (pp. 194-197, 431,440), Egg and Dart, Egg and Serpent, etc.

It will be noticed that the best known symbols begins with P and M, or contain M in the second word, such as Om, and the word Pyramid begins with Pyr (or Fire), the male element, which is the same as Pul, as y and u are the same letter, as are R and L, so it is possible that the word " pyramid " is the same as Pesel and Masekah of the Hebrews, the Pestle and Mortar of the Alchemists, Pyx and Monstrance, Pillar and d'Om of the church. Pyramid begins with Pyr, which is pur, puer (Lucretius), Pul, Pala, or Phallus, the male, or male organ, and equivalent to Zakar, the " piercer," used for male in Genesis i., 27; and its second syllable is the universal word for the female, Om, Am, Umma, or even Alma, original of Womb.

Pyrom was the two-sexed term applied to

the statue or monument of Kings or Priests claiming creative power or God-hood in early times, plural Pyromés, in Greek Pyramis, as the Greeks favoured the " is " terminal, writing Osiris for Osir or Osar, Seraphis for Seraph, and Isis for Ishi or Isha of Genesis ii., 23. Pyramis gives Pyramides in the plural, —hence our word Pyramid. So Pyramid is identical with the double-sexed creative power, the Three-in-One, Rod of God, and two stones in an Ark, four in all, the Tetrad, and the " incomprehensible mystery " of all nations, their most sacred symbol, creating or slaying like the Hebrew Ark, our Monstrance and Pyx, or the Square, Tetracht, or Tetracha of Pythagoras.

But other men other manners, and the time came when this ark of God was forgotten and neglected. It only flashed up for a time under David, then was entirely forgotten and lost under the oppulent reign of Solomon. " In those days no more shall one say, The Ark of the Berith of Iové neither shall it come into one's mind, neither shall we think upon it nor miss it, neither shall it be made again " (Jeremiah iii., 16). So their most sacred symbol was totally abandoned, and forbidden, perhaps, however, only by the reforming

Jeremiah, who wrote later " according to the number of thy cities are thy gods, O Judah " (Jeremiah xi., 29).

They had no wars then, and Solomon seems to have established great freedom of worship, as every sort of god was worshipped at Jerusalem, and Solomon built temples for the gods of his foreign wives, so Milcom, Chemosh, Ashteroth, and other strange gods or Als, including Egyptian gods, for Pharaoh's daughter; and even the dread Moloch was worshipped in Iové's sacred city without a word of protest. We read of Chemosh having his temple " in the hill that is before Jerusalem " (1st Kings, ii., 7). The Nabis probably knew that Solomon would give them short shrift if they publicly interfered in his efforts to please his foreign wives. So the great ark, which caused fifty thousand to fall dead at a stroke is now neglected, just as were their " Rocks " or stone pillars. " Of the rock that begat thee thou art unmindful " (Deuteronomy xxxii., 18); " Who is a rock save our god " (Psalm xviii., 31). All are forgotten in the splendour of Solomon's reign, unless as " old unhappy far-off things and battles long ago." They even repudiated the Rod of God and the stones in the Ark which constituted their

covenant of the circumcised phallus, as in
Judges viii., 33 : they say " the children of
Israel turned again and went a'whoring after
Baalim " (their Iové was once a Baal), " and
made Baal Berith " (called on the margin the
" Idol of the Covenant "), " their god."
Bagster's Bible tells us Baal-Berith was mercury or the circumcised phallus, as I have
shown, but disguised as the " covenant," so
there was no real change. It was the same
thing, as Iové's special covenant with the children of Israel was the circumcised phallus
(Genesis xvii., 10), and this " covenant," the
circumcised phallus, was to be " a god unto
Abraham " (Genesis xvii., 7). So the Berith
or circumcised phallus was a true god, and is
therefore included in the list of gods of the
Hebrews in the *Encyclopædia Biblica* (see p.
85). Here we have confirmation that they had
a real idol in the ark, the rod and stones of
God, and this idol was their god, and was the
equivalent of the phallic Hermes or Mercury
of the Greeks and Romans, or the ithyphallic
Osiris and Min of Egypt.

" And the children of Israel remembered
not the Iové of the Aleim . . . neither
showed they kindness to the house of Jerub-
baal, namely Gideon, according to all the

goodness he had shown unto Israel " (Judges xviii., 34-35).

In those three verses the writer condemns the worship of the Covenant Berith, once their most sacred Arcanum, and while condemning Baal worship, yet praises Jerubbaal, called also Jerubbosheth, the "shameful thing " or the Phallus. But we constantly find the Hebrew Nabis and their god bitterly condemning the very practices most universal amongst themselves, and Iové constantly breaks all the commandments except that about having "no other gods before me." He not only revelled in indiscriminate slaughter, but he complained when Saul did not exterminate the Amalekites (1st Samuel, xv.), man, woman, babe, with all their cattle to the last calf, kid, or lamb; and he praises David when he leaves not a living thing, and he invents all sorts of torture, as in 2nd Samuel, xii., 31, and other passages.

This brings to mind an error of many writers, including Gibbon, our modern Herodotus, who takes for granted that the bitter condemnation of crimes by the Hebrew Nabis proves that they were more moral than the surrounding nations, and showed us a good example. The very reverse is the truth.

They absolutely revelled in adultery publicly, openly, promiscuously, led off by the priests and Kadeshah or Temple women, and their god revelled in murder, theft, lying, adultery, and every crime in the calendar, as super-abundantly proved by his record in His own Holy Bible, a sample of which record I give later on. So the ten commandments story must be a late addition for the laity.

The *Encylopædia Biblica*, col. 2223, indicates that it was the Canaanites, not the Israelites, who were most highly civilised, and the " Israelites adopted all the Canaanite practices " (2237).

They changed their Gods according to the tribes amongst whom they dwelt, and when successful in war they stole the gods and women of the defeated clan and adopted both with equal gusto. This was easy, as most God-names were Phallic. Take the name of the Assyrian Tiglathpeleser (Greek, Tiglathphalassur). Ti is " God " all over Asia, also in Europe, as The(os), De(us), Di(o), Di(vine), etc.; and Lat is the Phallus (*e.g.*, Asoka's Lat in Delhi). Phallus needs no translation, and Sur is the " Rock that begat thee," so his name is " God of the Pillar, Phallus or Rock."

CHAPTER II

THE EARLY GODS

The Hebrews generally followed an intensely masculine cult. Their special tribal god, called Jehovah or Iové, is held to have been originally a Babylonian god Ia aVa (see my *Christianity*) or IV, if we cut out the " a's," which are like the Hebrew " h's," mere breaths; and his name was expressed in Hebrew as IhOh, IhUh, or IhVh, according as the Vav was pointed for O or U, or was left without points, when it is read as V.

Leaving out the " h's," that gives IO, IU, or IV, each of which was used in compound names, as the name of the most high god. With the H's, this was the sacred Tetragramatton or " four letters," to pronounce which was punished with death. There was a fourth rendering, IA or IAH, and although it is used only once as a name in the whole Bible, in Psalm lxviii., 4, yet it was employed more extensively than any of the others in compound names as meaning Jehovah, in such names as Jeremiah, Obadiah, Hezekiah, Nehemiah, etc.

The others occur in such names as IOseph, which we call Joseph, and IUpittar, the Roman Jupiter, while IV does not occur in a pure form, but combined with the IO form, as in Jehovah, really Iové or Yové, as the English Jeh are only equivalent to our I or Y.

The Hebrew priests or Levites gave him a terribly jealous and bloodthirsty character, with whole chapters of cursing those who served other gods, to keep the people faithful, so that the Levites might live; as the whole tribe of Levi had no other means of living but out of the daily sacrifices.

But before that they had other gods, and " Place aux dames," the first one mentioned was a goddess, as were the earliest gods of nearly all primitive people.

Early peoples followed nature, and they saw the creation of life out of the mother, so they held that all life comes out of the water and out of an ark, or Ruach, the universal mother (as did Moses), and the ark is woman, or the womb, as the word " woman " is simply the man who has the womb. Our word " ark " is in old languages this symbol RK or RCh, and becomes Ark, Arch, or the

" highest," or " holiest," as in Archangel,
Arcanum, and her symbol was the dove,
" love and peace." Dove is Iona or Yoni,
the female organ or womb, so we are round
again to ark. But, alas ! we only glimpse her
for a moment, and she is then hidden by the
terrible period of the masculine tyrant Iové,
who threatens to punish any serving of other
gods by fire, smoke, thunder and lightning,
pestilence and famine, rapine and slaughter,
pictured for us by the Levites as the rule of
their savage god—a picture of anger and vengeance calculated to keep their sheep in the
fold, and fill the Levites' coffers, as indeed it
did, as Abbé Loisy tells us that the more bitter
tongued Nabis often became wealthy through
the fears of their dupes.

Lecky in his history of morals writes of
this change even in artistic Greece, where the
female was so worshipped in art. In vol. II.,
p. 279, he says :—" It is one of the most
remarkable and, to some writers, one of the
most perplexing facts in the moral history of
Greece that in the former and ruder period
women had undoubtedly the highest place."
Later, on p. 280, Lecky says :—" The in-
feriority of women to men was strongly
asserted, and it was illustrated and defended

by a very curious physiological notion, that the generative power belonged exclusively to men, women having only a very subordinate part in the production of their children." Then :—" The woman Pandora was said to have been [like Eve] the author of all human ills." The change of worship from feminine to masculine is marked in the Hebrew Bible by the dream of Jacob of an interview with the masculine IO, in Genesis xxviii, 10-22; when he changed the name of his dream-place from Luz to Bethel—Luz being " almond," the symbol of the Yoni or Female all over the east, and Bethel bearing the meaning of the Place or house of El, the pillar or phallic god—purely masculine.

The Queen of Heaven's reign was quite different from that of Iové, in fact benign, as the Hebrews said that under her they " had plenty of victuals, were well, and saw no evil. But since we have left off to burn incense to the Queen of Heaven and to pour out drink offerings unto her, we have wanted all things and have been consumed by the sword and by the famine " (Jeremiah xliv., 17, 18, 19, 25).

This benign ruler is called in our translation the Spirit of God, but she is only the Spirit of God in so far as she is His female counterpart, and the ancients held that it was the female who spurred man to action, and hence his " spirit." Action in a god is creation of life, and man well knew that without the female he could not act or create life, hence the female is the " spirit."

Fig. 18.

That the Mediaeval Christian Church took that view is clear from this drawing from Didron, when the spirit or wife of God as a dove is doing the actual creation, brooding on

the waters (as women do in creating life) and
the god standing by, encouraging her with the
Orb of power in his hand. The orb of power
with its cross is the phallus or rather the
triple phallic emblem our male Trinity (see
my *Christianity*, pages 72-82, Fig. 72).

The first things created in this picture are
Churches. The Church is not over-burdened
with modesty, and evidently follows the
sarcastic Scottish prayer, " God gi'e us a guid
conceit of ourselves."

There were two accounts of the Queen of
Heaven and her creation—a dark, dismal,
wrathful, blood-thirsty story as in Babylon,
under the female dragon, Tehom, a baleful
destructive being—Tehom means " stormy "—
and a bright sunshiny happy creation by the
Ruach, the brooder, of the gentle "mothering"
type.   Ruach means " calm, peaceful," and
was the Mother of All, brooding on the waters
as a hen on her chickens and bringing forth life.
The chaotic state of the Hebrew Scriptures is
shown by the second verse of the first chapter
of Genesis, where there are three statements
drawn from entirely different sources and relating to three quite unconnected stories of
creation.   This is characteristic of the Old
Testament, it contains elements drawn from

Fig. 19.

widely divergent sources, giving the curious Hebrew colouring of making other nations' gods act like Hebrew men. As when they converted the Heavenly Sun God Hercules into the earthly hero Samson, whose name is still sun-god, or little sun, and, on the other hand, made all their own ancestors into gods— a habit copied by the Roman Church in declaring that all Mary's ancestors were " without sin," i.e., goddesses.   Mary is called by the Roman Church the Habitation of God, the Tabernacle or Ark of God, that is the Ruach of Genesis, and so she is Queen of Heaven. She is the Ark which we have seen in the introductory chapter was the habitation of God, in which He travelled about with the Israelites and in which He was represented by His rod and two stones, hence the incomprehensible mystery, the Three in One.   That the feminine is Unity is shown in another symbolical group, already referred to in pp. 55 and 56, Una and her lion. The lion is a very strong male symbol and is placed in that belt of Life the Zodiac, or Zion, in the great heat of summer, and hence is the energetic Male Trinity, while Una is the " One " or " Unity " as represented in this photo of the famous group (Fig. 19).   Here she is seen

holding the apple, the supreme erotic symbol
in her hand. The Hindoos have an identical
Tetrad in Maya on her lion (Fig. 20), some-

Fig. 20.   Fig. 21.

times a tiger; and the Egyptians had a like
Tetrad in their Kiun, Queen or Venus, probably Isis on a lion, which I show in Fig. 21.
This combination was very widespread, and is
a form of our " Incomprehensible Mystery,"
the Three-in-One, or Three and One, symbolised by the Hebrews in their most sacred
Tetragrammaton or Four Letters, IHOH.

The Queens of Heaven at one time held the
place which the male saviour or mediator took

in later times, and Mellita, the name of the Queen of Heaven of the Euphrates valley, means the mediatrix. But further, Manilius and Ovid tell us that Semiramis, a female Saviour, suffered death to bring salvation to man, and the story is told emblematically by saying the country was wasted and the people feared destruction by snake-footed Typhon, and he even pursued Semiramis or Venus, who, to avoid destruction plunged into the waters of Babylon and so sanctified these waters that they gave new life through baptism in them. Semiramis was also called Iona or the Dove, like Venus. We find Semiramis (or Melitta the Mediatrix) in the Bible, as Jonah the dove, plunging into the waters, and lying three days and three nights in Hell, or Sheol the dark grave (from the belly of hell cried I, Jonah ii., 2), and coming forth in order to bring salvation to Nineveh or the Ninevites. But the name used is Jonah or Iona, pronounced Yona, in Hebrew, which any Hebrew dictionary gives as " Dove " or Jonah, " son of Amitai the prophet," so the Hebrews brought down even the Queen of Heaven the Dove and made her into a Hebrew prophet. Jonah's father was Amitai, which is from the same root Matteh as the Rod of God,

p. 30, meaning a rod which swells or can erect itself—the phallus, which Moses held in his hand.

Jonah was the type of the later Jesus, who also suffered death (on the male cross, while Semiramis and Jonah suffered through female water), and Jesus also had the dove symbol; as a dove descended upon him when he was baptised in the Jordan by another Jonah, John the Baptist. He also descended into Hell, and came out in three days and three nights to the salvation of (at first), another " great city," Jerusalem, or the Hebrews, or the circumcised, although this salvation was subsequently declared by " Paul " to be world-wide, and not limited to the circumcised. I give this very inadequate account of the Queen of Heaven, Ruach, as she does not enter actively into Hebrew theology. But the reader may find her more fully treated in my book on the *Queen of Heaven and her Debasement* in this series.

Before entering on the long list of Hebrew Gods and their histories, it may be useful to illustrate the forms which the sexual symbolism took by a list of the principal symbols used for the male and female, and also to show the far-reaching character of this symbolism by the adoption of phallic words as the root-source of many words in all languages.

The male organ pala or phala—pul, pyr, or fire, as an element, is the same word—was symbolised by poles or pales as in " impaled," or " within the pale," a sacred place marked off or " palinged " off by phalli, gate posts, door posts, pillars, upright stones, tree stems, towers, peaked mountains (Ararat and Adam's Peak in Ceylon), rods, sceptres, Orbs of power with their crosses, serpents, tortoises, fingers, hands, feet, toes, heads, heels, lions, goats, rams, bulls (zodiac), and other male animals; sword, dagger, spear, arrow, especially any " piercer," such as the triple trident, Fleur de Lys, or broad arrow, the cross which is the sword and is a triple emblem or male trinity, the stauros, the pyx, spire, tongue of the bell, the bell tower, lotus bud, balance, tail, tongue, and many subordinate symbols derived from living things, such as pine cones, unopened rod-like palm leaves, and so on. The serpent was the most universal symbol of the Phallus or sexual passion, having been so used all over the world in every age. The Cross is one of the oldest and most universal symbols for the Phallus.

The female symbolism, with water as its

element, included all hollow or open things,
especially lens or almond shaped openings
called vesica piscis or fishes bladder, arks,
boats, or arghas, chests or altars, tabernacles,
dolphins (delphys-womb), whales, clefts,
mouths, rings, domes of churches, rounded
mountains, known as Omphs, caves, cups,
vases, bowls, crescents, coracles, rings, cradles,
shoes, or sheaths, the foot is the phallus and
the foot and shoe are sword and sheath,
pomegranates, almonds, windows, especially
lenticular or triangular, doors (the door of
life), arches, bows, horses', or especially asses'
shoes, as the latter is narrower and longer, and
both are adopted into Greek as the letter
Omega, Ω, which is not so much the great
O as the great Om or womb. Lotus flowers,
and more especially all over the East, the lotus
pod or seed vessel, which gives the circle and
triangle, as the cone-shaped seed pod is
circular seen from above and triangular seen
from the side, and its seeds sprout or
come to life in the seed pod or womb and
are dropped in the water alive with roots and
leaves. Besides the lotus is a water plant, and
water is woman. While there are very few
words directly derived from any roots denoting the female organ, the one word pala

denoting the male organ gave rise to a varied vocabulary.

In India the female of Pala is Palaki, just as the god Deva's female companion is Devaki, and Palaki means the Temple woman or sacred prostitute, or female companion of the Pala, Kadeshah in Hebrew. In our language we have Palladium and Apollo, the Pala gods, and such words as pole, pile, pale, pilaster, pillar, impale, pall, poll (a head), pollarded (of trees), peel (a round tower). From the Ph form we have Philip, the loving one, Phillis, philander, and when Ph is taken as F we have fall, fallacy, folly, fellow, false, no doubt also filth and foul, and so on, while there is a wide adaptation of the word in Greek and Latin as to priestly vestments, especially in phallic caps, phileolus, pilaeus, pillion, etc., used to imitate a bald head instead of the tonsure (see pp. 162 and 318).   Palace was once the holy place where the phallus was worshipped, and its German form, palast or pelesht, is used equally throughout the Bible for both Palestine and Philistine, or for Palestina and Philistia. The two lands are apparently one in the Hebrew Bible, Palestina is Phelesht in Isaiah xiv., 29, and Pelesht in verse

31; while Philistia is Phelsht and Philistine is sometimes Pilestim, and so on.

Having now some idea of Hebrew symbolism, we are in a position to understand their gods founded on that symbolism.

Not only did the phallus give names to lands like Palestine, Philistine, Phaliga, etc., but similar names were used all over Europe.

The Holy Hill of Rome is the Palatine, and the " Palace " of the Kings of Rome is on the Quirinal—from Quiris, spear, a phallic symbol (see p. 208), piercers being phalli. But Spear, Spar, and Spire may be derived from Pala, as S if often added to words, as tamp—stamp, pare—spare, kirtle—skirt. Now Pyr is identical with Pul, King of Assyria, written Phallus in Greek, and Pyr (the male element Fire) becomes Spire on a church, also Spar and Spear—all " Rods " or Phalli.

The home of the classical Gods, Olympus, was also double-sexed, Ol being the Phallic or Pillar God, and Om, Um, Ym—they are all the same—and Omph were used for the Great Mother or Womb, the double word signifying " life creation " or Lingam-yoni place, or simply Holy Place.

CHAPTER III

THE GODS OF THE ISRAELITES

The list of gods mentioned in the Bible as worshipped by the Israelites is a very formidable one, and includes Abir, Abraham, Adonai, Al, Alé, Ail, Alue, Allah, Alu, Amen, Asteroth, Ashera, Asher, Eli, Baal, Bamath, Berith, Iové, Io or Iah, El, Eloh, Jehovah, Elyon, Luithan, Nahathan, Oliun, Oli, Tsur, Sur, Selah, Sabaoth, Shaddai, Pahad, Adonai or Adonis, besides those foreign gods they occasionally worshipped, and whose names became family names, such as Anath, Belial, Chemosh, Chiun, Dagon, Gad, Queen of Heaven, Rimmon, Siccuth, Tammuz, Fortuna, Abraham, Isaac, Sarah, Milcah, Moloch, Laban, Samson, Jonah, a list I take from the *Encyclopædia Biblica*, col. 3320; and also Jacob, Joseph, Peter, Paul, Apollos, Barnabus, and others, in the New Testament derived from the Old Testament. Their god names and their religious practices were intensely phallic, as I have shown here and in my *Queen of*

Heaven. They created an alphabet and root words, and even the alphabet was symbolical of phallism.

Fig. 22.

Fig. 23.

Fig. 24.

The letter A, their Al-eph (Fig. 22), was originally a serpent wound round a pole, at one time their god, as here (Fig. 23), and this became the formal Aleph—" al," the god, post pillar or phallus, and " eph " or " oph," the serpent, the serpent god—the phallus. This was the brazen serpent of Moses, so long worshipped by the Israelites, and in truth by all other nations, as the tree stem caressed by a serpent (Fig. 24) was a universal symbol of the phallus, or creative power, excited by sexual passion.

Then Beth, the second letter, is a word meaning the house, tabernacle, or temple, as

Bethel (Beth-Al) is the house of god; so Aleph-beth, or Alphabet, was the house of the serpent god or phallus, and the student was thus told that by gaining the knowledge of writing he was entering the house of the serpent god or becoming a phallic priest.

But the Greek alphabet improved upon this. The Greeks adopted a phallic letter, Phi, which we pronounce " fie," and it is the ring and dagger of Persia, Φ, or the circle and pillar, exactly parallel with the Lingam-yoni altar of India. It is the " Alpha and Omega," as Aleph or, inverted, Alpha was an " upright " rod caressed by a serpent, the beginning of life.

We use this " shameful " letter, Phi, in reproving children, and say " Fie, for shame." But the Greeks created other new letters —amongst others the horeshoe or omega, which is the great O, or Om of Hindoo temples, the great mother or woman, just as Phalega was the Phallus. The Omega, Ω, or horsehoe was the symbol of good fortune or luck, and was embedded in church floors, and is still nailed on doors or hung up by ribbons. In Ireland the evil eye was evaded by putting a nude female, as the key-stone of the arch, exposing herself, so that the horseshoe or omega, the lucky symbol, might be made visible to all (see p. 96, my *Christianity*). So the Alpha and Omega were not only the beginning and end of the alphabet, but were the " be-all and end-all " of life, the two-sexed phallic pair, as is the Lingam-yoni altar of India (see Figs. 15 to 18; this Vol., pp. 402-404). In our religion the god is said to be the " Alpha and the Omega," the beginning and end of everything, but it also meant that the male and female organs were the cause of all life, and that all true religious symbolism was founded upon and bounded by the creation and continuance of life through these organs. Our Trinity in Unity is the same thing. So when we name the " alphabet " we are saying that the list of letters so indicated is the key that opens for us the door of the " house of the serpent god," or phallus; in short, the key to religion.

This word " Al " was the general title for " god " all over Western Asia, and the name varied in pronunciation from Al, El, Il, to Ol; and it got a prefix, Ba, said to have meant the God of the Land, but the Hebrews had phallic names commencing with B—Basar, Bosheth, Bom, Bamah, Bamoth, Behemoth, etc., and no doubt Baal, and no doubt Baal was a combination of such roots with Al, giving a very phallically named God. The plural of Alé was Aleim, and of Eli, on whom Jesus was said to call when deserted on the Cross— the plural was Eli-im, but written in the English Bible Elohim; as in Mark's Gospel Jesus calls him Eloi, hence Eloi-im for the plural, or with the neutral letter " h " to divide the word, instead of the second " i," and so we have Elohim, El-O two sexes.

This band of gods, Elohim, is mistranslated in the English Bible as " God," singular— with a capital G to give it holiness when it is applied to the Hebrew band of gods, but as " gods," plural, with a small " g " when it is applied to the other tribes' bands of gods. But they were identical, and this dishonest translation was done to bolster up a mono- theistic religion to which the real Hebrew writings give no support.

The Hebrews were polytheistic in their beliefs as to their own gods, and, as Dr. Cheyne, Oriel Professor of Holy Scripture at Oxford, and creator of the *Encyclopædia Biblica*, tells us, " the Israelites worshipped a small divine company under a supreme director." They also believed that every other clan and nation had a band of gods under a supreme director, as had the Greeks and Romans with their Hermes or Mercury, Aphrodite or Venus, Pallas or Minerva, and so on, under the supreme director Zeus or Jupiter, or Iové.

We therefore find in the Old Testament constant repetition of the phrase " Jehovah Elohim," falsely translated in our Bible Lord God, whereas it is simply " Jehovah of the Elohim," like Jupiter of the Olympian host.

Some editorial hand, perhaps following the fashion of the time, separated the two names, and treated Elohim as the personal name of a god, as we see in Genesis first; but the truth comes out by the scribe openly treating Elohim, when applied to all other Gods, as a plural noun, as it clearly is. It is the regular Hebrew plural—Cherub, Cherubim; Seraph, Seraphim; Alé, Ale-im; or as Jesus calls the god in Mark, Eloi, Eloihim, or Elohim, gods.

The form Jehovah Elohim persists through the entire Old Testament, although one scribe may represent the Elohim as speaking, while another assures us that the message comes from Jehovah; then each will suddenly say " Jehovah Elohim." There are hundreds of such passages. We may take one at random from Genesis ii., 4, " In that day that Jehovah of the Elohim made the earth and the heavens," or from Habakkuk iii., 18-19, "Yet I will rejoice in Jehovah; I will joy in the Elohim of my salvation;" then suddenly " The Jehovah of the Elohim is my strength," or in chapter i., 12, "Oh, Jehovah, my Elohim;" and constantly throughout the Old Testament or the equivalent phrase, Jehovah Sabaoth, Jehovah of the Heavenly Host, like Marduck, Zeus, or Jupiter. In fact, we shall see that Jehovah of the Hebrews and Jové of the Romans were identical, not only in their names, but in fables by which their histories are surrounded (see pp. 85, 109, 111).

The main difference between the Hebrew conception and that of the Babylonians, Egyptians, Greeks, and Romans was that they did not particularise the members of the band of gods. They seem to have addressed themselves almost exclusively to the recognised leader of the band whether it was Ba, Berith, Sur, Iové, or any of the others in their long list of gods; and to have grouped all the others into Aleim or Elohim, whereas in the other religions the Ale-im were all separately defined, and each one had a rôle to play.

The Christians followed the Roman method, but they called their minor gods or godlets " saints," and we find them absorbing all the " heathen " gods into their heavenly hierarchy as Saints—Tammuz as St. Thomas, Dionysus as Saint Dionysius, Bacchus as Saint Bacchus—and we even find the universal Womb, the Dolphin, adapted as a Christian saint in St. Delphin, adopted in French R.C. calendars for 24th December, when the sun was re-born out of the Dolphin, as detailed in my *Romance of the Hebrew Tabernacle.* See also my *Christianity*, p. 330, for the whole question of heathen gods as Christian saints. So we see that all religions are polytheistic, even when they repudiate polytheism by calling their minor gods saints. A saint is a true god, as he can create or perform miracles, and he lives for ever.

Some of the gods the Israelites adopted from other countries became very dim (had their Gotterdämerungen or twilight of each god), and only cast ghostly shadows on the Biblical scenes.

The Amen we apostrophise in our prayers is the great Amen of Egypt, translated in our Bible as the " God of Truth," as was the phallus in the India Lingam-yoni altar (*Chris-*

tianity, p. 52), but no doubt imposed on the Hebrews during one of their Egyptian captivities, or when they dwelt in Egypt for choice, and raised the ire of Jeremiah, where they probably also learnt the worship of the benign Queen of Heaven, Isis (Jeremiah xliv.). This Amen worship seems to have been eclipsed during the period of Babylonian influence, until the new revolutionary religion took its rise in Alexandria, as Christianity, when Amen once more received his invocation at the close of Christian prayers.

The Christ is called the Amen in Revelation iii., 14, and this god may have been the " Hidden " or " Unknown god " referred to by Paul, as Amen was the God " hidden " behind, but ruling, the sun, adopted by the Egyptians when their observations proved that the sun moved mechanically, ruled by a higher power, now called Amenti, the Amen God.

In passing we may note that amongst the rich and varied symbolism in Revelation, the equivalence of David and Peter are stated (Revelation iii., 7). David was Didi, the loving one, masculine, the " right hand " cult, replacing Saul's " left hand " worship, and was identical with all pillars or rocks, Sur, or Peter, and in this verse Peter is called " he that hath the key of David, he openeth and no man shutteth, he shutteth and no man openeth," a good description of the powers of a Pope, repeating the promise of Jesus to Peter in Matthew xvi., 19, or Isaiah xxii., 22. The rock Sur, so often referred to in the Bible and in my books, was by no means a decaying god, but one most widely worshipped, and included both solar and phallic creative ideas, changing from the Tsur into Tsar, Tur, Tyre, Tower, Tor, Ter, and Tar, when using the initial T, and into Sur, Ser, Sar, and even Sir (in Osiris), when employing the S as initial letter, just as S and T replace each other in water, wasser; street, strasse; kettle, kessel; out, aus; etc., in English and German. As all nations used R and L indifferently, the final R becomes L, and we have Sal, Sul, Saul, Sil, etc., as in Sulberg, Sulgrave, Silchester, etc.

The Tsur (Tzar) was a very widely worshipped stone pillar god, as is shown by its giving names to Suria (Syria), and with the prosthetic A to Assuria (Assyria), to Tyre, which is Tsor or Tsur or Sur in the Bible and in maps, and to gods of Egypt in Osar (Osiris) and Serapis, while Surya is a Hindu name of the sun. The Ashurim of Ezekiel xxvii., 6, are identical with the Fellahim of Egypt of to-day

—Phalla-im, worshippers of the phallus. Temple prostitutes were called Asheroth—feminine plural of Ser with the prosthetic A, S and Sh being practically identical.

Our Seraph or Seraphim is pillar serpent, as is the Teraphim which Rachel stole from her father. The Teraphim were no doubt lingas, as noted in Bagster's Bible, but they were more. They were Tur-Aphim, rocks or pillars with serpents embracing them to show their passion. Such was the Caduceus of Mercury, twin serpent symbols of life and healing, yet conducting mankind to Hell. It was similar to the violent two sex figures of India called Dakpo, Yaman Daga, Vajra-Bhairava, and other titles, showing sexual creation by the embracing of the two figures, while they, at the same moment, crush the living to death under their feet. This is to illustrate the fact that creation of life necessitates death, else the world would become overcrowded (see my *Christianity*, p. 340). So the Caduceus, although a life-symbol, conducts Euridicé to Hell or death. All the beautiful Earth maidens symbolising summer vegetation, such as Ceres, Proserpine, or Persephone, herself the " death destroyer," are drawn to Hell by serpents, and the whole structure of the Christian creed—man's fall and redemption—is founded on the serpent. It was the most subtle and wise thing—" Be ye wise as serpents." "In all lands and faiths," says Forlong in his *Rivers of Life*, I., p. 178, " the serpent is he who gives knowledge," as he did in Eden.

The Teraphim was represented by a tree stem entwined by a serpent, or by a serpent climbing the tree of life (Fig. 25), or by a true Tor or tower with a serpent, as shown in Fig. 26. This was a great favourite with the gnostics. The Seraph (plural, Seraphim) was the same thing, from Sur, Sar, or Ser, the

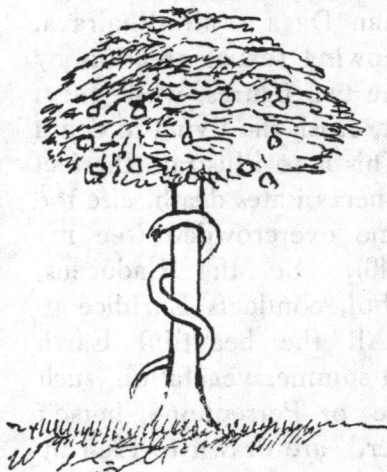

Fig. 25.   Fig. 26.

Tsur, " Rock that begat thee," and Aph, the serpent. It is a curious fact that the name of the calm, benign, digified god of Egypt, Serapis, whose portrait became that of Jesus, is the same word—column and serpent—symbolising creative power or the creator.

Pesilim or Pesselim were identical with Berith, the " covenant," or circumcised phallus, as shown on p. 35. Massekah was not a " molten image," as the translators misinterpret it, but a vessel to pour out libations to the Queen of Heaven (Jeremiah xliv.), and invariably painted as an " almond-shaped " vessel in church pictures of Mary Magdalene (Mary of the Almond). This aimond shape represented the Muliebre Pudendum, and represented the character of Mary as a temple woman who had " much loved " (see my *Queen of Heaven* or *Hebrew Tabernacle*). Rod and Almond, Makel and Saked, are symbols of Lingam and Yoni, as used by Jeremiah (i., 10), and carved on the holy seven-branched candlestick, and they appeared in the Holy of Holies at the bidding of the Rod of God (see my *Christianity*, pp. 234, 215, and 332; also Exodus xxv., 33; Numbers xvii., 8).

Another dim stone god similarly apostrophised in purely Hebrew prayers, and long forgotten till resuscitated as the Rock of Christ's Church, is the rock Selah, or Sela, an early form of Tzur, Sur, Sul, or Sel, the " Rock that begat thee," with the female affix Ah. We find Sela or Selah replacing Tsur as " Rock " in 2nd Samuel xxii., 2, and in 2nd Kings xiv., 7. In Lexicons Sela is Petra (in Edom), the Rock " Peter " of the Gospels. Selah or Sela is placed in the Psalms (which are prayers) as an apostrophic or vocative invocation, just as we use Amen in Christian prayers. To avoid such dangerous ground, Christian Hebraists tell us that it referred to an " upward " or " rising " tendency in the music. But this " upward," " upright," " high," " rising," or " swelling " or " extending " (see pp. 34-179), is common to the root meaning of all words signifying the phallus, just as the Hebrews also used the reverse, the " sinew which shrinks " (Genesis xxxii., 32). In Latin it was the Ruber (" red thing," identical with " Adam ") Porrectus (from porrigo, to " rise up," " swell," or " extend "). This rising or " extending " is the identical root-meaning of Matteh, the Rod of God (the phallus), with which Moses did all his miracles, and is the condition of the serpent which "went

erect " in Eden, and it is also translated as the
" marvellous thing " or the " miracle worker,"
as producing the greatest of all miracles or
mysteries, " Life."   Selah was therefore Sel,
the " Rock that begat thee," with the female
particle Ah, making it double-sexed, as was
IhOh, and many other creative gods all over
the world.   In a very old Psalm (89) we find
Ethan apostrophising both Amen and the rock
Selah when addressing his double-sexed god
IO, or IhOh, or Jehovah.

2nd Kings xiv., 7, shows us that Amen was
the same as Selah, and is composed of A or Ah,
the feminine determinant, and Men or Min,
the ithyphallic god or Rock of Egypt, so we
see why it was of a rising tendency like the
Ruber Porrectus of Horace.   So we see how
correct Bishop Colenso was when he wrote,
" The Jews worshipped precisely the gods of
the people among whom they dwelt."

We find the Israelites taking up, early in
their history, the Hindu god Bram or Brahm,
who was afterwards Bramah, adding the prosthetic A, and making the name Abram, who
was also afterwards named Abraham, inversion of Bramah, then taking up the Al or El
of Asia, as their god Eli, or band of gods Elo-

him, then the Amen of Egypt, changing to the Sur of Western Asia and again to the Selah of Edom, then adopting in turn the Ba Als of the Canaanites, Hittites, Amorites, Perizzites, Hivites, and Jebusites, Baals being Gods of the Basar, Bamah, or Bom, the phallus, finally worshipping a purely phallic conception, the IO, dagger and ring (male and female) of Persia, the rod and almond of Jeremiah, a life-giving god portrayed by the male and female reproductive organs in combination, and their whole religion, we are told in the *Encyclopœdia Biblica*, col. 1511, consisted in phallic hags (or orgies), in which the priests and temple women led off in the promiscuous sexual intercourse (*Encyclopœdia Biblica*, 2066).

An interesting god name is Hur, who assisted Moses in ruling the Israelites when Moses went up Mount Sinai. The *Encyclopœdia Biblica* says " a connection with the Egyptian Horus is very probable." The Egyptian Horus was the virgin's son, like Jesus. Josephus (*Antiq.*, III., 6, 1) calls Hur the Husband of Miriam or Mary. Here we have a dim reflection of Jesus and Mary, and the absorption of another great nation's god as a Hebrew man.

We have, then, the principal god of the

Hebrews, Jehovah, or more correctly Iové of
the Alé-im or Eli-im, and we may now glance
at the true meaning of these names. As Al,
El, Il, Ol, Allah, Alé, and all its numerous
forms was the god of Western Asia, while
Iové was the tribal god of the Hebrews, we
will consider Al first.

The root Al is used everywhere in the sense
of a post or upright thing, or a thing which
rises or has an upward tendency—its use as
" upright " meaning " just " is much later. It
is actually used in the Bible as an oak or terebinth, oak stem, pillar, post, or other up-
standing thing to swear by, and which was
always anointed, and which, we are told, in
the *Encyclopædia Biblica*, in column 2982,
the Hebrews believed to be alive, and which
Joshua declared heard all the words he had
spoken. This is the same symbol as was worshipped by the Druids in Britain, and which is
illustrated on p. 35 as the Dorsetshire Column,
a sort of god which was very common all
over the world at one time. When this was
anointed with oil to show its lively condition,
it was a true Hermes, Phallus, or living god.
Al also signified sexual force, and was constantly identified with a varied spelling, Ail or
A'l, a ram, the Zodiacal symbol of male fer-

tility. It also means strength, especially
sexual strength, and that strength found in the
rugged stems of the oak, pine, or terebinth
always indicative of the Phallus. It is very
suggestive of a Roman redaction of the old
Hebraic writings, when we find that the " oil
of anointing " for phallic pillars, priests, kings,
etc., is called " semen," the word used by the
Romans and our medical men for the fructifying liquid of the male.

Job calls his god Al or El Shaddai thirty-
one times; and the *Encyclopædia Biblica*,
after criticising and rejecting all explanations
of the origin of El or Al, says :—" We are
no nearer a solution of the divine name
Saddai " (column 3326). It was by this name
" that God revealed himself to the patriarchs." It is no doubt allied to the Arabic
root Sadda, as the " firm, upright thing," as
all god-word roots indicate this, and Ail means
to be strong, as does Abir, a stone, Sur, a
pillar, and so on; but it is quite probable that
it has a similar meaning to Ba in Ba Al, that
is the god of the land or field, or the god of
the special locality in which one stands at the
moment. Shad is the fertile field, so Al Shaddai may be the god of the land or field; but,
on the other hand, it generally has a fertilising

meaning, and he promises Jacob offspring, and shad also means the breast or pap, and shadah that which pours out, so that El Shaddai may be exactly the same as the original meaning of Aquarius or Jupiter Pluvius—the micturator or fertiliser—because when he is mentioned it is always with the promise of " fruitful and multiply," and Jacob promises Joseph that Shaddai shall bless him " with the blessings of the paps and of the womb " (Genesis xlxix., 25).

That Al or El represented the " Rock that begat thee " is shown by 1st Samuel, ii., 2, telling us that " other than Tsur-Eli-im " (the rock or pillar gods) " there is no god " (El). See p. 35.

In the Old Testament Al or El (plural, Ale-im or Elohim) is translated as God, gods, spirits, oaks, tree stems, rams, goats, posts, upright firm or virile things, pestles, etc., so we see that the idea was truly phallic. Names occur, such as Zuriel, " the Rock is our God," and reversed Elizur," " El " (or God) " is the Rock " (that begat thee), clearly proving the phallic nature of Al or El. Besides Al, El, Il, or Ol were the names for the " upright pillar," the " Rock that begat thee," or god, all over Western Asia.

In the story of Michal, David's wife, we have a little tale in symbolic language to show the equivalence of the Hindu Phallus or Pul with the Hebrew El.

Phalti, to whom David's wife was given by Saul, is Hindu for Phallus god, " Ti " (Anglicé, Tee) being the word for " god " all over Eastern Asia, from India to China, as Al or El was in the West. In 1st Samuel xxv., 44, Michal's new husband is called Phalti— " the phallus god "—but in 2nd Samuel iii., 15, he is call Phaltiel—" the phallus god is El." This is repeated in other names declaring the equivalence of the phallus with Jehovah, as in Pelatiah, " the phallus god is Jehovah." Pala or Pela, the root, means in the Hebrew code the " miraculous thing " or " miracle worker " (Rod of God in Egypt), also " consecrated," " dedicated," as all phallic men and women, Kadeshim and Kadeshoth were,—any direct word for the phallus is always avoided in Hebrew, strong proof of a thorough and careful editing at a very late date, probably by Roman direction. We have even the Hindu god (or his day), Ithar or Ithra, adopted into the Hebrew as a man, Jether or Ithra (2nd Samuel xvii, 25, and 1st Kings ii., 5-32), names which illustrate the inversion by which Assur-El was converted into Israel—the Asher or phallus god. First the A becomes by rule I, which is the sign of a proper name, and the Assur, Asar, Assyr, or Asher—for it is spelt in all these ways—becomes Isra by inversion, like Ithra, and so we have Isra El, the phallus god, or " the phallus is god," which it was all over Asia, and still is in India, where the Lingam altar is the " Maha Deva " or " Great God." The change may have been more direct—from Ithra to Isra, as S and Th are everywhere interchangeable, even in our children's lisping (see p. 94).

This sun god Ithra is identical in its root form with Jethro, the prince or priest of Midian (as J is I in Hebrew), the man who taught Moses his religion. So we have the Indian sun god as the teacher of their entire religion to the Hebrews. Jethro is Yetro.

There also occur the names Pela-iah and Pelatiah, which are also written Phalatiah, " the phallus god is Jehovah," and Phelaiah, " the phallus is Iah," or Jehovah, as PLA and PLTh, from which they are derived, mean that which brings forth or creates, and the miracle working thing, like the Rod of God of Moses

—showing another proof of the phallic character of IAH, Jehovah, or IoVé.

We now come to the Hebrews' special god, called by tradition Jehovah, but written in Hebrew IhOh, IhUh, or IhVh, but never pronounced; in fact, it was declared to be unpronounceable, and it was death to attempt to pronounce it. The tradition is that its pronunciation was governed by the vowels in Adonai, that is " o " and " ai," which is exactly the same as " é." The prosthetic "A" in Adonai is not considered important, because it was almost invariably placed before or after all consonants by Arabian and allied nations. For instance, Ram, a name in Ruth as an ancestor of Jesus, is called Aram in the New Testament, and an Arab at this day cannot say " good;" he says " good ah," just as he says Allah for Al; or some foreigners of to-day cannot say " this shop, " this street;" they say " this (or dees) eshop," this estreet." So Jehovah is incorrect; it should have an "ai" termination, as in Adonai, and be Jehovai or Jehové. But no language, except English, uses the soft G or J in place of I, or the Hebrew Yod, so it ought to be Iehové. But I, e, and h are the same letters, and are used indiscriminately, as in Jerusalem, Ierusalem, Hierusalem, or Herusalem, which was probably the " Salem " or " Shallum," heaven of the " Heru " or the Horus of Egypt, one of the original models on which the Jesus of Palestine was built up. Another illustration may be given. We write Joshua, which should be Ioshua, while the Hebrews in giving the names of their prophetic books write Jehosuah or Iehosuah, showing that Ieh or Jeh is equivalent of I or J only, so that Jehovai is really Iové. The equivalence of H and E is seen in the Greek, where the capital Eta is our H, and we write the sun Helios instead of Elios or Elias, as the Hebrews wrote, and on whom the Jews said Jesus was calling when he cried Eli, Eli, Lama Sabachthani. The Jewish assertion was quite right, as Jesus was, as I shall show, a sun god, and was calling on his father, the Sun, Helios, or Elias. The Greeks used the termination " os " as the Romans used " us " to represent the substantive, so Eli of the Asiatic nations, including the Hebrews, became Elios, or, as we write it, Helios—the Sun. Thus the Greek Sun and Eli of the Old Testament were the same god, although the Hebrews took the phallic side of this Solo-phallic cult.

By eliminating the H's in IhOh the real

name of the Hebrew tribal god was IO,
or IV, or IU, or IΛ (Greek IL), which are all
the same, and are written in the Bible Jeho,
Javé, or Iavé, and Jehu in such names as Jehu,
son of Jeho-shaphat, and Jehu-di; and we see
the changes in Joshua, Yoshua, Jehoshua,
Jeshua, Oshea, and Hoshea or Hosea, which
are all the same name. Jehu and Jeho are IU
and IO.

The IO is falsely rendered JO in our Bible,
as our translators slavishly followed the German Luther, whose J is our I. So the holy
name is IO, and names such as Joel should be
Ioel, IO is El; Jehovah is Elohim; and
Jonathan should be Ionathan, or in English
pronunciation, Yonathan, Joseph, Yosef, etc.

The IO is a famous phallic combination,
and doubtless had its first ecclesiastical prefer-
ment in Persia, where it represented the male
and female, called dagger and ring (the sword
and sheath or Zakar and Nekebah of Genesis
i., 27), with which Yima was commanded to
create all living things, the ring being the
" door of life." The Greeks created a new
letter called the " phallic letter," Phi (pronounced by us as " Fie "), Φ, the double sex
sign, ring and dart, " rod and almond," of the
Bible, pillar and cleft, Lingam-yoni, and we so

express its hidden meaning in saying "Fie, for shame" to children. It occurs in the Bible in the name Joseph, IOseph, signifying male, female, and serpent, or sexual passion, the name being a condensed epitomé of the Garden of Eden story.

To return to the true pronunciation of Jehovah, tradition says that it was governed by the sound of the o and ai of Adonai and as the " o " is pronounced as in " no " and the " ai " is the same as ai or Latin é, the original of Jehovah was, as I have shown, Iové, pronounced yové or eeovay, probably the same as the ancient vocative of Jupiter when appealed to in prayer, when the nominative was Jovis or Jovos. On adopting the Aryan or Babylonian form Iupiter, the vocative Iové no doubt gradually disappeared. The Italians still have Giové, or Jové, and their Thursday is Giovedi (*Christianity*, p. 106).

The extreme similarity of the sound of the two names even when spelled Jehovah and Jové has always been considered dangerous to religions founded on the Hebrew god, and this similarity is never alluded to in any religious publications, nor in parsons' sermons. The modern biblical scholars have even attempted to remove this similarity by spelling the name

as Yahveh, or still worse, Yahweh, as both Y
and W are modern letters, when used as in
Yahweh. The Romans said Yové for Jove.

But our A is often pronounced O, as in
" all," " raw," " war," " water," etc., the
same sound as o in not, dog, for, etc., so
Yahveh is identical with Iové, as Y and I are
identical; and the final " h " is quite super-
fluous or only replaces the accent (as I have
written it in Iové) required in the English to
make the " e " vocal. Without the accent
the English reader would and does say Djoav,
for Yové. Not only were the names of the
Hebrew and Roman gods the same, but their
characters and functions were identical, although the position of the Levites caused them
to paint a more savage, jealous god than that
portrayed by the Roman priests, and for a very
good reason, as we shall see.

The Roman Jové was the sun, and the
Romans held that the sun died on the 20th
December, or equivalent date, lay 40 hours in
the shades (sheol) during the solstice or standing still of the sun, and rose from the grave
" on the third day," the morning of the 22nd
December, as the Divine Babe. But the
Romans seemingly did not like the idea of
their great Jove's death, so they made Jové

have a son, and this son died annually, and, on resurrection, was reabsorbed in the great god, or lived on in Heaven, thus creating many sons of Jove. The sun myth has always been associated as much as the phallus with the creation of life, because the ancients represented the sun in spring as the bridegroom, with the earth as the bride, and as causing the earth to be " fruitful " and to " multiply," Iové's greatest commandment. So this annual marriage of the earth with Jupiter or his son gave rise to the birth of numerous sons of Jove, or sons of god, and the offspring became heroes or " men of renown."

In Genesis vi. it tells us that " the sons of God saw that the daughters of men were fair and they took them wives of all which they chose," " and also after that when the sons of God came in unto the daughters of men, and they bare children to them, the same became mighty men which were of old, men of renown."

This is an exact parallel with the history of the Amours of Jove and his sons with earthly maidens; and the " Mighty men and men of renown " were such as Hercules, born of Jupiter and Alcmena, Castor and Pollux by his intercourse with Leda, Perseus by Danae, and so on.

The Jove of the Romans resembled the Jove of the Hebrews in being a god of thunder and lightning, but although both were "fear" gods, the Hebrew god was portrayed in terribly savage colours. Not only was his character jealous, but, as he tells us, his very name was " Jealous " with a capital J in Exodus xxxiv., 14, " For thou shalt worship no other god : for the Lord, whose name is Jealous, ' is a jealous God.' "

As the Levites had no " portion " in Israel and engaged in no occupation but that of priests, and were entirely dependent on the offerings of the people to Iové for their sustenance, any defection from the worship of Iové would leave them to starve. Besides, as they not only had wives, but also concubines (see Judges xix.), and engaged neither in war nor in work, each of which takes its toll of deaths, they would naturally increase more quickly than the general population, and so become ever more pressed for the means to live, hence chapter after chapter of curses against anyone forsaking Iové and worshipping other gods, and warnings given out with " thunderings, lightnings, thick smoke, fire, furnace, earthquakes (Exodus xix., 16), and in " Leviticus," the priest's book, there are all

sorts of death penalties and long lists of curses
for disobedience, and in Numbers it is death
to touch any holy things. Even to come near
the Tabernacle of the Lord was death, while
running all through Leviticus are threats for
going after *other* gods, and the Hebrew is
told to " forsake not the Levite as long as
thou livest upon the earth." In Deuteronomy xiii., 14, the Holy Inquisition is instituted on behalf of Jové, and the death penalty
freely promised for even " doing presumptu-
ously " or " for speaking a word not commanded." Deuteronomy xxxii. to xxxvii. is
occupied entirely with cursing, and throughout the Old Testament, like a refrain, goes on
the injunction against serving " other " gods,
and all because the Levites " have no inheritance in Israel," but eat only of the " offerings
of the Lord made with fire," " the Lord is
their inheritance," and the worship of Jové is
their sole means of subsistence, hence the
curses for desertion. Jové was evidently a
bogey or special engine of fear created by the
Levites to coerce other people into paying
their temple dues.

Sacredness is a great theme also, and when
Jové thundered and trumpeted on Sinai
before giving out the Commandments, the

mount became so holy that they are warned
(in Exodus xix., 12-13 : "Take heed to yourselves that ye go not up to the mount or touch
the border of it, whosoever toucheth the
mount shall be surely put to death. There
shall not an hand touch it, but he shall surely
be stoned or shot through, whether it be beast
or man it shall not live." What harm were
the poor beasts doing? Where was the visible
boundary of the mount to let one know
whether the hand was or was not touching it?
All this is purely the Mumbo-Jumbo rhodomontade of an ignorant but cunning priesthood, and still terrorises ignorant and superstitious people.

Besides these formal lists of cursings, there
are stories such as that of the slaughter of the
Midianites and the immoral use of the women-
children by Iové, repeated more weakly, as all
bad things in Holy Writ are, in Judges xxi.,
12, where they utterly destroy the males with
the women and children, and keep all the
" young women virgins that knoweth not the
lying with man " for the Benjamites, and one
can compose a general account of the character of this god from memory of a general
reading of the Bible, which shows him in the
following colours.   Jové of the Aleim is a

hating, jealous, capricious, tyrant, pleased and then displeased with what he has done, and repenting alike of good and evil intentions (Genesis i., 31; v., 6; viii., 21; Jonah iii., 19), and he allies himself with lying and deceitful spirits, and is unjust, ignorant, and spiteful enough as to visit the sins of the fathers on the children—a cruelty Christianity has accepted in her leading doctrine. This god requires bloody sacrifices of man and beast, especially innocent victims without blemish, the first-born of man and beast. He glories in evil as well as in good (Isaiah xlv. 7; Amos iii., 6), and the smell of burning flesh is called the " food of God."

The Ale-im and Jové are seen in the ravings of madmen and the discourses of prophets, and they are specially terrible, jealous, wrathful, and demoniacal. It is a fearful thing to fall into the hands of Jové, and " no one can look upon him and live," yet " seventy elders went up with Moses and Aaron, Nadab and Abihu," " and they saw the God of Israel," and did not die. He abhorred even his chosen people, and was like a " fire which burns in the lowest hell " : he likes " heaping mischief upon them," and " darting arrows at them," in " burning them with hunger, and devouring them with heat and bitter destruction." He urges them to commit innumerable cold-blooded murders of helpless captive women and children, and to use examined virgins for prostitution (Midianites), and he sits in heaven throwing stones at the Amorites (Joshua x., 11). He sends upon his chosen people " the teeth of beasts and the poison of serpents," " the sword without and the terror within shall destroy both the young man and the virgin, the suckling also, with the man of gray hairs " (Deuteronomy xxxii., 25).

Iové " whets a glittering sword and arrows which shall devour flesh and be drunk with the blood of the slain " (Deuteronomy xxxii., 41-42). He sets " snares " for his erring children " to provoke them to wrath," so that they may be " destroyed and consumed with fire and everlasting burnings." Yahweh was identical with Yachweh, the Phœnician sun god, whose priests demanded hecatombs of human burnt offerings, and the Israelites' altars were equally gorged with human blood. " Passing through " meant burning their sons and daughters alive, and this was practised as late as the reign of Josiah. Ahaz, King of Judah, burnt his children in the fire (2nd

Chronicles, xxviii., 3), and the children of
Judah built high places of Tophet in the valley
of Hinnom to burn their sons and daughters
(2nd Chronicles, xxxii., 6).   Child burning was
" an ordinance in Israel," *i.e.*, one of the
Commandments (Judges xi., 31-39).   So our
present commandments are the result of much
editing at later dates.

Even as late as the middle of the sixth century, B.C., Ezekiel charges the Israelites with
sacrificing their sons and daughters to be
devoured (Ezekiel xvi., 20-21, and xxiii.,
37-39), and with slaying their children to their
idols and coming red-handed to the sanctuary,
the courts of which were filled with the blood
of the innocents.   Kings Ahaz and Manasseh
set the example by burning their own sons to
Jehovah or Iové, and the whole popular and
national religion of the Hebrews was a gross
sensual and cruel idolatry with worship of
phallic pillars, and serpent poles; and we see,
from the burning alive of their innocent children as a sacrifice for their own sins, where
the Christian religion got the basic principle
on which it is founded.   The just must die for
the unjust.   All these local Ba-Als were identical, as we see the followers of Iové falling
back from Mesha's fort when it was in their

power, because he burnt his son on the battle-
ments (2nd Kings, iii., 27). They evidently
thought that such a powerful fetish would
effectually protect Mesha from their assaults.
Iové seems to have delighted in the most cruel
bloodshed and commanded the Kings to spare
neither age nor sex, and the matter of fact way
these orders were given showed the same
delight in slaughter, especially of women and
young children, as the Roman ladies showed
in witnessing the death of a gladiator. Of
course, these were simply the high priest's
orders, as we see in 1st Samuel, xv., where
Samuel instructs Saul, in the name of Iové, to
" smite Amelik, utterly destroy all that they
have, and spare them not; but slay both man
and woman, infant and suckling, ox and
sheep, camel and ass;" and because he took
Agag their king alive, and the Israelites saved
some of the best of the cattle in order to
sacrifice to Iové, Saul was condemned to lose
his kingdom. But Samuel demanded to bring
Agag to him. " And Agag came unto him
delicately, . . . and Agag said, ' Surely
the bitterness of death is past.' And Samuel
said, ' As thy sword hath made women childless [a curious charge for Jové to make, as
this was his constant occupation], so shall thy

mother be childless among women.'   And
Samuel hewed Agag in pieces before the Lord
in Gilgal." So Saul lost his kingdom for
showing mercy to one man, having really carried out all that was necessary of Jové's order.
But David, " a man after Iové's own heart,"
left neither man, woman, child, nor animal
alive, so Iové condemned for too little murder, never for too much. The phrase, " after
the Lord's own heart," applied to David does
not mean devout, but carries the meaning, a
man who will do as Iové (the priest) bids—
murder, thieve, etc.—popularly, " the man
for my money." A point may be noticed
here as an instance of what I have pointed out,
that every important statement in the Bible is
directly contradicted in some other passage.
Verse 29 says :—" Also the Strength [God] of
Israel will not lie nor repent, for he is not a
man that he should repent;" and verse 35 :—
" And the Lord repented him that he had
made Saul king over Israel;" or Jeremiah
xv., 6 :—" I am weary of repenting."

In that terrible slaughter of the Midianites
to get " women-children who had not known
man by lying with him," it may be calculated
that to get the thirty-two " women-children "
for Jové's use there were slaughtered about

half a million of men, women, and little children by the express command of this " god of love." If such things were openly stated and approved of in a novel for public reading it would certainly be suppressed; yet this is our great book of " moral teaching." This is a portrait of Iové as reputed by the Church to be drawn by *himself* for our *instruction*, and he has had apt pupils in the Junkers of Germany. Notice that no punishment ever follows these awful unprovoked crimes against inoffensive people; in fact, in another case the Danites, to get a land for settlement, send out spies, and they locate Laish, where the " people dwelt careless, quiet, and secure, and had no business with any man," and yet " a place where there is no want of anything that is in the earth " (Judges xviii). Surely an idyllic people who might have been left in peace. But no. First the Danites stole Micah's carved image, ephod, teraphim, and molten image, idols of divination no doubt to give them good fortune, or gods necessary to success in war, like the Field-Marshal's baton, which, as the " Rod of God," gave Moses victory over Amalek. All are phallic. They even commandeered Micah's priest, and " came unto Laish, unto a people that were at quiet and secure, and they smote them with the edge of the sword and burnt the city with fire." And there was no deliverer, " because it was far from Zidon and they had no business with any man." A sad end to an idyllic existence. Iové seems, by his repetition of the description of the good and inoffensive character of the people of Laish, and of their having no deliverer, to emphasise his devilish joy in this wholesale murder of innocent people; but I cannot see that any moral lesson is taught by this tale. It is on a par with the action of the Germans murdering in Belgium in order to intimidate France, when they had no cause of quarrel with the Belgians. Yet it is a fair sample of Old Testament teaching so admirably followed by the German Kaiser, and the Old Testament should be disavowed as a moral teacher by the Church.

Here we may glance at the idols which were common to the Hebrews for over a thousand years.

The carved images which the Danites stole from Micah are called in Hebrew Pesselim, often translated graven images; and in the singular Passil or Pessel, a masculine carved image, the point being that these Pesselim were works of art, not mere unhewn stones

set on end, such as Joshua set up, called
Mazzebah. Pesselim were carved Phalli.

These are related to the Pessah or phallic
dance, and also to the Pascha or Passover celebrations, which were everywhere intensely
phallic rejoicings at the return of the Bridegroom Sun. The Pesselim were no doubt
important adjuncts of such dances, probably
similar to the Ruber Porrectus, the ruddy one
which extends itself, which Horace tells us
was worn in phallic dances. (See *Christianity*,
pp. 40-41; *Encyclopædia Biblica*, col. 2976; or
my *Passover and Crucifixion*.)

The Pesselim was often coupled with
Masekah (*Encyclopædia Biblica*, col. 2148),
translated as molten images; but this is, as I
have said, a feminine word derived from the
root meaning to pour out libations—a pouring
out always connected with the Queen of
Heaven or with water, the female element,
and the subject of the most intensely phallic
celebration known to the Hebrews (see my
Queen of Heaven), so the Pesselim and
Masekah were the old Hindu combination—
the Lingam-yoni, or our Pyx and Monstrance,
or Pestle and Mortar, the double-sexed
symbol of eternal life.

The Ephod is Hebrew for " serpent

witness," and was no doubt the entire male organ, as the Rod of God was a serpent, Eph, and Ed, Od or Oduth were two stones. The Ephod was often described as a short cloak, embroidered with male insignia, in which David " danced."   Finally, the Teraphim or Tur Ophim, pillar serpents, or a serpent on a pole, Moses' brazen serpent, which we know were worshipped for generations by the Hebrews, were lingams, as the *Encyclopædia Biblica* tells us, or as Davidson's *Lexicon* says, " the penates " (the Roman male emblem). Fig. 26.

The Pesselim were specially carved, and we know that Phalli carved out of every sort of material, from wood and precious stones, up to gold, have been found in the ruins of all ancient Eastern cities, as deep as the fourth layer of debris forty feet under ancient Troy, so the Hebrews were only conforming to the worship of other contemporaneous nations.

The crass idolatry and low religious status of the Hebrews are well told by Hosea (iii., 4), who tells us that the Ephod, Teraphim, and Massebahs were " essential to the religious observances of his people; in their absence religion would cease " (*Encyclopædia Biblica*, column 4974).

In his ungovernable fury Iové sometimes

goes so far as to threaten to extirpate the human race and depopulate the earth by slaying all, " from one end of the earth even unto the other end of the earth, and to leave the dead bodies as dung on the ground, there being no one left to bury them " (Jeremiah xxv., 33).

In one very important aspect the Jewish hierarchy differs most materially from those of the nations around them. Although they use the word Elohim or Eli-im, gods, for the creative power in Genesis i., they never separate these gods, as did the Babylonians, Greeks, Egyptians, and the Romans, hence the text has much more of dignity, conveying better the feeling of one central power than do the religions of the much greater nations by whom they were surrounded. They had their band of gods, Elohim, but that band was never divided; they acted together. The nearest to this is the Babylonian gods, who also formed a united council, and delegated the power of a Gee Urge (George), or Earth Creator, to Marduk. Jové and Marduk play parallel rôles, and so do their Elohim; but the Hebrews treated their Elohim as though it was of one mind, and indeed as a unit, as they never name any individuals. Such ideas as were held by the Greeks, of different gods taking sides against one another, as in the Trojan war, seems to have been unthinkable to the Hebrews. Probably this monotheistic tone was introduced by a thorough modernising of the fragmentary Hebrew writings by the Romans in setting up the Greek and Hebrew " Testaments " by the aid of the Masoretes and " harmonisers," who, like Eusebius, produced a text which was " needful and apt."

The Hebrews, however, believed in the existence of many bands of Elohim—every tribe having its own, with a Ba-Al as chief god, so they had Iové fighting for themselves, while Milcom, Chemosh, or other god fought for the other tribes and against them, like the Germans to-day with their " good old German god." Another very advanced point in their view of a god-head was that their Iové had no father. He was, like Brahm, self-existent and eternal, whereas the Roman Jupiter and all the other nations' gods had a genealogy and a childhood like Jesus, whereas the Hebraic gods are simply in the story without beginning or end, as is so well said of Melchisedec in Hebrews vii.—" Without father, without mother, without descent, having neither beginning nor end of days, nor end of life "—a true god.

It was probably this unique view that determined the Romans to make the Hebrew scriptures the basis of the official religion of Rome. On the other hand, a view sometimes presented itself to me that this monotheism and the miraculous creation from a void or vacuum in Genesis i., as in Chinese, are the work of those late writers, like Jerome, who, under the Romans, edited the scriptures in the most drastic manner (see *Christianity*, pp. 199-200), and then declared what he had written to be the only true word of God. No one knows what went on before the official decision was given as to what writings constituted the official Bible, and we must not forget that it was the very human characters attributed to the Greek and Roman gods that caused their downfall; so the Romans probably instructed their " harmonisers " to remedy that.

It may be that the monotheistic colouring, in order to form a basis for more advanced religion, was given at a date as late as 200 to 400 A.D., and it might even have been introduced by the Masoretes under orders from Rome or Constantinople as late as 500 or

600 A.D. We have no MS. earlier than 1000 A.D. I mention this, as it is difficult to imagine how a people with such a high idea of their " Ancient of Days " could have symbolised him, as does Moses, with his Ark, with its " two stones," and its " rod of god "— purely phallic. The symbolical idea was borrowed in great part from Egypt, although their idea of the Heavenly Hierarchy was, as Dr. Cheyne now admits, that of " a small divine company [Elohim] under a supreme director " [Iové] (see *Encyclopædia Biblica*, cols. 3323-4).

The Hebrews had a well-defined sun god in Noah, whom they treated in their literature as a patriarch. But he is the Author of a new creation and new " generations " (see my *Seven Stories of Creation*), and he is represented as planting a vineyard.

All sun gods are vine, or wine gods, or Dei Vini gods of wine, our word divine ; and when Ham is said to have " uncovered " his father's nakedness when he was weak or drunken (the sun in winter), the Rabbis held that Ham really castrated him, and he dies soon after. The drunkenness and castration were symbolical of the sun's loss of fertilising power in winter, and all sun gods were made to die in that way.

When Moses, as a youth in Egypt, felt so strongly the degradation of his people in Egypt that he slew an Egyptian for beating a Hebrew, he fled into the land of Midian and obtained there the " rod of God," and latterly his " two stones," and put them in the female ark, as I have detailed in pp. 13 to 33. I have already shown on page 40 that Moses and Aaron were equal to Elohim and Jové; in fact, they were " gods to Pharoah." The name of Moses is said to be derived from Moseh " draw out," as he was " drawn out " of the waters, but drawn out has another meaning of extension, and the true root of Moses's name is Moseth or Mesech, the " th " or " ch " being rendered " s " in other languages, just as Benoth in Hebrew is Venus in Latin; and this Moseth word means " a rod," also " that which extends itself or swells up," and also " that which is anointed "—a true definition of the Phallus, with its rock representative, " the Rock that begat thee," and said to be connected with god's anointed, the Messiah. Moses is thus identified with the Rod of God he found in Midian.

It is the same thing as Matteh (root Nattah), the Rod of God, a rod which swells up and becomes a serpent. So Moses is the life bringer, the phallus, or a masculine god. Now, the word Aaron actually means the Ark or Ruach, so Aaron represented the female or left-hand cult, a cult always condemned by the Hebrew prophets, as their Jové was a very masculine god, and they had abandoned the Queen of Heaven and had no female in their Hierarchy, and no word for goddess.

There arose a great quarrel between Moses and Aaron. When Moses was absent getting the " stones " of Iové to put in his ark, Aaron made a golden calf, which is generally represented as a bull calf, and therefore representing the phallus. But the *Encyclopædia Biblica* tells us that the golden calf, eglel or Eglah, was a young cow (*Encyclopædia Biblica*, columns 711 and 1202), so Aaron was setting up female worship, as he had seen it widely followed in Egypt. The cow stood in Egypt for Isis, Queen of Heaven, and was called Hat-Hor, the house of the god, just as is our Virgin Mary so called by the Catholics at this day, and the worship of the female was always accompanied by promiscuous sexual intercourse (see my *Hebrew Tabernacle* and *Queen of Heaven*); and, as the highly orthodox Dr. Adam Clarke long ago told us, where the Israelites, whom Aaron had " made naked to their shame, rose up to play " round the golden calf, it meant public sexual intercourse, led off by the priests and temple women, a practice still common in tropical savage tribes (see also *Encyclopædia Biblica*, column 2066). Moses threw down and broke the stones of god, and commanded a great slaughter of those who had joined in female worship. This breaking the stones of god I believe to be symbolical of the " Benefit of Clergy," to indicate secretly that the clergy were outside the " law," and in no way bound by the ten commandments. So we see that Moses or Moseth and Aaron were the old, old symbol of life, the Lingam-yoni of to-day in India, the Rod and Almond of the Hebrews and Egyptians, the ring and dagger of Persia, the Ankh or handled " cross of life " of Egypt, or the Zakar and Nekebah of Genesis, and were, as the Bible tells us, true gods (see pp. 18, 19, and 40).

Passing over in the meantime the various Ba-Als exactly similar to their own Baal Iové, (as the *Encyclopædia Biblica* says, column 3327, Baal was used as a designation of the god of Israel), the next gods requiring our attention, according to the *Encyclopædia Biblica*, column 3320, are Abraham and Isaac, and, as

I shall show, Jacob and his son Joseph, who was made a god in Egypt.

The *Encyclopædia Biblica*, column 24, says that " Abram was not so much a historical personage as an ideal type of character. This theory alone will account for the dreamy, grand, and solemn impression which this patriarch makes upon us." (Elsewhere his name is classed as that of a deity.—Column 3320, footnote 2.) This description is exactly that applied to the first Great God of India, Bram or Brahm. So wrapt was he in contemplation that no creation could be made by him, so a second god was invented, Bramah, who was sufficiently detached and active as to create.

A similar change is made in the name of Abram by putting an H into the name and changing it from Abrm to Abrhm, the Ab, according to Hebrew dictionaries, meaning " ancestor, author, or maker," and so he is indicated to be a god. But another root, ABR, means the " strong " or " upright thing," so Abraham conforms to the universal derivation of all early gods, and is the phallic creator. Like Bram, Abram's name had to be changed before he created his heir Isaac.

I am inclined to think that he is really the

Hindu Brahm, as Jové's definitions of both names are the same, "Father of many nations," so the name looks like an attempt to import Bram and Brahma as Abram and Abraham into the Hebrew patriarchy. There is the same indistinctness in the differentiation of the Hindu Bram and Bramah. The placing of the prosthetic A before the Bram or Bramah to make Abraham or Abram is of no consequence, as it was the custom of all Syrian and Arabian tribes, as we see in the name Ram mentioned in Ruth as an ancestor of Jesus, but written Aram in other parts of the Bible. It even appears in Hindu and Greek. Pala becomes Apollo, Syria becomes Assyria, Thenen, Athené, and so on. So the Hebrew patriarch or god is probably the supreme god of India reduced to this demi-god of the Hebrews.

The god Isaac is simply the phallus. His name means he who " sports " or plays, and when Abimeleck looked out of the window he saw that Isaac was " sporting " with Rebekah, and so he knew that she was his wife, not his sister as he had stated. The same word is used where the children of Israel rose up to " play," when Aaron had made them naked round the golden calf, and the *Encyclopædia*

Biblica tells us that " rose up to play " was pairing off for sexual intercourse. So if we use Isaac, or in Hebrew Isachk, untranslated, as a proper name, we ought to use " play " also untranslated, and say Abimelek saw Isaac Isaacking Rebekah; or, if we translate, we have, he saw " the thing which sports (the phallus) sporting with Rebekah;" so Isaac is simply the symbol for the creative organ or a god so named. This is the same as the name of the King of Assyria, whom the Hebrews called " Pul," the phallus, or that of Assurbanipal, which means the " Phallus, son of the Phallus."

Isaac's son Jacob was identical with his father, as was Assur-bani-pal, as his name given as Jacob or Iakob, and said to be to " take by the heel," was really AKB or Akob, which is the word used for the phallus, euphemistically heel, in Genesis, " Thou shalt bruise his heel." The Greeks called it Iakos, finally Bacchus, and Iakos was a nude ithyphallic man inclosed in a phallic line or box, as in Fig. 27, with a sword or piercer like Paul on the great door of Amiens Cathedral, in his hand to indicate his nature —our Jack-i-the-Box who erects himself or springs up. Akab is a very common

Fig. 27.

From Forlong's Rivers of Life.

word in the East : we have the Gulf of Akab
bounding the land of Midian, and Akab or
Akub is a name frequently used in the Bible,
as was Assur or Asher in Babylonia, or as
" Linga " is still used from the Red Sea right
round to Singapore. Ahab the king, of whom
we read so much in the Old Testament, is
really Achab or Akab in Hebrew, and as he
is given the sacred A or Aleph in both halves
of his name, his is a god name or the phallus,
although it is given in dictionaries as " brother
of the father;" but it is truly phallic, as all

god-king names were. As to the I in Iacob,
the Hebrews put the I or yod before common
words to distinguish them when used as proper
names. But Jacob had another name which
occurs about nine hundred times in the Old
Testament—Israel. The story of how he came
to be called Israel seems to indicate a change
of worship from the left hand to the right
hand sect. He was at Luz the " Almond "
or Yoni, indicating female or left-hand worship, when Aleim, the gods, changed his name
to Isra-el, the upright or erect god, and he
erected a pillar or upright stone as a
phallus, and anointed it with oil for fertility
and call it Beth-El, the house of the male
god El, thus changing to the worship of the
male organ, the Asher or " Ishra El," his new
name, which was, however, only a change in
the roots used, the meaning was the same.
Assur, Asyr, and Asher are all names for the
phallus, called " groves " in the Old Testament, and Jacob or heel was simply a
synonym for the same thing, and he was
originally called Iacob-el, the heel (or Phallus)
god. The change from Asher to Ishra is a
common inversion, and is illustrated in 2nd
Samuel xvii., 25, where the name Jether is
rendered Ithra ; but in " Israel " the A of Asher

or Assur is by rule replaced by I, the prefix
for a proper name, hence Asher or Assar El
becomes Israel, the phallus god or pillar god
(Genesis xxxiii., 20).

Many stories in the Hebrew scriptures are
told in two forms—first, a seemingly plain tale,
such as the " revolt of Korah," but the names
used (absolutely artificial names) are a running
comment for the priest, telling him much not
comprehensible to the ordinary uninstructed
person. Such is the rebellion of Korah. We
are told in the *Encyclopædia Biblica* that
" each of the many names of persons in the
Bible must, of course, originally have had
some special meaning." The writer might
have gone further, and said many of them
were specially composed as an esoteric
explanation of the story the scribe was
writing; so that the story bears two meanings,
one for the people and another for the priest.
That a great number of these names were
phallic is evident, and as the Hebrew alphabet
and language were a sort of " zend " specially
created in which to write a scripture unreadable by the uninitiated, and composed of
really a small number of roots built up in a
very ingenious way, it was quite incapable of
expressing all the shades of meaning which

occur in any natural language. Hence the constant admission of obscurity throughout all works on the Bible. Professor Noldeke, for instance, says (*Encyclopædia Biblica*) :— " Very much still remains obscure, far more than was supposed by Genesius." " The Hebrew language is but imperfectly known." " Untrustworthy," " inconsistencies," and like words and phrases, are freely scattered through the greatest and most recent work on Biblical criticism. Take a few out of the hundreds in the *Encyclopædia Biblica* to show our most learned scholars opinions :— " Our knowledge of the Hebrew language is very imperfect " (column 3274). " Its meaning is often unintelligible " (column 3274). " An interpretation which is barely possible " (column 3274). " The grammatical form presents great difficulties " (column 3283). " Explanations do not agree—the question at issue is difficult " (column 3320). " A primitive name that had long since become unintelligible, far too abstract to be by any possibility correct " (column 3322). " There is just as little proof . . " (column 3325). " There is no less difference of opinion . . . " (column 3326). " We are no nearer a solution " (column 3326). " There is much difference of opinion " (column 3324). " It is not to be denied, nevertheless it seems precarious " (column 3323). " Difficult to explain " (column 3309). " The sense is obscure " (column 3290).

I cannot but think that if these learned Professors would really grasp the fact proved by the temple practices of the Hebrews that their religion was based on phallic worship of male and female emblems, and even of actual sexual relationship carried out at the religious festivals, as their famous compendium, the *Encyclopædia Biblica*, amply proves (see pp. 282-292, or my *Queen of Heaven and Her Debasement*), they would more easily arrive at a true meaning of the names employed.

But while these learned heads of religious colleges will admit any practices, " however vile," against the individual Hebrews, they are extremely unwilling to admit that their " Word of God " is written tacitly admitting that such practices were part of the ordained religion, as proved on pp. 69-70, 114-117, and were embodied in the holy names and commanded by the Hebrew God.

To illustrate this use of symbolical names there is this " Rebellion of Korah." detailed in Numbers xvi., of which I have never yet seen a true account.

We must remember that all nuns and religiously consecrated women were used for prostitution for the profit of the priests. Now, in all countries up till nearly the nineteenth century the priesthood have been charged with the utmost licentiousness, and with the early use of young communicants for their own enjoyment and the general body of the priesthood has ever been the most immoral part of the population, with, of course, a few very fine exceptions. Again and again the people have protested against the abuse of the confessional and the exercise by the priests and prelates, from bishops to neophites, of the very secret and privileged position the priest holds in his intercourse with young girls. The access of members of a congregation to the Kadeshas, and to join in the various feasts, such as that of Tabernacles (see my *Romance of the Hebrew Tabernacle*), in which promiscuous intercourse was the bait, was one of the great inducements to join the " congregation." But when the practices became more secret, and the privileges of the clergy, still echoed in " Benefit of Clergy," preserved for their own body, constant complaint was made

that the clergy " broke in " all the young girls
so that ordinary men could not obtain a virgin
wife. This breaking in, or sacrifice of virginity was described by Herodotus as a sacrifice
to Melitta, made in a semi-public manner by
all virgins. (See my *Christianity*, pp. 225-
227).

Now this revolt of Korah was a protest
against the special and privileged position
which all priests have in regard to young girls.
We see from the story of the Midianites how
Moses and the priests kept the virgins amongst
the captives for their enjoyment, killing all
other women, and this rebellion (it was no
rebellion, merely a protest) was an expression
of their opinion on this subject. It is told by
the priest in symbolical names so as to tell the
story his own way as a warning of the terrible
doom awaiting anyone attempting to curtail
the privileges of the priests, and he symbolically declares the protestants to be much
more immoral than Moses and the Levites, he
even narrates the details of their punishment
in a purely phallic way. He begins first with
the names of the rebels or protestors, and it
was in reading these names in Hebrew that
I recognised a very phallic passage. The very
first name, Korah, arrested my attention as in

studying old Missals and Books of Hours, of which I obtained some very beautiful specimens many years ago from Bernard Quaritch, I noticed the constant protrusion of a bald head or tousured head through the feminine side of the Egyptian Crux Ansata (see *Christianity*, pp. 75-76) used by our Church as a decoration on the pallium or phallic priest's cloak. The Crux Ansata is, as we know, the " rod and almond " joined and made into a handled cross (Fig. 28). The creative rays are made later into a mere ornament (Fig. 29), and finally into (Fig. 30) the handled cross. The priest here shown (Fig. 31) on a missal of 1509 has his tonsured head through the yoni on the cloak and hence makes the symbol of the double sexed god or that of eternal life.

Fig. 28.   Fig. 29.   Fig. 30.

The tonsured head represents the circumcised phallus.

Fig. 31.

The name Korah means a tonsured one— one " made bald," and also bareness or " nakedness " and we know the priests had to wear breeches to hide their " nakedness " when going up to the altar.

Now Bacchus, Adonis, Tammuz, and all sun gods were like Noah (see p. 127) put to death at the end of the year by mutilation (symbolised by circumcision) and were lamented by bitter weeping—" there sat women weeping for Tammuz " (Ezekiel viii. 14)—and lamented him in India as " Rosh Gheza," the mutilated prince.

But " Rosh Gheza " also signifies bald or shaved head, the tonsure, so it represented the circumcised phallus and probably took its rise in India, as Gotama Buddha, 540 years before Christ, insisted on its practice, and was himself called " shaved head."   So Korah was the circumcised phallus, and Korah was the lewd epithet which the children applied to Elisha when jeering him (2nd Kings ii., 23).   That Bald-head means the phallus is proved by the Greek word Phalakra, which means the end, point, or top of the Phallus.   But this is given in all dictionaries as " bald-head."

We often get a clear statement of obscure phallic symbolisms from the very honest and direct expressions used by the Greeks.   Korah was the son of Ishar, meaning one who presses out oil, our Pyx, again the phallus; and Ishar was son of Levi, the serpent or phallus, the thing that " joins itself to anyone," as given in any Hebrew dictionary.

The next man is Dathan, who holds the " balance " of justice which once was the phallus, as shown here by a drawing from Webster's Dictionary.   The Hebrew for balance is Peles, the phallus.   Then his brother Abiram.   Ram means the unicorn or erect " horn," also bull or buffalo, and is a purely

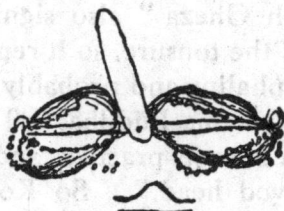

Fig. 32.

phallic word, so Abiram means the erect
father, or Dad of Egypt, or the Sur, " of the
rock that begat thee thou art unmindful," of
scripture, sons of Eliab. Eliab means " Eli,"
the erect thing or " pestle " is his " father."

Then another of the rebels is called " On,"
the " strong " or " vigorous one," a constant
euphonym for the phallus, son of Peleth (or
Palas), simply a Hebrew rendering of Pala or
Phallus, as he is called Palu or Phallu in other
texts, and his name also means the swift
messenger, the name of Mercury or Hermes,
the phallic god par excellence, son of Reuben,
whose name means the " miracle worker," or
what Moses called the Rod of God—again the
Phallus. Here we see the same nomenclature
as Assur-Bani-Pal, " Phallus son of the
Phallus," in Assyria. These men are all
entirely phallic, and they say, according to
the authorised version, that they are quite

as holy as Moses, Aaron, and the Levites, and they complain that these priests take too much upon them. But the Hebrew Bible does not say this. It says that all the congregation are Kadeshim, equally with the priests. Kadeshim is a word which any Hebrew dictionary will tell us means male prostitutes, the masculine form of Kadeshah, temple prostitutes, also translated Sodomites, but it was used here no doubt in referring to the privilege the priests claimed of having the first of the " women children " as Moses called them.

Having carried on the tale so phallically the priest had to make a phallic ending, and in telling that the earth swallowed Korah and his associates up he says that the " Adama," the female Adam, or female " red one," mother of all, the earth, opened her " mouth," or more accurately made a " cleft " under them —again phallic—and they were engulfed. Moses thus makes this thing,—the yoni, which they wanted to share with the priests,—the instrument of their punishment by swallowing them alive, and further we read that fourteen thousand seven hundred people who subsequently repeated Korah's protest, died of a sudden plague; so this plague was the

Ophalim, or woman-man disease called
" emerods on their secret parts "—syphilis,
and which I have treated very fully in *The
Queen of Heaven and her Debasement*. The
word for plague is made of two different
genders, masculine first, negep (Number's xvi.,
46), then feminine Magepah (Numbers xvi.,
48), derived from the same root, to make a
declaration that the disease was that of the two
sexes.   So syphilis was threatened for any
interference with Moses, Aaron, and the
Levites in their privileged relation with
women.

We see how careful and minute in their
symbolical imagery are these priests, when
they write symbolically, quite the contrary of
their constant contradictions when writing
" history." The inaccuracy of their history
arose from the fact that they had to adapt their
" history " to the phallic tales they were telling and their secret language was neither rich
nor flexible, and frequently had no roots to
accurately express ideas which had to be conveyed, so some roots are given a wide variety
of contrary meanings, in order to cover
new points.   That the whole tale is a fable to
illustrate a doctrine is clear, and we have a
modern example of the same kind of composi-

tion in Bunyan's *Pilgrim's Progress* with its Giant Despair, Slough of Despond, etc.

Another symbolically told story is that which details the birth of Joseph. The conception and birth of Joseph affords a good example of what I have elsewhere pointed out, that the Bible teaches the immoral doctrine that great men were born through murder and adultery, as David begat Solomon, or incest, or in some irregular way. It also illustrates the use of " Testes " (the Bible testimony or witness) in place of " phallus," as the reproductive power. We are told in Genesis xxx. that Reuben found mandrakes in the field. The *Encyclopædia Biblica*, col. 2928, on mandrakes says " the belief still survives in Palestine that the fruit when eaten ensures conception. A quite distinct tradition is that which rests the use of the plant as an aphrodasiac," or lust producer. All dictionaries say it is a cure for barrenness and an aphrodasiac. But the word in the Bible is, as pointed out in the *Encyclopædia Biblica*, Dudai or dodai, which is love, and it is also written Doddaim and M'dodai. One form of the word means " love " and another " baskets," although they all come from the same root, " dud to love," hence the basket

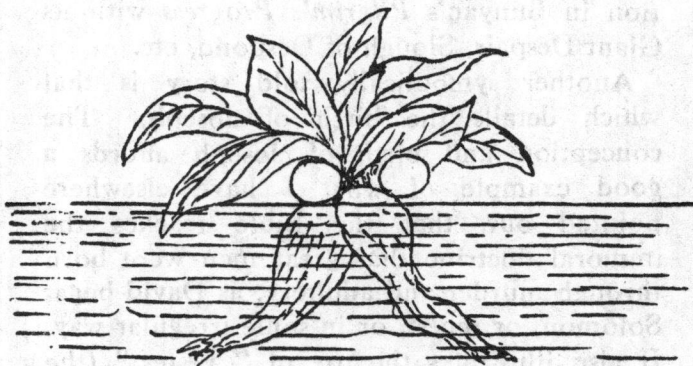

Fig. 33.

must have a " love " or phallic meaning.
Now Mandrakes would tell the tale the priest
wishes to tell quite well, as we see here in this
drawing of the actual Mandrake, it has two
stones and a human form, but these scribes
were very accurate in their symbolism, and
there is another plant, much used in ancient
drawings, of a " love " type.   It is most
significantly called "Archis or Arkis Masculi,"
or Orchis—Greek for testicle, our orchid—
the male Ark, and here is a rough drawing of
nature's imitation of the scrotum with its two
stones in their basket, vulgarly called, even
yet, the " dudai," and we remember the great
sacredness of the Ark which Moses made for

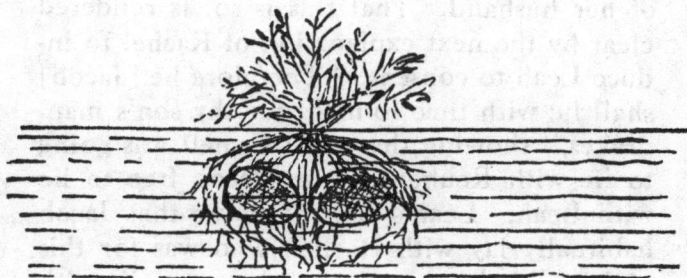

Fig. 34.

the two stones of the Iové. So far the symbolism used, but see pp. 258, 444. Reuben had these " dudai," as, of course, all males have, which ensured conception, and a sure cure for barrenness, and as Rachel was barren she demanded the use of Reuben's "dudai"—Reuben now being grown up—to remove her reproach of barrenness. The Bible words in Genesis xxx., 14, are—" Give me, I pray thee, of thy son's mandrakes " (love apples, Dudaim, or orchis Masculi), a fruit frequently shown as being presented by lovers to Venus in Pompeian and other ancient sculptures. The Bible makes Leah answer—" Is it a small matter that thou hast taken my husband? And wouldst thou take away my son's Dudai also?" so the son's dudai were the equivalent of her husband. That this is so, is rendered clear by the next explanation of Rachel to induce Leah to consent, "Therefore he [Jacob] shall lie with thee to-night for thy son's mandrakes," showing that she (Rachel) was going to lie with Reuben, setting Jacob free to lie with Leah. Leah's remark shows that Jacob habitually lay with Rachel, who was for this night making a special arrangement to lie with Reuben. This is the secret teaching of the Bible as to the conception of Joseph, who was, as we shall see, a god, and was finally to become symbolically the father of Jesus. After this incident Rachel says, "God hath taken away my reproach" (barrenness), and she called his name Joseph.

This story is corroborated in Genesis xix., 4, where Jacob on his deathbed says to Reuben, "thou wentest up to thy father's bed; then defiledst thou it," and then seems to mumble in his beard piteously, "he went up to my couch." So Reuben was the father of Joseph, yet by admitted parentage his brother. This position arises in the birth of all immaculately conceived saviours, where a member of the brotherhood of gods impregnates a virgin and so he is the father of the

child and yet that child is one of the brotherhood.

Reuben is represented in his character as
Joseph's father or protector when his brethren
wanted to slay Joseph through jealousy. He
seems to use every means to protect him
(Genesis xxxvii., 21-22), and when he thought
that his brethren had, during his absence slain
Joseph, he calls out in an agony of fear and
remorse, " The child is not, and I, whither
shall I go.?"

This is exactly parallel to the remorse and
fugitive position of Cain when he had slain
Abel, so that Reuben felt that he was as bad as
a murderer in failing to prevent the murder of
his own son, whom he calls the " child."

The above was the story as told for the
priests in the Bible, but was by no means intended for lay consumption, as it was veiled in
symbolism.   At Genesis xxxv., 22, it says,
" And it came to pass when Israel dwelt in
that land, that Reuben went and lay with
Bilhah, his father's concubine [Rachel's maid]
and Israel heard it." This with its condemnation in Genesis xlix., 4, is a common story of
adultery (and no child was born), and its discovery, and is told in plain language, while
the incestuous conception of Joseph is told in

phallic symbolism for the priest's private ear.

That Joseph is a god is told in the Old Testament in the plainest language and also by a wealth of symbolical language. In fact it is told the sacred seven times. First his name Ioseph. The letters IO are the same as IhOh, the most holy name of the Hebrew god, and are the dagger and ring of Persia, with which Yima created all life, or the Zakar and Nekebah of Genesis i., the rod and almond of the Hebrews, the Lingam-yoni of India, or the phallic letter of the Greeks—phi, Φ— in fact the universal creative or god sign of all nations. The second part of the word "seph" means serpent, so, in this word we have an epitome of the Eden story, man and woman urged on to the creative act by sexual passion—the serpent.

Again Jacob says his son Joseph is a fruitful "bough by a well." Here again we have a universal symbol for the two sexes used in all Eastern lands, or a god symbol—a tree and a well—symbolising Joseph's divine character. But in more enlightened nations all gods were sun-gods, and as the sun, after its birth at the winter solstice to save mankind from deadly grip of winter, has to pass through the worst part of the cold season—January and Febru-

ary—it seems to be passing through a dangerous time when its young life is threatened. So
constant is this myth in the lives of all gods,
Asiatic and European, that a phrase has been
coined to give expression to the fact, and they
are called " dangerous children."   Joseph
falls into line with all the others when his
brethren propose to slay him, but finally put
him in a pit to die of hunger and thirst; but of
course he is rescued, and he narrowly escapes
hanging in Egypt. So in his name, his father's
description of him and in his adventures he is
always portrayed as a god. Then he goes to
Egypt and after additional dangerous adventures there is taken into the favour of Pharaoh.
Now the Pharaohs were all gods, born in
immaculate conception by the converse of
their mother with the god, in fact they were
the originals of Jesus and his mother both in
story and as statues—the first statues of the
Virgin and Child in Italy being those of the
Isis and Horus brought from Egypt.   The
long lists of Egyptian kings written in such
beautiful hieroglyphics declare them to have
been sons of God, sons of Ra (the sun), Beneficent God, and so on, shown to be applicable even to females in an example Maspero
gives of the birth of a princess whose father

was Amen Ra the supreme god (see *Christianity*, p. 295). Nebuchadnezzar says in an inscription, " The god Bel himself created me, the god Marduk engendered me and deposited himself the germ of my life in the womb of my mother," so we see all kings were gods. In fact, even in Europe, kings and parsons are still divine—it may be gods of wine. The generic name of the Kings of Egypt is ample proof of this. The name in hieroglyphics is Para-O, or in the Bible Phara-Oh; but as Egyptians had the same sign for R and L, it was Pala-O or Phala-O, the lingam and yoni, which was used in a reversed form by the Hebrews in describing the woman-man disease syphilis, O-Phala, or plural O-Phalim, as seen also in the double-sexed Amazon-Queen Omphalé. So Pharaoh was a creative or double-sexed god. His crown was the Lingam-yoni altar of India made to fit the head (see my *Christianity*, p. 31).

We see the indifferent use of P and Ph and the double and single L in the phallic name in the Old Testament sometimes written Phallu or Palu and sometimes Phallu or Phalu. Phala-O is identical with IO, the first part of the name Joseph, and the name of the Hebrew god.

Now this Phallic Phalaoh made Joseph ruler over all his household and over all Egypt in exactly the same way as Jesus gave Peter power in the New Testament (see p. 248, Part II.). Pharaoh says that " the spirit of God is in Joseph " and he gave him his ring (Peter has also a ring) and put a gold chain about his neck and made everyone " bow the knee " to him, " and Pharaoh said unto Joseph I am Pharaoh and without thee shall no man lift up his hand or foot in all the land of Egypt " (Genesis xli., 44).   Similarly to Peter Jesus said, " And I will give unto thee the keys of the Kingdom of Heaven; and whatsoever thou shalt bind on earth shall be bound in heaven; and whatsoever thou shalt loose on earth shall be loosed in heaven " (Matthew xvi., 19).   So we see that Joseph and Simon Peter were both made into gods.   In the margin the Rabbis have given another interpretation of Joseph's name as " added " or the " additional."   This is no doubt one of the interpretations called in the *Encyclpædia Biblica* "an artless attempt " and of "no more scientific value than the etymologies of Plato " (col. 3271).   But if so, then the Rabbis took care to provide a sign from which it is derived, yasaph, from which comes Joseph, and this

root means " to increase," " to add to," so
Joseph is according to the Hebrew the additional one. It plays a very important part in
binding together the Old and New Testaments. Certainly the ingenuity of the
grammarians has been taxed to find a root for
Ioseph, and the name is referred to the root
ISPh, which means " added " or " additional," while it is really derived from no
root, but is the phallic god-name IO (the
Persian dagger and ring), written in Greek
or Roman character, meaning the creation
and continuance of life, or life eternal,
symbolised by male and female under the
influence of " Seph," the serpent of passion.
However, the derivation from " additional "
is extremely important, as Jacob describes his
son Joseph as a god (" Tree and well "—identical with IO), and Pharaoh made him an
additional god in Egypt, and finally, in
Genesis l., 19, Joseph tells his brethren " not
to fear," for he is " in the place of the gods."
Some editor, afraid to admit such an assertion on Joseph's part, gave the sentence an
interrogative form, saying " Fear not, because
am I in the place of God?" The word
" because," coupled with the interrogative
"am I," makes the sentence nonsense. and the

" am " is not in the text, which reads, " Fear not because I in the place of the gods," and so in the original it was probably not interrogative, but a plain formal statement, " Fear not because I am in the place of the Eli-im " (gods).   By adding a single letter H (the Hebrew hei) to the Hebrew word for " in place of," the positive statement is converted into an interrogative, and the sentence is rendered meaningless.   There are hundreds of similar passages in the Hebrew Bible, where the Rabbis, or perhaps Jerome (see *Christianity*, pp. 199-200), altered the sense by juggling with a letter or two, making all obscure, where he was afraid to change the " Word of God " by rewriting or deleting the sentence.

Lastly, the Egyptian form of Joseph's name was, as Dr. Sayce tells us, Osarseph. Osar is the true reading of the name of the Egyptian god, corrupted by the Greeks to Osiris. It is identical with Joseph, and is composed of O, the Yoni, the female organ, or " door of life," and Sar or Sur of the Old Testament, " the Rock that begat thee," the male organ, and Seph, the "serpent" or " passion," so as he was given a true god-name in Egypt, he was, in fact, the additional god, Pharaoh being the principal god. A god consists in little else than a name—change the name and you change the god.

So Joseph is declared to be a god by seven different methods of symbolic description. The seven repetitions is to emphasise its extreme importance; just as in the case of Christ being a "priest after the Order of Melchisedec," repeated seven times in Hebrews, an attempt to reconcile the Hebrews to the imposition of a Sun God (p. 332, Part II.). But he is not only a god, but the additional god. The reason why is not far to seek. In Matthew we find the last two names in the genealogy of Jesus are Jacob and Joseph, the same names as the last two phallic gods of Israel, and certainly in the New Testament Joseph was the additional god or father in the case of Jesus, the god-head or Holy Ghost being the first father, as we are told, " when Mary was espoused to Joseph before they came together, she was found to be with child by the Holy Ghost." We thus see how important is the interpretation of the Old Testament Joseph as an added or additional god, so often symbolised in Genesis. This points to a careful editing of the ancient Hebrew manuscripts in more recent times to give support to the double fatherhood of the Saviour, and indicates a very artful preparation of the ground work for the introduction of the New Testament story, the official religion of the Roman Empire—priestly composition, not history.

To clearly understand the terminology of many of the list of gods whom the Israelites worshipped at one time or another, we must glance at the Hebrew roots from which the names were formed.

The *Encyclopædia Biblica* says, column 3271 :—" Each of the many names of persons in the Bible must, of course, originally have had some special meaning;" and in column 2973, " From a critical consideration of the Old Testament references to these names, it would seem that they played a far more important part in the early traditional history of Israel than appears on the surface."

The first thing which strikes one is the very great proportion of these roots which bear a phallic meaning.   For instance, under the first letter of the alphabet, " Aleph," there are about 100 roots, and of these 40 bear a phallic significance.   In all languages the phallus is called the " Strong One," " Strength," or the " Bull."   Out of the 40

160 GODS OF HEBREW BIBLE

phallic roots, 12 means to be, or to become,
" strong." It is not only the word " strong "
which indicates the phallic nature of the
words, but " strong " is accompanied by
other interpretations, such as " tree stem,"
" creator," procreator," " idol," " to be
fleet " [Hermes], " to cover," " fruitfulness,"
" fertility," " the happy one," " images,"
"grove," which indicate the truly phallic
nature of the roots. The roots were evidently
invented to express the ideas of a phallic
religion. Then to " desire " or to lust has
two roots in this small part of the language.
Roots meaning to have an upward tendency,
to stretch out, expand, extend, to sprout, to
spring into blossom, to have a rising tendency,
said of a rod or staff (often the same root),
are especially phallic. " P " words are nearly
all phallic.

We remember Hermes or Mercury is the
" fleet one," and the cause of fertility. Some
roots mean all these things, " to be
strong," "vigorous," "active," " fleet," and
" strength." All upright or straight things
are phallic, and we have asher, the happy one,
the straight one, upright, lucky, fortune,
grove, image, idol, shrine, and tree stem—all
phallic allegories—and asher is, as I have

shown (p. 41-42), the phallus. Asher or Assur is the same as Sur, " the Rock that begat thee." The story of Eden made the Hebrews regard woman as the author of all evil, and the Bible tells stories of terrible sexual diseases through men's sexual contact with Peor or woman (Numbers xxv., 9-18), so one root, ANS, means " incurable," " mortal ' (syphilis), " man woman," " concubine," " widow," " wife," and " one another " or "together," pointing to all conditions of women being dangerous, and " one another " or " together " points to sexual intercourse of man and woman as the cause of the incurable disease. The word " know " or " knowledge " is generally phallic in the Bible, the " tree of knowledge," " the phallus," and " Adam knew his wife and she conceived and bore Cain," and so on; and we have Abida (Genesis xxv., 4), " father of knowledge or knowing," a son of Midian, Midian being, of course, " in the midst," where the tree of knowledge or of life is situated in man.

Lastly, we have the first of the list of subsidiary gods, Abir, meaning to be strong, or strong ones, or bulls, or chief of the shepherds. The strong one or bull we understand, but "chief of the shepherds " puzzles one, till we

find that this god Abir of Jacob is the source
of the "Shepherd, the stone of Israel"
(Genesis xlix., 24), and we must not forget
that Jesus is the "good shepherd," and the
"chief stone of the corner," again coupling
up the Old Testament names with the New
Testament allegories.

It would take several volumes to go fully
into the nature and histories and etymologic
derivation of all the gods of the Hebrews in
the Old Testament, so I can in this sketch
only touch lightly on the remaining unimpor-
tant ones, as we have much to study in the
New Testament gods.

We have next Adonis or Adonai translated,
as in the case of Iové, as "Lord," a name
without personality, which can be applied to
any of the thousands of gods of China, India,
Babylon, Egypt, Greece, Rome, or Europe.
They were all "Lords" of something, if it
were only of war or hell. There is little to
chose between these, as has been most brutally
demonstrated by the Kaiser. We have even
our noble House of Lords, for which its worshippers are constantly thanking God. This
word was originally plural, like Elohim,
Adoni as in Adoni-zedek (Joshua x., 1), which
in early times meant the "Lords of the up-

right or erected thing," or better, the spirits
of the upright thing, the Lords being a band
of gods or spirits like the Elohim, showing
that all the gods were symbolised by the
Phallus.   The term "upright" gained a
moral meaning, and so it became the upright
or righteous lords or gods, and finally the
singular form lord of righteousness.   But
Adonai originally means to judge, plead, or
to punish, and it was connected with a column,
pillar, or phallus, on which oaths were sworn.
Now the Scales which blind Justice holds in
her hands were originally the triple organ of
man, as shown by a drawing on page 144, out
of any dictionary, and in Egypt the phallus
sometimes meant a just character, one who
was strong enough to stand erect and do
justice without fear; and "balance" is in
Hebrew Palas or Peles, the Pala or Phallus;
so again we see the original of Adonai was
phallic.

The phallic nature of the balance is shown
in Fig. 35, a symbolical representation in
bronze from the Capitol.

Another god-name which at first sight seems
to be free from phallic significance is the great
Egyptian god, the Amen, which Christians
apostrophise in their prayers; as this god was,

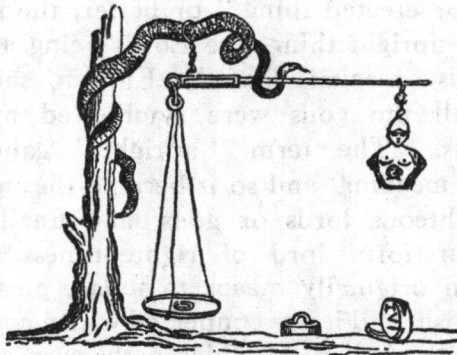

Fig. 35.

to the Egyptians, the great hidden one, who created, directed, and upheld the universe. The sun Ra was a great god, but the Egyptians saw that the sun moved according to law and had no " free-will," so they postulated Amen as the greatest god of all, but entirely hidden from man.   Amen-ti is Amen the God (p. 93).

The Hebrews, in adopting it, brought it down to the phallic level, and Christians have further disguised it by calling it the " god of truth."   But Amen means the firm or strong thing, the right hand or masculine one, the creator, and finally the covenant, which we know was the circumcised phallus kept in the ark, so we see it is as phallic as are all the other Hebrew gods (see p. 52).

Baal was a god common to all Semitic tribes. Ba is a root word for the erect phallus, as in Bam, Bom, Bemoth, Bamoth, Behemoth, etc., making with Al, Ba Al, " the phallus god," while Berith is the ring mark of circumcision, a feminine symbol making the dagger and ring, piercer and womb symbol of creation.

We have in the Behemoth or Bamath, an ancient god of the Hebrews (probably while they were still in Arabia), who was chief of the ways of Al, that is, he represented the creative power—an early god. This is treated fully in my *Seven Stories of Creation*. This is also written Bamah, translated high place or hill top. But they could not place a hill top " in every street " (Ezekiel xvi., 24), nor could hills or rocks be " burned and stamped into powder " (2nd Kings xxiii., 5). The Bamah was undoubtedly a wooden, stone, or clay phallus. Burton draws a modern picture of Jerusalem when he tells us " in Dahomey it is uncomfortably prominent, every street from Wydah to the capital is adorned with the symbol, huge Phalli." Then we have Jonah, who is simply Yoni or Iona, the Dove, and feminine, still used in the East as the symbolic name of the female organ, and hence meaning the same as Ruach or Uma, words widely diffused over the ancient East as the mother of all, or the womb of Time. But, as usual, the Hebrew Nabis would have nothing feminine in their religion, and they made the universal mother into a Hebrew prophet, and used this feminine noun in a masculine sense, but as he was the prototype of Jesus—being a sun god three days and three nights in the sea, or the grave or hell, " out of the belly of Hell cried I "—so he was truly a Hebrew god, the prototype of Jesus. He was son of Amitai, from the same root as Matteh, the " rod of god " of Moses, so he was son of the Phallus (see pp. 79-80).

There remains a number of foreign gods whom the Israelites worshipped, such as Astoreth, whose names, being quite foreign, have no definite Israelitish meaning; that is, although in dictionaries they are located under the root sign of their consonants, they have no philological connection with that root, and no symbolic meaning. Astoreth is, of course, Astarte, Venus, the goddess of love and patroness of the feast of tabernacles, Succoth Benoth (Venus), when promiscuous intercourse was not only allowed, but commanded, and its practice meritorious. As the B and the Th of Benoth have no dot or dogesh they are soft, so the word is really Venos, and as O and U are both Vav, Benoth may be actually written " Venus," as in Latin.

Then there is Chemosh or Kemos, the Iové of the Moabites, whose temple was " in the Hill that is before Jerusalem," and we have Milcom and Molech of the Ammonites, and even Milcah, daughter of Haran (of the High Place or phallic shrine), names given in the dictionaries as identical with Malak or Melchi, usually held to be " King " or " Queen," as Melchizedek was King of Righteousness or Upright King, or King of the Upright Thing, so these " idols " were merely king-god worship. I might extend the list to very wide limits, as the Israelites used god-names both of their own worship and of that of foreigners, very freely as personal names in their purely imaginary genealogies.   For instance, we have such names as Palu and Phalu also spelt Pallu and Phallu, just as the Hindu word Pala has one " l " and uses the hard " p," while the Greek corruption Phallos, or Latin Phallus, have two " l's," and use the Φ or Ph form of " P." These words, of course, are the phallus, the god symbol most widely worshipped of any in the world. The Hebrews also gave it the form Salu, to indicate the

" left hand " or feminine form of Phallic worship, and these names are symbolical indications of the real but hidden meaning of Saul and Paul (pp. 264-266).

That Zur or Sur was as much a god as Al or El or Iah, Elohim, or Jehovah, the God and Lord of our English Bible, is shown by the parallelism of their use in names. The *Encyclopædia Biblica*, column 3281 (note), says Sur or Zur is " a genuine divine name." Peda means " redeems." Then we have Pedah-el, Pedah-iah, and Pedah-zur, all meaning the same, " God redeems ;" *Encyclopædia Biblica*, 3281, using Sur as the equal of our God and Lord. The *Encyclopædia Biblica* says that Zur, Rock, is a synonym for God (column 5442). We have Beth-el and Beth-zur (Joshua xv., 58), both meaning " house of god " (or of the phallus), and names like Pedah-zur, Eli-zur, Zur-iel, Zur-shadai, meaning " the rock redeems," " God is a rock," " the Rock is our god," " the rock is the fructifier," showing that Zur the Rock was the equivalent of all the other gods (*Encyclopædia Biblica*, 5444). In fact, Zur was the one constant god of the Hebrews, right down to Peter and Paul (see pp. 245-259 *et seq.*). Others might change, but they were all Zurs or stone Phalli; in fact, the phallus was their god. This is the rock illustrated on p. 35, called in Dorsetshire the Christ-in-hand (there are many " Christs-in-hand " in England), the phrase meaning " the Christ as represented in the hand "—hand being a euphemism for phallus, as yad, its Hebrew form, meant rod and became our measuring rod or yard.

The intimate connection between all the words used to indicate the Hebrew Phallic god is shown in other directions. For instance, the serpent in Eden is Nachash, but changing one vowel, as Nechash, it also means brass or brazen. Now, Nechash and Bosheth mean the same thing, the organ of shame, or " shameful," while " brazen " is up till this day freely used in the same sense. But when we come to the brazen serpent or the shameless or shameful phallus we find the word is Necheshtan or Nechesthan. Here the serpent has an entirely different name, Tan or Than, as in Levi-a-Than, or Luithan, the great monster serpent of Job, the Edenic Nachash being employed in this case for brazen. "Than" is a widely used word for serpent, and we have it in Greek, Thenen, serpent, and in the Greek name for wisdom, " Pallas Athéne " or "the phallus, the serpent," usually portrayed as a female figure endowed with all the male attributes, the spear, the helmet, and so on, and sometimes with a snake on her shield; the snake and shield being the male phallus and female belly, or O, sign of woman, giving again the Lingam-yoni or Omphallic creative pair. Another example of the phallic character of the god-names is given in Genesis xxxi., 42, where Jacob says "except the God" (Alleh) " of my father, the God of Abraham, and the Fear " (Pahad—equivalent to a god) " of Isaac, had been with me, surely thou hadst sent me away now empty. God (Elohim the gods) hath seen my affliction," etc. We see here the varied form of the word translated God, and the identity of Pahad and Alleh.

But the word Pahad means thigh, on which at that time oaths were made, and by " thigh " was meant the reproductive organs of man, as Abraham said to his servant, " Put, I pray thee, thy hand under my thigh," and so makes him swear an oath. So the " thigh " of Isaac was equal to Aleh, or the upright thing, or stones, or God of Abraham. Pahad is translated " stones " in Job xl., 17.

The Arabs,—direct descendants of the Abrahamic tribes,—still swear in this form, as do the Hindoos on the Testes or " Testimony " of Siva's bull Nanda (Fig. 5, p. 43), or we on our " Testament," and this constitutes their most sacred oath. So we see that the supposed spirituality of the original Hebrew Gods was non-existent,—the more sublimated ideas having been introduced by commentators at a very late date, whose marginal notes also slipped into the text. (See 141-151, my *Christianity*, and the *Encyclopædia Biblica* throughout.)

The Hebrew priests adopted creative gods modelled on the physical facts relating to creation or reproduction of life as known to them in nature, and we shall see in Part II. that the Romans modelled the New Testament Gods on the same basis, with the sun as supreme ruler,—a cult which had long been dominant in leading nations all over the world.

END OF PART I.

THE GODS OF THE HEBREW BIBLE

PART II

NEW TESTAMENT GODS

CHAPTER I

GROWTH OF THE SUN GOD IDEA

When we pass from the Old Testament to the New Testament we find an entirely different world.

The terrible Iové has entirely disappeared with his huge retinue of names of men dedicated to him with their Iah termination (see Part I., p. 58), Jeremiah, Obadiah, and so on; or with their IO, or in its more complicated form Jeho, where the Jeh is equivalent to our I or Y. For instance, we have IO-nathan, which we call Jonathan, instead of Yonathan; and this is spelt Jehonathan, as in Jehonadab or Jehosaphat, where all J's, I's, and Jeh's should be pronounced as Y. IO was even called Yahu, our term to this day for a blatant, rude, bloodthirsty, angry individual, as Iové was. In the New Testament all this is changed, and a mild, meek creature, son of IO, but founded on the Hindu Buddhas, replaces the implacable

IO, Iové or Jehovah, and an entirely new set of names is introduced. The father god is now called Kurios, the sun, but we may remember that in Exodus xxiv., 10-17, Iové or IhOh was symbolically the sun (see this volume, pp. 31-32). But the old savage god must be abandoned, so a complete change of names was required. This shows the artificial character of the New Testament. It is utterly unthinkable that the universally used names founded on the god of the nation could in a century or two completely disappear, and their places be taken by a totally different class of name. The *Encyclopædia Biblica*, col. 3271, tells us that "each of the many names of persons in the Bible must, of course, originally have had some special meaning." As the Rabbis wished to tell a story in symbolic language, they had perforce to invent names which would convey the interpretation they desired, and the *Encyclopædia Biblica* often remarks that names like Abraham, Isaac, or Jacob are quite unknown until suddenly coined by the writer of the scripture. The Old Testament was written round Iové, a phallic god, so they had to choose phallic names, but as the New Testament was written to introduce a religion based on the Saviour idea derived from the Sun-

Saviour cult, which was the basis of most
Asiatic religions and even of European druidical myth, a new set of god-names was
required.

But the old phallic cult could not be thrown
off, because it was the religion of the people,
so it was included, and the Old Testament
symbolism and names retained, although they
were sometimes expressed in their Greek
equivalents. Although the atmosphere is entirely changed, we shall find that the book is
only a new chapter added to the tale of the
Hebrew gods, as the old heroes still play the
principal parts under Greek or Græco-Indian
names. The New Testament miracle play is
still played by the same Old Testament gods,
so I include its gods under the general title of
the " Gods of the Hebrew Bible."

The incidents and tone of the New Testament are moulded on the lives of the Hindu
Christna and Siddartha the Buddhas who were
sun gods : the miraculous tales from Christna,
and the gentle teaching from Siddartha, and
nearly every word of the Gospel is copied
directly from the lives of these Buddhas and
from Hindu writings, such as Manu and the
Maha Bharata, of course taking only the best
parts of these complex books.

The sun gods of Northern nations were nearly always of a benign and gentle character, as the sun is the great friend of man, ripening his food and wine, and bringing man every blessing. The sun's weak condition in winter was always mourned as the death of a benevolent god, as we see the Israelitish women copying the Syrians, and weeping for Tammuz, who was killed by being wounded in the reproductive organ by the tusk of the boar of Winter, or by the thorn of Winter, as the sun's fructifying power was lost in Winter. The Egyptian women tore their hair and wept similarly for Osiris (see p. 281, this volume). When the sun was re-born at Christmas after the winter solstice, or after lying in the grave for forty hours, he was acclaimed joyously as the " Saviour," " the Light of the world," as without his resurrection the universal death of winter would reign.

So the main theme in the Gospels is the death and resurrection of the sun to the salvation of mankind, exactly as played by the high priest in the Tabernacle (see my *Romance of the Hebrew Tabernacle*). But the tone of the Gospels is absolutely opposed to that of the Old Testament. while it is exactly the same as that of the life and teaching of Siddartha, the prince who renounced a throne to teach goodness and humility in India, and who was, after death, recognised as the embodiment of the Great God. All the great nations, China, India, Babylonia, Assyria, Egypt, Greece, and Rome, reached the higher plane of natural religion, and held the sun to be the benevolent god, the bringer of all blessings, and they mourned the death of the sun at the Winter stolstice as the death of man's greatest benefactor, but rejoiced that he was born again, after lying in the grave or sheol over the solstitial day. His early years, the months of January and February, were full of dangers, as he was still too feeble to dispel the cold and darkness of winter.   When, however, on the 22nd of March he crossed over the equator and entered the Northern Hemisphere, he was hailed as having accomplished the act which was the salvation of mankind. These ideas were quite true as physical facts, because, if the sun did not cross over, universal death would reign in the Northern Hemisphere.

These were the ideas held by the more intelligent nations, and their priests were often good practical astronomers.   The sun was called the Saviour, and the Saviour idea is generally coupled with sacrifice, so the legend that the Saviour died to save the people from the penalties for their sins was nearly universal. Astronomically, the death of the Sun Saviour took place at the same season as his re-birth, and that was at the Winter stolstice, while the salvation of man from the death of winter was not accomplished till the Spring equinox, when the sun was supposed to be the Bridegroom of the Earth, as is dimly told in Genesis vi. (Part I., pp. 110-111).

The death was therefore not directly coupled with salvation by the astronomical myth, and several nations, long before Christianity, made the joyous passing over, crossing over, or crossification into a painful crucifixion, and thus joined his death at the equinox to his rôle as Saviour by bringing in the Summer or Paradise part of the year to the salvation of mankind. His death and re-birth at Christmas were, therefore, separated, the birth remaining at the Winter Solstice and the death passing over to the Spring Equinox, when it was coupled with a revival or resurrection. The joyous Spring marriage time was thus converted into a time of gloom, our Easter. The weeping, at the

Winter Solstice, for the death of Tammuz, the Syrian Christ, was thus abandoned, and we only keep the rejoicing for the young sun's birth at Christmas, when we rejoice by bearing in to the feast-table the flaming ball of the sun as our plum pudding. The Hebrews held their great phallic Hag or Pessah dance in the joyous feast of spring, as did all other nations, and as the Hindus still do, executing phallic dances with ithyphallic members, called by Horace " Ruber Porrectus," the Red erected one, and by the Hebrews, " Pesselim," Phalli.

But the Hebrews were a very ignorant, savage nation, and they held fast to the purely phallic religion. We find in the Old Testament two attempts to introduce the higher solar religion. The first was the miracle play, for which the Tabernacle was supposed to have been constructed—a miracle play treating of the death and resurrection of the Sun.

As I have described this in my work on Christianity, and more fully in a special volume on *The Romance of the Hebrew Tabernacle*, I will deal here only with the essential points. All scholars are agreed that this Tabernacle was a myth, and never was, and never could have been, constructed, as the minute descriptions given are really solemn nonsense, and the structure could never stand if its erection were attempted. This is dealt with fully in the *Encyclopædia Biblica*, and the famous Tabernacle is dismissed as entirely the work of some scribe's imagination. But a purely negative criticism is unsatisfying. One is entitled to say, here is an elaborate description using clearly specified and peculiar materials of symbolical significance, frequently repeated, and therefore considered very important, and to ask " for what purpose was this elaborate description written?" The answer is : it was the basis of a proposed miracle play portraying the story told by many Greek medals, viz. : the annual death of the old sun, which from the position of Greece and Palestine was thought by the inhabitants of these lands to be culminated by the sun's descent into the sea, and thence to Sheol; and its re-birth from the dolphin (delphys—womb), sometimes called Ked or in the Old Testament the whale, or great fish, of the Jonah myth. The Tabernacle was described as made of rich materials and gold and silver in masses unobtainable even in great kingdoms, and impossible to a small tribe of leprous slaves in a desert, where such things were unknown. The truth about the famous Exodus was that the Hebrew slaves had sunk to such a woeful condition that they were the cause of pestilential diseases, which were spreading all over Egypt, so they were hastily expelled—" thrust out " is the phrase used in the Old Testament.

All the great historians of ancient times agree in this—Manetho, historian of Egypt; Lysimachus, Diodorus Siculus, Tacitus, and Herodotus, the father of history—all agree in stating the true cause of the Exodus.   The Hebrew scribes take their revenge for this cruel expulsion into a desert without food by writing the " medicine-man " account of the plagues and the final overwhelming of the Egyptians by the help of the phallus of Iové (see pp. 53-57, Pt. I.).   Then, when starving in the desert, they were supposed by the scribes to have erected their fabulously rich Beth-El, house of God, tabernacle of Iové, " little tavern of IO," in which they kept the two stones and Rod of God, the symbols of their covenant with Iové, which covenant was to be carved on every man's body by circumcision. The circumcised phallus and two stones of Iové in the ark were their most sacred arcanum, to touch which, or even to look into it, or to go near it, was punishable by death.

This ark, with its inclosed phallus, are the originals of our Monstrance and Pyx, to touch or look into which was punishable with death by being hanged, drawn, and quartered, according to the laws of England at the time of Richard II., about 1400. The imaginary Tabernacle was used as a house for their double-sexed symbol of Iové, and at the same time some priest with a knowledge of the universal myth of the Sun's birth and death made an attempt to engraft Sun-worship upon the Hebrew religion. I have detailed the ritual so fully in other works (*Christianity* and *The Romance of the Hebrew Tabernacle*) that I can merely summarise it here. The Womb of Ked or the Dolphin form of Tabernacle, was specially characterised by coverings emblematical of Sun worship and the death and re-birth of the Sun in this fashion. The inner covering was purely astronomical, being designed with the signs of the Zodiac, and over that were dolphins' skins (delphys— womb), and over that rams' skins dyed red to imitate flesh, the "flesh of her nakedness." Over that was some kind of fabric made of goats' hair, "long and silky." The goat and the ram were both specially phallic animals, the ram having the same name as the God.

At the East end of the Tabernacle, the end of
the Holy of Holies, these fabrics hung down
to the ground, but were looped up into a
cleft, representing the vulva of Ked or Virgin
of Israel, out of which the Sun was re-born.
The play showed the High Priest clothed in
all the life symbols, bells and pomegranates—
bells, the double-sexed symbols of god, and
the only symbol with a " voice;" and pomegranates, symbols of the fertile womb. He
entered by the West end at sunset on the 20th
December, or equivalent date, and put on
grave clothes and showed himself to the
people as the dead sun. He then lay forty
hours in " sheol," the dark Holy of Holies,
till the morning of the 22nd, when he thrust
himself through the dolphin skin-lined cleft,
and with great rejoicing was " born again."
This being born again was a universal idea,
and practised all over the world. In Eastern
countries rich princes had cows made of their
own weight of gold, with appertures large
enough to crawl through, and they were thus
re-born. In every country, split trees, holes
through rocks, and all such natural vulvæ,
have always been used for the " born again "
ceremony, especially to cure disease or restore
a chronically ailing or weak person to health.

In the Old Testament and Josephus all this is detailed, save the re-birth, which was perhaps never written, or considered too near Sabaenism and cut out, so another scribe wrote the Jonah story where Jonah is re-born out of the whale's mouth, and he is held up in the New Testament as the prototype of Jesus. Some later scribe put this allegorical miracle play into the usual Hebrew form of telling it of one of the Hebrew prophets, and he uses or portrays a live great fish or ked, and completes the tale by making the swallowed prophet issue from the fish's mouth after the astronomical forty hours, exactly identical with the tale of many Eastern Sun-gods. So we find Jonah or Iona (the Eastern masculine of Ioni), son of Amittai, put forward to act this miracle play. Jonah clearly means the male reproductive organ, and Amittai is the same as Matteh, Moses's rod of God, the firm or upright thing or phallus; so Jonah has a pedigree like Assur-bani-pal, " The Phallus, son of the Phallus." This Bacchus-like Hebrew prophet falls into the sea, is swallowed by a great fish or dolphin, the womb of creation, and after " three days and three nights," really forty hours, is re-born or suffers resurrection to the salvation of the people Nineveh

—a local salvation, as was that of Jesus at first, simply a salvation of Jerusalem or the Jews, afterwards declared world-wide by writers creating a religion for the Romans under the phallic name of Paul.

Like Jesus, " from the belly of Hell cried I," and in the New Testament the question is asked, " Can a man enter a second time into his mother's womb and be born?" "And Jesus said, Unless a man be born of water, as was Jonah " (John iii., 4-5). Jonah is therefore used as the Hebrew method of illustrating the universal Sun myth, and as the archetype of the later official Roman Sungod called Hesus Christos, and who also lay in Hell for " three days and three nights," really forty hours, like the High Priest in the Holy of Holies in the Tabernacle miracle play. So the complete story was told in the Old Testament, and although not told consecutively, and possibly adopted from two different sources, and coloured according to Hebrew idea, yet it sufficed to lend authority to Christna's Indian story when applied to the Christian hero, Iesu.

It will be noticed that, although Jonah is spoken to and commanded to go to Nineveh by Iové, the part relating to the Ninevites and their king is not about Iové (the Lord), but about Ale-im or Elohim, " the gods," or God.

As I have shown, all tribes had their band of Aleim or Eli-im, with a leader—that of the Hebrews being Iové—while the Ninevite was probably at that date Ninus, or it may be Marduk, so they, the Ninevites, did not acknowledge Iové after all Jonah's preaching, as he carefully used the universal Asiatic word Ale-im, quite orthodox in Nineveh. But the story is, of course, apocryphal, and it is the usual method of the Hebrew scribes to boast of converting, or ethically conquering, a great nation at whose hand they had so often and so grievously suffered. Those minor books, like Daniel, Jonah, and others, are so defective in their knowledge of history, and so errone-ous as to dates that they must have been written by scribes at a late date, and for a purpose far other than that of recording true history.

Here we have two attempts to introduce the world-wide religion to the ignorant Hebrews, but they remained steadfast to their Iové and purely phallic practices, and were in conse-quence considered an " obstinate nest of vipers " by all surrounding nations.

CHAPTER II

Let us glance at their status, numbers, beliefs, and the emblems through which these beliefs were materialised, as drawn for us at the zenith of their history—that fine imaginative historical composition, the building of Solomon's temple. These beliefs and their symbolical presentment persist, as we shall see, down to the present day, and even form the " incomprehensible " basis of Christianity.

The Three-in-One symbolism pervades all Hebrew literature, religion, and phylacteries from the earliest times to the present day. It is embodied in the name of the god IhOh, where hOh signifies to " breathe," to " live," " Eve," " life," " desire," " lust," " fall," and " calamity." This, coupled with Adam, the red one, and the serpent of sexual passion, gives us the whole story of Eden—male and female in the presence of sexual passion, all summed up in the most holy tetragrammaton

IhOh. Woman is symbolised by O alone in all ancient symbolism, while H, as a " breathing " letter, or aspirant, is " Breath " or " Life." so the H's on each side of woman mean that she is that which is fertilised, or life (see Fig. 6, Part I.), where Hercules fertilises woman, and declares her to be the mother of all living. When the pillar I is added, we have the complete life-creating combination or the male triad (or trident) and the female monad (or una), four in all, symbolised by the most sacred and secret tetragrammaton IhOh. Moses creates it also in the rod and stones of god in the ark, copied from Egypt, and in the old tabernacle composition—the male priest in the womb or ark of dolphins' skins, long forgotten and abandoned, and again in the pillars called Jakin and Boaz minutely described in another literary fable—the great temple of Solomon.

The account of this temple given in Kings and Chronicles is a good example of the two great characteristics of Hebrew literature— the phallic nature of all Hebrew worship and the ridiculous exaggeration of their writers.

They gloried in huge numbers, whether as to population, slaughter, or wealth, finally an enthusiastic account of half a million slain in one battle (2nd Chronicles xiii., 17), when the whole of Palestine could not support more than a fifth of that number in men, women, and children.   Smith's *Concise Bible Dictionary*, p. 391, 1874, says " the Jewish exaggerations (about popuplation of their little tribes) are so ridiculous that it is surprising anyone could have repeated them."   All serious statisticians agree that " whole Palestina " could never support more than 110,000 to 120,000 people, giving at most 37,000 men capable of bearing arms scattered through some twenty tribes, or about 1500 fighting men on an average to each of the " nations greater and mightier than thou " (Deuteronomy vii., 1; ix., 1; and xi., 23). so that, if, as some authors suggest, the " thousands " are a late addition to the text, and we take the first numbers without the " thousands," we have about the right numbers.   The half-million will then read as five hundred, and that is probably the greatest number ever killed in these little local battles.

We know that the great Babylonian monarchs registered as few as 16, 30, or 40 killed in some battles, so the armies were small. The Hebrews magnified the foreign armies also, declaring that Zerah came up against them with a host of a million men (2nd Chronicles xiv., 9).

The Hebrew part of Palestine was only 1120 square miles, and we know that the Hebrews were not the principal inhabitants, as even in Jerusalem they merely " dwelt among " the real owners of the soil (Judges iii., 5), and even if the Hebrews numbered 20 to the square mile (the maximum of which such a country is capable), we have only 22,400 Jews as the whole Hebrew population, and we are told again and again that the " nations " amongst whom they dwelt were " greater and mightier than thou," so they could not have even that number.

Josephus is another priestly composition containing a little history padded with fiction written to support the scriptural view of the importance of the Hebrews. Its falsity is apparent when it states that a million perished at the siege of Jerusalem, when the whole city could not hold 20,000 people.

The Hebrews dwelt among the Aborigines of Palestine on sufferance, exactly as they do in Europe to-day, although they had been commanded to " utterly destroy " and exterminate the native races and to take their land and houses (Exodus xxxiv., 16; Deuteronomy vii., 1-3).   But in Judges iii., 5—" And the children of Israel dwelt among the Canaanites, Hittites, and Amorites, and Perizzites. and Hivites, and Jebusites, and they took their daughters to be their wives, and gave their daughters to their sons and served their gods;" in fact, as the *Encyclopædia Biblica* says in column 3214, " a tribe must adopt the religion of those amongst whom they sojourn or dwell," and we have ample evidence that this was the case.

The Israelites inter-married with and served the gods of all tribes "from Mount Baal-Hermon unto the entry into Hamoth " (Egypt), so they were never a pure race, as they also inter-married with the people of the lands of their numerous captivities, and conquerors sent their own subjects to form colonies in Palestine, still further to dilute the race.

In Ezra iv., 4, the phrase, " people of the land," shows that Judah and Benjamin were not the people of the land, but lived in the country on sufferance, as at verse 23 we find the " people of the land " were able to prevent the building of the temple " by force and power."   Jerusalem was inhabited by the Jebusites, " and the children of Benjamin did not drive out the Jebusites that inhabited Jerusalem;" " but the Jebusites dwell with the children of Benjamin in Jerusalem unto this day " (Judges i., 21). All the surrounding tribes and nations utilised the Jews as slaves, and there are texts showing this, such as 1st Chronicles v., 25, rebuking them for going after " the gods of the people of the land," or Exodus x., 11, " separate yourselves from the people of the land;" or Ezekiel xxii., 39— " The people of the land used oppression," and we find the Babylonians picking out the Hebrews as slaves and leaving the " people of the land " in peace. Their condition was always abject—even under Solomon they were subject to their ancient enemy Egypt.

Yet they continually boast and exaggerate, as is exemplified in their statements about the gold and silver used in the temple. Some gold had been collected by David, and was given to Solomon to decorate the temple, and the amount was expanded till in a burst of boastful exaggeration David is made to tell Solomon (1st Chronicles xxii., 14) :—" I have prepared for the house of the Lord an hundred thousand talents of gold and a thousand thousand talents of silver." This would amount to 5848 tons of gold, worth six hundred million pounds sterling, and to 52,232 tons of silver, worth in those times about four hundred million pounds. Of course such fabulous sums did not exist in the possession of all the nations of the world at that time, and looking to the small size of the temple, such a quantity of gold and silver would have sufficed to build the whole temple of these precious metals. So we see they varied their statements as to facts in the most reckless and shameless way, but their phallic symbolisms remained fixed, and were repeated verbatim sometimes three or four times without the change of even one word, except where, in more enlightened times the copyists softened down the nudity of the phallic language, or our translators dishonestly invented new words which had no meaning, to prevent us from knowing the truth about " Holy Writ." Let us look at the symbolism of the temple.

I have already treated very fully the symbolism of the tabernacle, the fabulous forerunner of the temple, in my *Romance of the Hebrew Tabernacle,* so I shall only touch on the new symbolism introduced into the temple to replace or to amplify that of the tabernacle.

The Alpha and Omega of the description of the temple furniture are, first, two great pillars

with elaborately described details mentioned in
1st Kings vii., 15 ff., and last the " hinges of
gold " (verse 50) for the golden doors (2nd
Chronicles iv., 22) of the main entry of the
house and those of the " most holy place."
There is also an oracle or speaking place mentioned, our pulpit, which merits attention. As
the Holy of Holies was used in both tabernacle
and temple, I will treat of these curious hinges
of gold on the golden doors. The Holy of
Holies in both structures contained the ark of
the covenant, or more fully the ark of the
Berith of Iové; that is, the ark of the circumcised phallus of Iové. In the tabernacle the
entrance was closed by a curtain, and in the
temple by golden doors. The whole description of the tabernacle, repeated four times, was
that of the womb out of which the sun was
born every year, a fable often stamped on
Greek coins. This was indicated by the use of
dolphins' skins, as the young sun god was
born of a dolphin (delphys, womb) annually.
So the tabernacle was feminine, as are all
churches, and as the " most holy place " in
the temple seems to have taken the place of
the tabernacle it had to have female symbolism, as the dolphins' skins were no longer used.

We are specially told in the English version

that these golden doors had golden " hinges."
To tell this was quite unnecessary, because the
hinges are part of a door needing no special
mention, and naturally would be of at least as
good material, besides the golden hinges are
included in a long list of special sacred golden
vessels, utensils, censers, etc., and having
nothing to do with doors, were a part of the
ceremonial or symbolic ecclesiastical furniture.
The word used in Hebrew is Pitoth, plural of
Pit or Put, and when we look up Pit or Put we
find that it means " nakedness " or the
" muliebre pudendum," so that the plural,
which the translators disguised as " hinges,"
were really models of the female organ in gold
to indicate that the temple and its holy of
holies were feminine, or the womb in the belly,
just as is the case at Mecca, where the Kaba in
Macca means the womb in the belly, or in our
own churches, where the nave under the d'om
is also the womb in the belly. Probably the
translators knew the true meaning of the word,
and translated it as " hinges " to avoid the
danger of a truthful translation. But it has
no possible relation to hinges, and the only
other mention of hinges in the Old Testament
employs another and the correct word,
" zirah;" while in Isaiah iii., 17, the word Pit

or Pitoth, from the same root, is given as
" secret parts," " will make naked their
secret parts," speaking of the " daughters of
Zion," so there is no doubt that Pit means
yoni, the female organ. This symbol, which
may have been realistic or only one of the
horse-shoe order, was placed there to declare
that the holy of holies was the womb or female
member of the Three-in-One, or the Ark,
Ruach, Mother of All, dwelling-place of the
gods, like our Virgin Mary, who is called the
habitation of God, " in whom dwells the god-
head bodily." These Putoth were fixed on the
outer doors also, as churches or temples all
over the world are female.   Our bishops on
their appointment wed their church with a
ring, calling her " Mea Sposa," my bride. The
entrances to the churches in Ireland had this
same symbol, but more realistically expressed
by a nude female figure exposing the muliebre
pudendum, carved on the keystone of the arch
of the great church doors. It was supposed
to keep off the " evil eye " (see my *Christianity*, p. 63).

Similar churches all over Europe had the
horse-shoe either on the door, or threshold,
or pavement of the church, to indicate the
church's female nature. This symbol had to

be very secret in the Hebrew practice, as the female was taboo in their religion.

In the new temple there was an oracle or speaking place, and this is still called a pulpit, a name which has not changed from very early times. This is another ecclesiastical double-sexed temple structure, its name being derived from Pul, the Hebrew name of a King of Assyria, whom the Greeks called Phallos, and therefore the male organ, and Pit, mistranslated hinge, the Hebrew for the lingam and yoni. It consisted of an *upright column* supporting a platform in the shape of an *open bowl* or *lotus flower,* from which the priest spoke; so here is a word for the Lingam and yoni in English, through the Latin pulpitum, which has descended unchanged through thousands of years.

The word used for pulpit in the temple is also a double word, Migdal-Ez, which in Hebrew lexicons are given as (M)GDL, flourish or flower, and Ez, tree or tree-stem— the word used for the trees of life and knowledge in Eden—the phallus. GDL is given as pulpit or tower, but that is only a guess from the context, as are so many meanings given to Hebrew words. MGDL means several symbolic things, such as the fringes on the Hebrew prayer dress and altar furniture, and the " platted chain work " on the pillars of the temple we are about to consider; but pulpit in Migdal-Ez form is identical with the English word (also derived from Hebrew) meaning a female thing supported on a male pillar—an open flower on a tree stem, as so many beautiful pulpits are to this day. It is significant that MGDL is also Magdala, and it means almond, a female symbol. We speak of a mineral as being amygdaloidal or almond-shaped, so Migdal-Ez may mean " almond and tree stem," or the " rod and almond " of Jeremiah i., 11, the secret sign of a double-sex religion. Mary of Magdala was called Mary of the Almond to symbolsie her as a temple harlot. Such play upon words has been a characteristic of priestly writings from time immemorial.

Mary as a name is generally supposed to be derived from Maya, her Indian prototype; but all the Queens of Heaven were known as those who stirred the god into action, as without the female no creation could be made, and Mari (Hebrew mem, ayin, resh, and yod) is derived from AUR (ayin, vav, resh), meaning " to excite," or " to stir into action," and the feminine word, Mari or Mary, means " she who stirs (the god) into action " or the wife of God (see my *Christianity*, pp. 48, 187).

We see here the linking up of the elements of the principal religions and carrying the female Luz (almond) of Jacob, and the Saked (almond) of Jeremiah, right into the New Testament symbolism. We now come to the chef d'œuvre of Solomon's temple, the two famous pillars, Jakin and Boaz, which have puzzled so many scholars, but which were simply the embodiment of their symbolic IHOH.

I shrewdly suspect that, after Jacob's clear declaration that the stone phallus, pala or pillar, he erected and anointed, was " El the god of Israel," many scholars knew that all sacred columns were of the same nature— creative columns, but they, like Nelson, mentally turn their blind eye to all such deductions.

Twin pillars were common all over the world, *e.g.*, Pillars of Hercules and of Palés, god of flocks, who was double-sexed, represented by twin phalli, called the Phalikoi, twin sons of Zeus by Thalia, goddess of green or vegetation. The space between the pillars represented the door of life, the female, and the pillars male, hence double sex. Egypt

had twin pillars as shown in Fig. 1. These
were twins of the Dad or Father shown in the
right of Fig. 5. But it was reserved for the
Hebrews to express the complete creative
group, accompanied by a wealth of creative
symbolism on each of the pillars, Jakin and
Boaz in their impossible Temple.

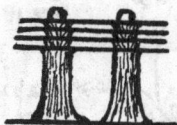

Fig. 1.

Probably Jakin and Boaz were mere
creations of the pen; but I have endeavoured
to draw a column exactly as specified in 1st
Kings vii., the two were identical, of which
there are three repetitions, in 2nd Kings xxv.,
13-17; in 2nd Chronicles iii., and iv.; and again
in Jeremiah lii., 17-23, four in all; but the
first account in Kings, from which the others
were no doubt copied, is a little fuller than the
others, and I follow that description. Note
that the columns form a tetrad or foursome
symbol, and they are described four times. I
need not go over the whole specification here,
as on my drawing I have indicated and identified all details, and quoted the verse from
which these details are taken.

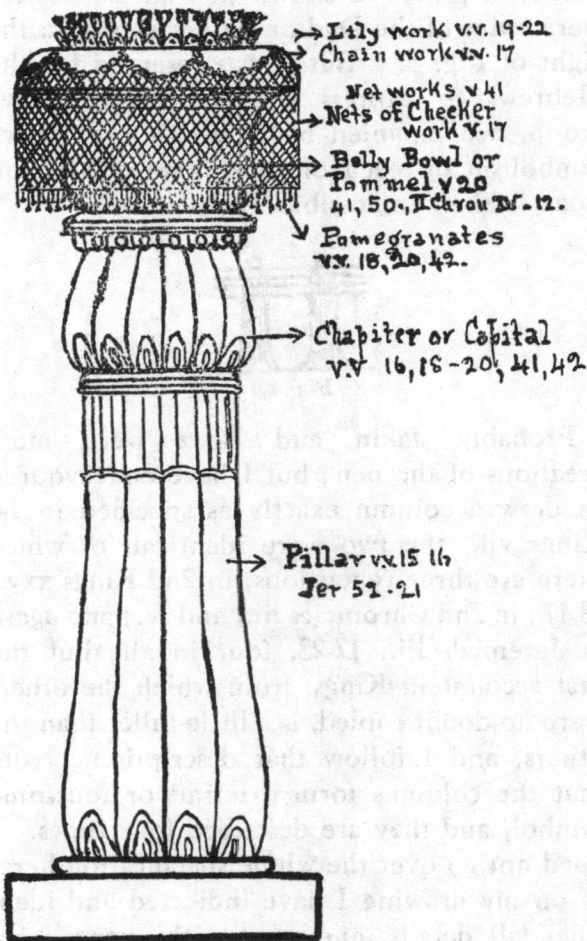

Jakin and Boaz
I Kings VII, 10-14, 20-28

→ Lily work v.v. 19-22
→ Chain work v.v. 17

Net works v 41
Nets of Checker
Work v. 17
Belly Bowl or
Pommel v 20
41, 50·, II chron IV. 12.

Pomegranates
v.v. 18, 20, 42.

→ Chapiter or Capital
v.v 16, 18-20, 41, 42

→ Pillar v.v. 15 16
Jer 52·21

Fig. 2.

Whether a temple in the least degree approaching to the description of Solomon's Temple was ever erected, or whether it had its Jakin and Boaz, the " establisher " and the " strong one," we do not know, as no serious historian mentions Solomon or his temple, but we do know that its predecessor, the tabernacle, was a pure myth, or a pen creation, and that the vast riches of the new tablernacle or temple are equally fictitious. The pillars with their fruitful bellies, symbolised by the pomegranate, may also be a pen creation, but we may be sure that a nation living in a land mostly composed of barren mountains would erect just such a bare church as one may see to-day in the mountains of Switzerland, Norway, or Scotland.

The two pillars are known as the " establisher," or that which is erected, and " alacrity," or " fleetness," both phallic (see the erection of the Dad or phallus in Egypt in my *Christianity*, p. 81), and alacrity or " fleetness," which is the name or attribute of Mercury or Hermes, also the Phallus. Jakin or Yakin is the same as Iaccos, the early name of Bacchus, and is the original of our Jack-in-the-Box, which springs up or erects itself

(Part I., p. 134). So we see both pillars were phallic by name.

As most of the Hebrew symbolism came from Egypt, and the Pharaoh's daughter had an elaborate house built for her as Solomon's wife near the temple before its erection [the *Encyclopædia Biblica* says she was probably there to watch over Pharaoh's interests] we must look to Egypt for the model on which such pillars were constructed. Egyptian symbolism was acutely phallic, and they used both the Lotus and Papyrus stems and buds to represent the phallus. We see most of their temple pillars have the proportions of the natural phallus, and although they were produced with great art, as at Phylae (Phalli), the proportions are not chosen for grace, but were symbolical. I have therefore applied the Egyptian type of pillar, and find it fits the specification given in the texts as to height and girth and general proportions. But the Hebrews did not slavishly follow Egypt, they broke out into an original form of symbolism, which I do not remember having seen in any other country, unless it is India.

As will be seen from my drawing, there was a pillar composed of a lotus stem and bud to represent the circumcised phallus, and on that stood a bowl, belly, or pommel, draped with network and hung round with pomegranates (fruitful womb), and crowned with lily-work (virginity). The chain-work, from which was hung the network by which the " belly " was veiled, was evidently a symbol and not a mere means of hanging the net works. Chains always mean serpents, so this is most probably the symbol for the sexual passion accompanying the production of life, as on tree stems.

These pillars will be found to have the same proportions of height to girth as the Dorset Column at p. 33, Part I., and are therefore drawn for the same purpose of symbolism. The Egyptian carvings are openly phallic, and are associated with ithyphallic gods.

The word translated bowls in 1st Kings vii., 41, and then changed to pommels, has evidently given the translators anxious thought. The article which was above the chapiters or Capitals is called a belly in 1st Kings vii., 20, and the Hebrew word used, Beten, does mean belly or womb, but means also almond, the symbol for the muliebre pudendum, and also for temple women, as Mary Magdalene is Mary of the Almond; so that which was on the top of the pillar was a belly with the yoni or almond, no doubt plainly indicated. It is associated

with a word EBR, not included in the English
translation, but which is intimately connected
with Hebrew history and symbolism, as it is
the root of " Hebrew " and " passover," and
has a meaning of "impregnation " or immaculate conception, which is the whole significance of the column.   The word for what was
over the chapiter when next mentioned in
verse 41 is " Gulloth," translated " bowls " in
Kings,   but   " pommels "   in   Chronicles,
although it is the same Hebrew word in both
cases ; and Gulloth is closely allied to Gullulim, possibly derived from the root GLL, and
much used by Ezekiel for " idols," but whose
etymology is uncertain (*Encyclopædia Biblica*,
col. 2149).   As Gulloth has not the recurring
L, like Gullulim, it is probably derived from
GLH, instead of GLL.   GLH means to
" make naked," or the " naked thing," and
in certain circumstances " carnal intercourse,"
which, again, is what the pillars indicate ; so
we are in presence of one of those passages
mutilated by ancient editors to muddle or
conceal its true meaning.   But the English
translators seem to have had a shrewd idea of
the true meaning, when they coined a word
pommel as the equivalent of Gulloth in
Chronicles.   Pommel is in no way related to

a bowl, but it is related to pomum (apple), and the bowl was surrounded by rows of another apple, the pomegranate, the apple with the many seeds or grains, and pomegranate signifies the fruitful womb. We are told that at the very phallic feast of tabernacles the women carried pome-citrons in their left hands (see my *Queen of Heaven*), and we know from Eden that the apple is the erotic fruit or, as the *Encyclopædia Biblica*, col. 269, says, " the whole classical history of the apple is saturated with erotic suggestion," so the pommels or apples were a euphuistic term for belly or womb, and we know that later writers always toned down any phallic suggestions. So we see from these time-worn relics what an extremely phallic symbolism saturated the ideas of temple construction among the Hebrew scribes. I say " ideas among the scribes," as I doubt if any such combinations were ever erected, as in some of the four descriptions the articles are named and arranged haphazard, differing in each text, and strung off as from a catalogue, not part of a scheme understood by the writer. But we see that their supreme efforts were reserved for the bisexual combination, the male triple organ and the female unity, making four in all, or the tetragrammaton. They even repeat the description of the temple phylacteries four times, as they did also with the details of the tabernacle materials, thus making even the description fourfold or a tetrad. The Jewish practice was full of such superstitious precautions, and a volume could be filled with the elaborate precautions as to handling of writing sacred things or texts, and all tied up in a most elaborate manner so that if any error or slip were made the whole had to be begun anew, exactly like children's games. Probably all religions are simply childish make-believes played by children of a larger growth.

A curious point in the arrangement of these columns is that, although they are specially arranged to symbolise the impregnation of a female, and so creating life, they are crowned by the emblem of virginity, lily-work. But it is not so strange when we remember that all Kings, whether of Africa, Asia, or Europe, were the result of the converse of their ever virgin mother with a god, so all their ideas of divine motherhood were those of Royal or Divine mothers crowned with virginity or immaculate conception, as I have shown, symbolised by Jakin and Boaz, and continued in the Story of Mary.

We see from all this that the phallic idea reigned supreme in the Hebrew religion, and although Eli, the triple male god, was the most universal god common to all Asia, and hence used in the New Testament, which was adapted so as to be acceptable to all nations, IhOh was the complete creative double-sexed tetragrammaton, infinitely more sacred than Eli, and is still held to be so by the modern Jews.

The English translators seem to have understood something of this, as they gave the three-letter god, " Eli," a three-letter name, " god," and the four-letter god, " IhOh," a four-lettered name, " Lord."

I mentioned that such an elaborate combination as the pillars of Solomon's Temple was perhaps only to be found in India, and I have noticed two constructions, at Puri (a centre of intensely erotic phallic worship) in the temple of Lakshmi, the goddess, meaning also a very lucky thing or a preservative from evil, and so connected with the female, yoni, or horseshoe. They are (1st) a pillar like Solomon's, but caressed by a serpent, like the tree of " knowledge " in Eden, as shown in Fig. 3.   The upper part is the same idea as the " belly " veiled in a network. The serpent's head is adoring or penetrating the network. The same idea has been expressed by savages all over the world, by dressing their spear with

Fig. 3.

Fig. 4.

hair, as shown in Fig. 4. The Latin for spear, Quiris, gave its name to the holy Quirinal at Rome. The Hindu symbolism is either extremely sexual, as at Puri, Elephanti, and other places, as in the Surya Deul, at Ronarak, near Puri, and unfit for publication in an open book, or so highly conventionalised and beautifully decorative as to seem to be only a lovely piece of sculpture, and at Puri we have both, and my second illustration (Fig. 5) shows the idea of Solomon's pillars beautifully conventionalised. It is the same as the Tat or Dad of Egypt, a true phallus (see my *Christianity*, pp. 73, 81). If the reader will compare the pillar form with the serpent penetrating the " fringes " of the " bowl," he will see its identity with the bowl with its checker-work and fringe of pomegranates, the Jewish symbolism being much more complete. But at Puri this refined symbolism is accompanied with a commentary of nude figures, some in coitu, some illustrating all sorts of erotic sexual excesses, so the meaning of the more refined symbolism is clearly indicated.

I am indebted to the India Office Museum authorities for being allowed to study the magnificent collection of photographs and drawings of Hindu temples, and my sketches are from *District Puri*, Black Pagoda photos 361, 364, 385, etc. In Fig. 5 is shown the Hindoo (left) and the Egyptian (right) forms of the Tat, Dad, Father, or Phallus highly conventionalised. I have in my possession a series of drawings by the late Mr. Alexander Simpson, the well-known artist, from paintings and sculpture of the insides of Hindu and other temples (also unpublishable), which show the riot of erotic suggestion common to all early outbursts of emotion on contemplating the creative energy so fully illustrated in the Hebrew Bible.

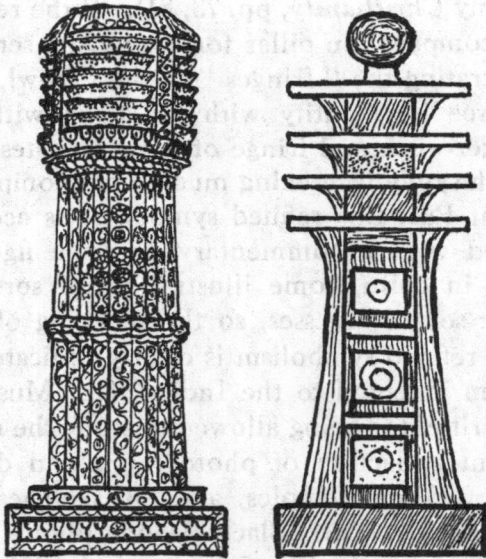

Hindoo Phallus.   Fig. 5.   Egyptian Dad.

I must now touch on similar symbolism still extant in modern Judaism, and embodied in Tephilim or " appendages of prayer." They belong to a class of articles found wherever religion exists, superstitiously believed to have the potency of the god in interfering with the course of nature and preventing the happen-

PART II.—NEW TESTAMENT GODS 211

ing of disagreeable or evil things or events,
which without their influence would happen.
(The most intelligent people have some belief
in the miraculous effect of mascots.) They are
called through Greek derivation phylacteries,
but we see that both words, Tephilim and
Phylactery, contain as their basis the word
Phil or Phyl, love, derived from Phallus, the
love organ, and in all countries the sexual
organs of either sex were held to be the source
of and embodiment of all good, and, in fact,
were the symbol of the god. In short, the
Phylactery represents the god in giving those
who wear it everything for which man prays
to his god. It is a charm, spell, token, amulet,
preservative, talisman, or safeguard against
disease, danger, bad luck, evil eye, or the
machinations of evil spirits, and the bringer of
good luck, health, and wealth. When divorced
from religion is called a mascot. It is the
universal religion, dearer to savage and
civilised alike than any creed, prayer-book, or
church service. It is the Ankh or Egyptian
cross, the Cross, the Rosary, the Crescent, the
lingam-yoni altar of India, the dagger and
ring of Persia, and all their varied relatives
which are worshipped wherever man thinks of

212 GODS OF HEBREW BIBLE

" life," and uses models of his own " life producer " to symbolise such ideas.

In Italy and in the East at this day mothers
hang a phallic charm on their babies' arms to
protect them from the evil eye, disease, and
death. It is sometimes a realistic phallus (or
phylos), but generally the combined male and
female organs in the form of a clenched hand
with the thumb protruding through the
fingers, called the " phallic hand;" and I have
shown in my *Christianity* that up till 1790 the
keystones of the church doorways in Ireland
were sometimes decorated with the sculpture
of a nude woman exposing herself to bring
good luck to, and keep off the evil eye from
those entering the chapel. This was a true
mascot or phylactery, but the horseshoe is now
substituted for the " natural " exhibition.
The Tephilah or Phylactery is described and
illustrated in most good dictionaries, and in a
book on *Modern Judaism*, by John Allen
(1816), a clear illustration is given of how it is
worn, and also of how it is made.

The phallic nature of the Judaic and Christian religions is clearly shown in these names,
as the Christians wore phylacteries also. In
Hebrew Tephiloth (feminine plural) is the
word for prayers, and Tephilim (masculine

plural) is the word for prayer-things or sexual symbols, and the word " palal," to pray (the Indian pala), shows to what the Hebrews prayed. The Christian phylactery was the bell a phylactery still used in the Catholic churches to frighten away evil spirits in the church service (see pp. 14, 249 in my *Christianity*). It is, as I have shown on p. 69, exactly the same as the Maha Deva of the Hindus, the great creative god as symbolised in the creative organs of the two sexes. So we see the practical identity of all religions, an identity long known to scholars free from church bias.

The tephillin, or in modern books tephilim, are of two forms, one for the hand or arm and the other for the head. These tephillin are made " of a piece of skin or leather manufactured from the skin of some ' clean ' animal, well soaked and stretched on a block cut for the purpose, sewed together while wet, and left on the block till it is dried and stiffened into the requisite form." When taken off, it forms a stiff leather box, and it has a loop of leather formed on one side, through which the band which binds them to the worshipper is passed.

The phylactery for the hand or arm is

fastened by the worshipper by a very long band
to his left arm, near the elbow, with the skin
satchel or capsule pointing to his heart, and
the long band forms an elaborate binding down
the arm, and five times round the fingers. The
capsule formed of skin, as above is shown in
Fig. 6, is identical in form with an old phallic

Fig. 6.

pillar and base in Ireland, which is shown in
Fig. 26 in my *Christianity*, and as Allen says
(p. 310) it has as a box or capsule a " hollow
piece of skin like the finger of a glove "—a
true phallus. Into the finger-shaped cavity is
placed a strip of parchment, with four quotations referring to binding something on the
arm and on the brow between the eyes. The
texts are Exodus xiii., 1-10; Exodus xiii., 11-16;
Deuteronomy vi., 4-9; Deuteronomy xi.,
13-21; and are supposed to contain the divine
tetragrammaton, IhOh, a greater number of
times than any quotation of equal length—23
times.

The tephillah for the head is more elaborate, and contains both structural and written signs, of which that for the arm has none; in fact, the information is all applied to the seat of intelligence—the head. It is made in the same way, with wet skin, as that for the arm, and is of equal length and breadth, about an inch and a half square, and of nearly equal depth, but instead of the phallic capsule, as shown in Fig.

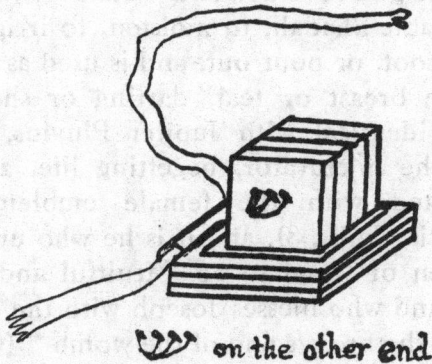

on the other end

Fig. 7.

6, it has four rectangular receptacles, in which the above four texts are separately placed. It has the same sort of attachment for binding it on the head as that for the arm. On one side (the right) is stamped the letter Shin, with its triple points or prongs, and on the other

a new form of Shin with four prongs. The
knot tying the head capsule is tied at the end,
so as to form the letter D or daleth, while that
for the arm is made to form I or Yod at the
end.   These with the Shin stamped on the
brow capsule give SDI, which stands for Saddai or El Shaddai, called the Almighty in the
translations, but having nothing to do with
" might " or " mighty," as " El " is, as Jacob
said, the god of Israel, and " Shaddai " is from
the Arabic Shadah, to moisten, to irrigate, to
cast, shoot, or pour out, and is used as a word
for the breast or teat, darting or shedding.
He is identical with Jupiter Pluvius, and is
truly the micturator, begetting life, as he is
associated with the female emblem, Luz
(Genesis xlviii., 3), and it is he who urges the
children of Israel to be " fruitful and multiply," and who blesses Joseph with the " blessings of the breasts and of the womb " (Genesis
xlix., 25).   He is, in fact, the god of procreation, and so is the god fit to be associated
with the female in any creative god symbol.
The phylactery on the head is such a symbol,
and the Shin on the right-hand side (masculine
side) is the symbol for the male god, and his
name in Hebrew has three letter SDI (like
Eli), as a triple form is required for all male

gods. But on the left-hand side the Shin has four prongs, so the " three " god has joined the female " unity," the fourth prong being the Hebrew O or Woman, and we have again the fourfold creative couple, male and female, IhOh. This four-ness is signified by the division into four cells, while the fact that a male god forms the basis of this creative combination is indicated by dividing the base of the phylactery into three layers, as is shown in all the drawings given of the Tephillim.

The box-like base is an Ark or Ruach, " in whom the God-head dwells bodily," and its square form indicates its completeness as a Three-in-One or Foursome Creative Symbol.

That the Three-and-One or Tetrad was considered necessary for creation and for the formation of a complete god is shown by the universality of the symbol. The phylactery is considered so holy that it is kissed on being unbound, and is placed in a special and beautifully decorated bag, into which no other article is ever put, and this is covered by another outer bag. The decoration on these bags is very interesting, and is still symbolic, as I shall show in one example from the *Jewish Encyclopædia* (Fig. 8). Here we have two triangles, one such as I noted on the Church of

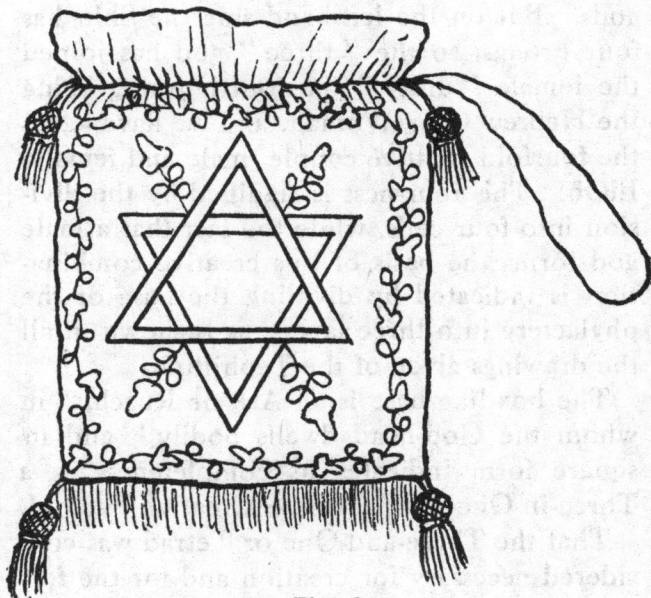

Fig. 8.

the Holy Trinity as being the symbol of the complete male organ, and the other being inverted to indicate the female, derived from the Lotus seed-vessel (Part I., p. 82), the two forming a tetrad. This is still used by the Jews as a symbol of the highest good, as witness this cutting from the *Daily Chronicle* of 31st August, 1916:—" Montreal, Aug. 30.—Mr. Doherty, the Canadian Minister of Justice, in recognition of the assistance he has given in recruiting for the Jewish company for overseas service, has been presented by the company with a gola watch bearing the regimental crest and the symbolic double triangles."

The foursome nature of the Phylactery symbolism is further emphasised by placing four phalli or serpentine stems in four of the six angles of the crossed triangles, and by decorating the four corners of the bag with four tassels, and finally by the square form of the bag itself (compare Assyrian priests' bags, Figs. 47 and 49 in my *Christianity*). These four tassels are called Arba Kanphoth, meaning the four corners (of the earth, *e.g.*), so they represent Kosmos as the supreme creative power. Arba (AlBa, L for R, inverted, BaAl), or Erva, involving four objects, and this was called the Arba El or "four-some god," often spelled Arbil. Erva-El is the same as Erva-Min—Minerva—El and Min being the ithyphallic gods of Asia and Egypt, and Minerva was the "complete" or double sexed god. The ArBaAl, God Baal, was embodied in a vase of a mortar and pestle-like form (Fig. 9), fitted with serpentine handles, and having a Linga protruding through it, similar to the Hindoo Lingam-Yoni altar (Fig. 11). The vase, which represents the female, is producing fruit (Fig. 9). For a very beautiful Greek expression of this symbolism, see Fig. 38, p. 63, of my *Christianity*.

Finally, to bind all these symbolisms together the scholars who created Hebrew and composed the Bible made Arba explain its ecclesiastical significance by giving it a meaning of to " copulate " and to " lie with," and this idea was, and still is, the incomprehensible Mystery of all great religions.

Fig. 9.   Fig. 10.   Fig. 11.

Fig. 12.

I place side by side with this God Baal the Christian phylactery—the Bell, used in Romish services to drive away evil spirits, the Hindoo lingam-yoni altar, and the ubiquitous mortar and pestle in its Hindoo and Egyptian forms —to show the identity of the " Blessed Mysteries " of all religions as explained to us by Bishop Hippolytus early in the Christian era (Figs. 9, 10, 11, 12, 13).

The Hindoos put four mortars and pestles under Christna to express their tetradic nature, while the Egyptians represented the complete four-some combination—the Ark (mortar), the Rod of God (Eli or Pestle), and the Eduth or two Stones, exactly as did Moses with his sacred Ark combination (see p. 64, Part I.). The nature of the two stones is shown in Fig. 13 under the Bull carrying the dead Osiris.

One last point in relation to Jewish phylactery practice. We know door-posts held a very high position in their symbolism, as their

Fig. 13.

Lanzoni.

god was a pillar or post, so they nailed to their
door-posts a sort of monstrance and pyx, as
commanded in Deuteronomy vi., 4-9, and
Deuteronomy xi., 20. This phylactery was
called the Mezuza or door-post, and the texts
relating to this and the hand and head tephillin
as above, were written on parchment, and
rolled up and put in a lead tube. The word
Shaddai was written on the roll, and a slit cut
in the lead so that it could be read, and this
was nailed to the door-posts and gates. It was
kissed like the Cross or Pyx or Pope's toe by
anyone passing in or out, and was as powerful
to influence the course of events as the tephillin, which were extremely holy, *as they were
worn by God himself.* The head tephillah was
always put on last and taken off first, as being
more holy than that of the arm. The tephillin
were as powerful and holy as the scriptures.

Allen says (p. 310) that the Shin with four
points or heads is affirmed to contain " recon-
dite mysteries," which he excuses himself from
specifying, and we remember that Hyppolytus
assured us that after being initiated into the
mysteries of many creeds he found that the
mysteries were all phallic, as is our incomprehensible mystery, the three in one, and the
four-pronged Shin.

CHAPTER III

FRUITION OF THE SUN GOD IDEA

When the Romans felt the power of their old gods crumbling, as had been the case in Greece, and were looking about for some universal religion through which to rule their great and unstable Empire, they seem to have found in the Jewish scriptures the only writings which were declared to be the actual message of god to man, and they saw in them the best basis for a universal religion. The Hebrew scriptures had one great advantage in view of the growing intelligence of the nations. All the gods of Greece and Rome were of a very human type, and, so far from being built on the idea of eternal gods, they actually had fathers, so that their reign seemed quite on the lines of earthly kings, whereas the Hebrew Iové and their band of Eli-im were apparently eternal and self-existent—true gods—being, like Melchisedec, " without father, without mother, without descent, neither beginning of days, nor end of life," a conception also held of Brahm in India, but peculiar to the Hebrews of all Western Asiatic people. So when the Romans felt the feeble nature of the bonds which held their fluid empire stretching from the Indus to Britain and France they no doubt realised that a religion common to all these nations would be the strongest cement with which they could solidify their very diverse conquests. They tied up the New Testament with the Old Testament by making the last two progenitors of Jesus (Jacob and Joseph—Matthew i., 16) bear the same names as the last two patriarchs of the miraculous period of the ancient Hebrews, as I have detailed at pp. 158-159, Part I.

The new form of Judaism, freed from all the irksome ritual and "works," demanded by the old Levite rules, and founded on the world-myth of the Saviour Sun, seems to have been favoured very early by some of these "powers behind the Throne," which are always the determining factor in the march of history, and which become insoluble puzzles to future generations. The very name of the Sun Saviour, "Jesus Christ," shows astute manipulation very early in the history of the cult.

Jesus or Hesus was the name of the European Druidical sun God, called "Hesus the Mighty," so the name Hesus or Iesu, or, as we erroneously spell it and pronounce it in Britain, Jesus, was one quite acceptable to all Europe. The other name, Christos, was supposed to be derived from Chrio, to anoint, or the Horn, in Hebrew, another very phallic word, and to replace the name Messiah, said to mean the anointed one, both names, if so derived, being phallic. Messiah was really derived from "Mess," son of, and "Iah," Jehovah, as Jesus was called Ben Yah in tales of his childhood. It was a son of Jehovah who was to raise the Hebrew clan to the leadership of the whole world. Christos derives itself from Chrio, but is also the direct Greek form of Christna, the Hindu Buddha, and the life of this Hesus Christos is identical in every particular with that of Christna, copied word for word down to the minutest detail.

I therefore lean to the opinion that the Romans, while being compelled to depend on the only scriptures claiming to have been directly dictated by a true god, and that god having the same name as that of the Romans' Iové, incorporated in the name of his Saviour son the two names most acceptable to Europe and Asia, in the hope of establishing a universal religion, the dream of most conquerors.

In my work on "Christianity, the sources of its teaching and symbolism," I have given a full list of the incidents in the life of Christna, which have been copied into the life of Hesus. The Christna legend dates back to 800 years before the Christian Era. The reader will find in my book the authorities for every incident related of Christna. The two names are very often differentiated by spelling, the one Krishna and the other Christ, but the latter is, on the other hand, often spelled Kristos; and Christna may be spelled Kristna, so that except for the terminations peculiar to each country of " na " and " os," the two names are identical. The English, in fact, reject the termination, making the name Christ, and so complete the identity.

But the whole story of the life of Jesus and his position as Saviour had been the common property of Asia for thousands of years before the Christian Era; the story being always the same, no matter how the names of the Saviour might vary. This was inevitable, as the story was that of the annual Sun. His lowly birth in winter, his struggles with the cold and stormy January and February, his Pass-over, Cross-over, Crossification, or Crucifixion at the Spring Equinox, when, by his crossing over the Equator and ascending into the Northern half of the sky, he ensures the salvation of mankind from the deadly cold of winter, and the Northern hemisphere is, by his crossing over, converted into a paradise or garden. In fact, his history was the history of the Sun. In my *Christianity* I give a list of twenty-six Saviours before Jesus, with identical histories as to the main features. But as his physical history was evidently copied from one of these—Christna—I give here a list of the identical incidents in the two lives. For confirmation I must refer to my *Christianity*, as there is not space in this small sketch to quote all the authorities which are given in detail in my larger work.

Identical incidents related of both Saviours which are proof of the identity of Christna and Christ. Each was :—

1. Born of a chaste virgin chosen by the God on account of her purity.
2. Real father was the Spirit of God.
3. Had an additional or earthly father.
4. Of Royal descent on earthly father's side.

5. Varied and contradictory genealogies given in both accounts.
6. Deity in human form.
7. Angels hail the Virgin.
8. Birth announced by a star.
9. Virgin's name the same (Maya and Mary).
10. Miraculous father.
11. Birth announced by pleasing sounds in the sky.
12. Born in poverty in a cave, also inn or farm.
13. Cave or stable filled with light (re-born sun).
14. Angels sang at night.
15. Spoke to his mother immediately on birth.
16. Adored by cowherds and shepherds (men depending on sunshine).
17. Magi guided by stars.
18. Earthly father carpenter (maker or creator).
19. Costly jewels and precious substances given by wise men.
20. Born poor, but of Royal descent.
21. Father away from home paying taxes.
22. Shown in a manger.
23. Mother on a journey at an inn.

24. Preceded by a fore-runner.
25. Rulers (Kanza and Herod) sought fore-runner's life.
26. Stayed at Maturea or Mattura. (A town in India; no such town in Egypt.)
27. Very learned when young.
28. Chosen King by boy companions.
29. Son of father's old age.
30. Father warned in a dream that Ruler sought to kill Babe.
31. Kings were Kanza for Christna and Herod for Jesus.
32. Father and mother fled.
33. Slaughter of innocents, but babe's life preserved.
34. King slays fore-runner.
35. Babe's life preserved.
*36. Made fish ponds (apocryphal gospel).
*37. Struck boy dead who broke fish ponds.
38. Miracles: Every kind of miracle common to both.
39. Beginning of religious life—Fasted.
40. Tempted of the devil. Offered Empire of the World.
41. Reproves Satan.
42. Anointed by a poor woman.
43. Twelve apostles or disciples.
*44. Chose two fishers. Simon and Andrew.

*45. Chose two more fishers, James and John.
*46. Two ships.
*47. Chose Simon, James, and John fishers.
*48. Miraculous draft of fishes.
*49. Fishers as apostles.
*50. Feeds 5000 men, besides women and children, on five loaves and two fishes.
*51. Tribute money from fishes' mouth.
*52. Fed 4000, seven loaves and a few small fishes.
53. Bruising head of serpent.
54. Transfigured before disciples.
55. Meekest and mildest of men (Siddartha).
56. Alpha and Omega.
57. Crucified with arms extended, marks on hands, feet, and side.
58. Sun darkened at Crucifixion (consoled thief and hunter).
59. Pierced.
60. Descended into hell.
61. Rose from the dead.
62. Ascended into heaven.
63. Many saw him ascend.
64. Will come again, warrior on horse, sun and moon darkened, stars fall.
65. Judge on the last day.
66. Had beloved Disciple Arjuna and John (same names).

67. Creator of all things.
68. Transfigured with shining light.
69. Second person in the Trinity. Brahma Christna Vishnu; Iové, Christ, Holy Ghost (Ruach).
*70. After Resurrection eats fried fish.
*71. After Resurrection causes miraculous draft of fishes.
72. Light of the world.
73. True vine.
74. Predicts his own death.
75. Walks on water.

This list needs no comment. It is utterly impossible that 62 coincidences, including all the important facts of his life could occur by chance in tales of two individuals. One must have been copied from the other. Christna must have been the original and Christ the copy, as he is eight hundred years later.

Those incidents, 13 in number, marked * refer to fishes, and there is little doubt that the Romans introduced sun worship at the time there was a change of the sign of the Zodiac in which the sun " dwelt " at the spring equinox. The change was from Lamb to Fishes.

That Jesus was a true sun god is shown by

the attempt in the Epistle to the Hebrews to get the Hebrew people to accept Jesus as their redeemer. In Hebrews v., vi., and vii. the phrase is seven times repeated that " Jesus is an High Priest for ever after the order of Melchisedec."

Melchisedec, a Canaanitish god, is described as being without father, without mother, without descent, having neither beginning nor end of days, nor end of life, a description very similar to those addressed to Ra, or the sun in Egypt (see *Christianity*, p. 260). The writer in this Epistle was asserting that Jesus was really an eternal god going on a round for ever as does the sun, although Jesus was known to have had two fathers. The argument is for a deathless intercessor; but the language is that used in cryptic descriptions of the sun. The attempt is very cautiously made, but even then it was summarily rejected by all Hebrews.

St. Crysostom, writing at the beginning of the fifth century A.D., says, in Hom. 31 :— " On this day " [25th December] " also the birthday of the Christ was lately fixed at Rome " [his true birthday being quite unknown]. " They call it December 25—the birthday of the invincible one Mithras—the sun, and who so invincible as the Kurios."

The Christians called it the " Birthday of the Solar Pyx." So the early Christians identified him by birthday, name, and symbol as the sun.

St. Augustine and Justin long ago declared that all other lands had this sun religion, and the earliest of which we have historical evidence was about 6000 B.C., when the sun was in Gemini the Twins. " Twin " worship was then universal in the great nations, and the names were ever after held sacred and have come down to us in legend—Romulus and Remus for the Romans, Typhon and Osiris for Egypt, Tammuz and Nergal for Syria, Ahura Mazda (or Ormuzd) and Ahriman or Rimmon for Persia, Python and Apollo for Greece, and later Castor and Pollux, etc. Then about 4500 B.C. the sun passed from Gemini to Taurus the Bull, when we have the period of Bull worship illustrated by the sacred Bull Nanda in India, the great man-headed winged bulls of Nineveh in the British Museum, the worship of the female Hathor the cow in Egypt at Thebes (a name which also means cow) and of Apis the bull also in Egypt.

The slow shifting of the direction of the earth's axis called the precession of the equinoxes caused the bull to pass away from

the position of the sun's house at the spring
equinox and the ram took its place. We have
then ram or lamb worship; and finally about
the time of Jesus the sun passed into Pisces
the fishes, hence the fish miracles in the New
Testament, which I have marked with a * in
the list of incidents, pp. 227-231. Jesus was
called " Ichthys," the fish, for about 400 years,
but the fish cult did not take with the people
and gradually died out. On many ancient
Christian grave stones, however, the fish was
sculptured as an emblem of the saviour. A
fish was sculptured at the head of the monument exactly as the Lingum-yoni was cut at
the head of all monumental or proclamation
stones in India, as shown by the hundreds of
photographs in the Library of the India
Office, or as the Cross in its phallic form has,
for ages, been cut on tombstones (see *Christianity*, Fig. 2, p. 30).

A great deal of useless discussion has taken
place as to the historicity or partial historicity
of Jesus, but we know that nineteen-
twentieths of his supposed acts and teaching
were attributed to various gods all over Asia,
hundreds of years before his time, and therefore it is of very little consequence whether or
not the remaining twentieth pertains to some

real but obscure Hebrew minor prophet. The tale of Jesus is the work of the priesthood, and was written for a purpose, and the gospels are just as much fiction as any of the popular semi-historic or mystic novels.

It is a curious coincidence that two great teachers were inculcating the humane principles attributed to Jesus at nearly the same time, Confucius in China and Prince Siddartha in India. Confucius was the first to clearly teach the Golden Rule, not only saying, " Do unto others as you would that they should do unto you," but in order to make it very clear, he also taught it negatively, " What I do not wish men to do to me, I also wish not to do to them."

He held that the golden rule was all one needs to guide one's conduct and re-states it three times, saying it is " The principle with which, as with a measuring square, to regulate one's conduct." He had other fine phrases, " Virtue has an irresistible charm and will not stand alone, but will find neighbours."

He had a healthy and virile outlook and did not believe in the ultra peaceful doctrine of " turning the other cheek," or suffering evil without correction. He held that injury should be recompensed with justice, and kindness with kindness, and warned his hearers never to let a small injustice go uncorrected " else it will become a great injustice one day and overwhelm thee and others."

A little before Confucius, but nearly contemporaneously, Siddartha, the Prince who renounced a throne that he might follow goodness, was teaching the opposite of Ezra's " Eye for an eye, tooth for a tooth " doctrine and saying :

" Let a man leave anger, let him forsake pride, let him overcome evil by good, let him overcome the greedy by liberality, the liar by truth."

" Let a man leave anger, let him forsake pride, let him overcome all evil bondage."

" He abused me, he beat me, he defeated me, he robbed me ; in those who harbour such thoughts hatred will never cease. For hatred does not cease by hatred at any time ; hatred ceases by love."

It took some hundreds of years for this gentle teaching to penetrate the western mind and to be reproduced by the priests, as the teaching of the Mess-Iah, the new son of Iah, Jesus.

Sons of God were as numerous as kings in

those days. Every Pharaoh was a son of God, and Gibbon tells us Constantine in the fourth century A.D. actually proclaimed his father a god after death, and Faustina, the wife of the Emperor Marcus, a woman utterly insatiable in sexual intrigues, was actually at the request of Marcus declared to be a goddess.

So gods, goddesses, and sons of God by immaculate conception were as plentiful as blackberries, and our New Testament simply fell in with the prevailing fashion.

So, under the guidance of the Romans, arose this new religion, attempting to combine the main points of all important European and Asiatic religions. St. Augustine said, " The same thing which is now called the Christian religion existed among the ancients. They have begun to call ' Christian ' the true religion which existed before," so that Jesus did not create Christianity, and Justin Martyr wrote : " By declaring the ' logos ' the first begotten of God our Master Jesus Christ to be born of a virgin without any human mixture, we Christians say no more in this than that you pagans say of those whom you style sons of Jové (Gen. vi.). As to the Son of God called Jesus, we should allow him to be nothing more than man, yet the title of the Son of God is very justifiable on account of his wisdom, considering that you (Pagans) have your Mercury in worship under the title of ' the word,' a message of God (Logos)." [Mercury was Hermes the Phallus, and was also called logos, hence the Phallic character of the Logos or " word," the Christ of John's Gospel.] "As to his (Jesus) being born of a virgin you have your Perseus to balance that." So the Fathers claimed nothing for Christianity which was not contained in the Pagan religions, in fact Tertullian about 230 A.D. bitterly laments that Christians adopted all the Pagan Festivals, showing great fickleness compared with the fidelity of the Pagans, who adopted nothing from Christianity. There was nothing to adopt, as Christianity was made up of the essence of pre-existing fables and beliefs.

I have dealt with this fully at pp. 135, 327, *et. seq.*, of my book on *Christianity*, and I must refer the reader to that volume for a full treatment of the subject. Outside of the very comforting though demoralising idea of some innocent person having had his blood shed for your own personal sin, and that by this sacrifice you could enjoy eternal felicity quite regardless of your life's conduct, the origin of the Son of God idea was purely astronomical.

Take, for instance, the Western Asian and the Roman idea. Their Sun god was slain annually by the tusk of the Boar of Winter and born again as a babe. But the idea of the Grand Old Jové or Jupiter being slain annually became abhorrent, and they substituted Sons of Jové as the Sun god, and these were slain annually and passed through Sheol and rose again, ascended into heaven, and were re-absorbed into the God-head exactly as in the case of Jesus in the Christian dogma.

The selfish and debasing doctrine of the innocent suffering for the guilty is very old, and we see in the Old Testament how, down through all their history, the Hebrews continued to burn their children alive as an expiation of their own personal sins.

Under Roman influence Greek philosophy was used to instal a true Sun God in place of the old Tribal Gods with their bands of Eli-im, which, up till that time, every nation set up,—pure Ba-Als, gods of the land—and at that time men changed their gods with change of country, thinking they must do homage to the god of the land in which they were even temporarily staying. " Do in Rome as the Romans do." But the sun remained the same in all countries, and could be made the basis of a universal religion.

But we must not forget that the whole world was interested in, and engaged in a sort of worship far removed from, the Solar idea, a worship symbolised in man's own body, and portraying an idea of eternal life which he could appreciate to the full, and in the practice of which he became participator in the act of the great Creator. The Phallic cult always did and does still retain the most absorbing interest for mankind, and we know that its practice with its great temples of sacred prostitution was universal about the time of the rise of the Christian cult.

Many people think that Christianity condemned all these phallic rites, and brought in a pure spiritual religion. Far from it. Just as in the Old Testament where the priests imposed the law of ten commandments on the people yet secretly inculcate the doctrine that the priest, as instructed by Old Testament examples, may indulge all his passions, murder, adultery, and theft, without any punishment— a liberty called in later times " Benefit of Clergy," in fact the priest portrays Iové or God indulging in all these pleasant pastimes, and exulting in them; so the New Testament, while establishing a Sun God, relegates his sphere of action to heaven, and sets up the representative of the Phallus, i.e., the priesthood, as having all power on earth, and as having sole power of giving or refusing the joys of heaven to men.

This is secretly taught in the New Testament by naming the opening writer Matthew, Matteh (Mattai or Mattheus, Greek and Latin), which is Hebrew for the Rod, Serpent, or Phallus which Moses received from IhOh (Jehovah), and which was the *font et origo* of the Mosaic religion. This rod or phallus of IhOh was exactly the same central symbol of the Hebrew religion, as was the phallus of Osiris in Egypt, where Moses was trained. Both were kept in Arks. The use of Matthew as a name was a statement that, although a sun god was to be worshipped, the phallic practices from which the priests drew their revenues were to be continued. Matthew is still written Matteh in Hungary and in the East.

Here we have a Gospel written by some one who wishes to declare he still adheres to the pillar worship of the Zur, " the Rock that begat thee," and in the genealogy of Jesus he concludes with Jacob or I-Akab (the I being indicative of a proper name and Akab is the

heel or phallus), and Ioseph, a name, as I have
shown, meaning the male and female organs
coupled with the serpent of sexual passion,
and declared to be a god, thus coupling up the
Old and New Testaments.

The supreme symbol of Christianity was the
Cross. The Cross was always and everywhere
regarded as the phallic symbol, par excellence,
or the triple male creative organ, a stem with
two protuberances, and all oaths were sworn
upon it as in earlier times they were sworn on
the actual organ or on the " Rock that begat
thee," and was used as a symbol of the god in
religions all over the world.

Abraham for instance said, in swearing his
servant, " Put, I pray thee, they hand under
my thigh." The cross handle of the sword or
any piercer was the same thing, and oaths
were sworn upon it, as in earlier times they
were sworn on the actual organ; and the
writer of the first and fifth chapters of Genesis
uses the word Zakar—sword—as signifying
male, with the sheath as female (Part I., p. 8),
and then commands the pair to be " fruitful
and multiply " (Genesis i., 27-28). All male
children are called Zakars or piercers in the
Old Testament, and to this day in Palestine,
where, Major Candor says, that peaks on which

the natives hail the new moon are still called zickers, piercers, or Phalli. The phallic nature of the Christian Cross is also shown by its use as our letter X (St. Andrew's Cross) in phallic words. The Pyx is the phallus, modelled after nature in India (pp. 500-501), the " Miracle Worker " or Rod of God of Moses, and is the "miraculous stone" for "testing" gold at our Mint, while the cloth in which it is wrapped by the priests is called the " Pyx Cloth " or the "Corpus Christi Cloth," so Christ is the Phallic God, as was Christna, The Onyx, a stone similar to Opal (admittedly " female-male," with its " water and fire " gleams, and Fornix, prostitute (fornication), and even " Pox," an old name for phallic diseases called Ophalim (pp. 437-443), and Pollex for " finger " when placed to the mouth to make the double-sex sign, and " Matrix " for womb, and even the word " sex " itself, and finally Crucifix, the prime Christian phallic emblem.

The literary and religious drama unrolled in the New Testament tells us the tale of the introduction of sun worship as the official centre of the religion, and describes the struggle between this pure religion and the old phallic cult with its unfortunate penalty of disease, and clearly details the compromise made—a compromise which was at the time a triumph for Phallism, in this world.

The Cross was adopted at a late date in Christianity. Everywhere a simple phallus of stone or pillar (pillar being simply the Hindu pala), or Lat was erected for worship or prayers for health, safety, or good luck, at all crossways or centres of villages, and at ferries, where there was some danger in crossing, hence they came to be called crosses. Latterly the two cross arms were added, making the male triple organ. Nearly all the ancient crosses still existing are simply pillars (Hindu Palas) or Lats, like those shown on pp. 33, 46, 47, or Figs. 4, 7, and 8 on p. 235, Vol. III., and have only been replaced by crosses in modern times. The Cross was a Hindoo phallic symbol long before Christianity, as seen in ancient Hindoo Temples, one of which I show at p. 404 (Queen of Heaven Study).

CHAPTER IV

PETER OR THE ROCK

The narrative detailed in pp. 76-80 begins with the sun myth, birth of a son of God by a virgin, exactly as detailed by the Romans of the other Iové, of the birth of Perseus by Jupiter (Jové), and Danae, and foreshadowed in the Old Testament, where we are told in Genesis vi., "that the sons of god saw the daughters of men that they were fair . . . and the sons of God came in unto the daughters of men and they bare children to them, the same became mighty men which were of old, men of renown," the precise history of the Roman Jové and his sons (see Augustine, p. 237. Then after the stormy solar youth of Jesus and his active campaign had begun we see a struggle between him and Simon Peter, to whom he yields the keys of heaven.

The name of this principal Apostle, to whom the son of God yielded up all his power on earth, and his judgment as to who should enter

heaven, is a mixture of Greek and Hebrew.
In the first place he is simply called Simon, or
Simeon, then Simon Peter, or Simon Barjona,
and finally Peter or Cephas.   The name
Simon is unknown in any language, but it is
the same as Simeon son of Jacob, founder of
the tribe of that name, and the Rabbis gave
the meaning of the name as " Hearing," and
that is the interpretation given in the dictionaries, as derived from the root S M A, to hear ;
the second name Peter or Petros, the Greek
for Rock (as we say Petroleum, rock oil), so
his full name is the " hearing stone " or rock.
We remember that Joshua " took a great
stone and set it up under an oak tree . . .
and said it hath heard all the words of the
Lord (Joshua's own words) which he spake
unto us " (Joshua xxiv., 26-27).   This was the
universal system, and is largely prevalent still
in Eastern countries ; and the ancients believed
that any stone so set up became a god, or the
dwelling-place of a god, and heard their vows.
This was the Zur of the Old Testament, the
" Rock that begat thee " (pp. 33, 94, 168, Part
I.), with a capital R for Rock, and in Hebrew a
capital Tzadi for Zur, indicating its god-ship.
So the old custom was to be continued, the
" hearing stone " being symbolised in a man

who was invested by the Son of God with a god's powers. Jesus after eulogising Peter as Simon Bar Jona, Simon, son of iona, the male organ, says to him, " Thou art Peter (Greek Petros) and upon this rock (Greek Petra) will I build my church." Here we see the man's name and its real meaning are revealed just as was Isaac's in his " sporting " with Rebekah (see p. 132, Part I.). Peter is the old Zur, Tsur, Sur, or Sul of the Old Testament, who was the Hebrew's god " who is a Rock (Zur) save our God " (or gods, eli-im) " 2nd Samuel, 22-32). " Make a joyful noise to the Rock of our salvation " (Psalm xcv., 1). That the Simon Peter or " hearing rock " was believed to be alive and to hear vows is stated in the *Encyclopædia Biblica* at col. 2982, and that this superstition was common to other nations is clear from the writing of Arnobius, " When I espied an anointed stone or one bedaubed with olive oil as if some person resided in it, I worshipped it, I addressed myself to it and begged blessings."

" Their rock is not as our Rock," in Deut. xxxii., 31, illustrates the same dishonesty, which was practised in the case of the word Elohim or gods, plural and small g for gods when it is other tribes' Elohim, and the

use of the singular and capital G—God—when
it is the Hebrew Elohim. The other tribes'
rock has a small R, while the Hebrews' Rock
has a capital. " Where are their gods, their
rock in whom they trusted?" (Deuteronomy
xxxii., 37). We find then the son of God
giving all power on earth to this humanised
phallus, " And I say unto thee, That thou art
Peter (the rock) and upon this rock I will
build my church . . . and I will give unto
thee the keys of the Kingdom of Heaven;
and whatsoever thou shalt bind on earth shall
be bound in heaven; And whatsoever thou
shalt loose on earth shall be loosed in
heaven."

Here is the active member of the Godhead
Creating another god upon earth with power
to admit whomsoever he liked to heaven in
spite of the Judgment day, in fact Jesus dele-
gates to Peter all power as far as the connection
of this world and heaven is concerned, as did
Pharaoh to Joseph—the additional god (Part I.,
p. 155). He declares, in short, that although he
is the god ruling over all, yet he will restrict his
rule to heaven (as does the sun), and he creates
an earthly god who has the entire say as to
who is to enter heaven or be denied eternal
bliss, and this earthly god is the Phallus or

" Rock that begat thee." This is, of course, the verse on which rests the whole fabric of Popery, the most baleful influence which has ever appeared in history. Some of the artists employed by the Roman Curia carried out this idea in bronze, and there is still preserved in the Vatican museum a statue illustrated and described by Payne Knight thus :—" The celebrated bronze in the Vatican has the male organs of generation placed upon the head of a cock supported by the neck and shoulders of a man. In this composition they represent the generative power of the Eros, the Osiris, Mithras, or Bacchus. By the inscription on the pedestal the attribute thus personified is styled ' The Saviour of the World,' ' Soter Kosmoi ' [or Kosmou], a title always venerable under whatever image it be presented."

But let us see what the modern church critics think of the truth of the story of Peter. The *Encyclopædia Biblica*, the most authoritative publication we have—compiled by Church Professors of all the great colleges—tells us, column 4564, the " Acts [of the Apostles] is seen to have little claim to our confidence in anything it has to say about Peter. . . . " If the Acts was composed about 100-130 A.D., its sources may easily have been late enough

to be legendary in character." I assert that
the whole New Testament is legendary and
symbolical. Column 4565—" The main thing
reported . . . cannot be regarded as historical. . ." " The case of Aeneas, moreover, shows how little the author of the Acts
felt it necessary to form himself any concrete
image of what he was relating." . . " The
story cannot possibly have come from the
mouth of an eye-witness; . . its historicity
becomes questionable;" . . " the credulity
of his [the writer of Acts] narrative is rendered
questionable by the circumstance that within
the compass of a few verses he sets forth two
wholly irreconcilable views." [This is the
character of the whole scriptures, Old Testament and New Testament included, and they
are simply " views."] Column 4567—" Observe, moreover, that a main point in contents,
the proof of the resurrection of Jesus drawn
from Psalm xvi., 10 (Acts ii., 27), is possible
only when G [Greek version] (not M.T.)
[Massoretic Text] is followed, and would thus
have been impossible in the mouth of Peter."
[So we see that there are two " words of God,"
Greek and Massoretic.] " Thus it appears
that on the whole the Acts adds extraordinarily
little of a trustworthy character to what we

already know about Peter from the Pauline Epistles [which are shown to be entirely apocryphal, see pp. 109-110]. The walking on the water is discussed as follows :—Column 4569—" Critical investigation demands that it be given up as a statement of prosaic matter of fact ; . . the desire of Peter that Jesus should bid him to come on the water is, literally speaking, simply childish."   " There are other narratives also which require no detailed proof of their unhistorical character " (column 4569). The angel speaking to Peter at the Tomb is also declared to be untrue, and the withering of the fig tree (column 4569). The phrases, " must be given up," " this second fact would rob the other of its value," " doubtful, even text-critically," " the historical character must be given up, " cannot be regarded as historical," are sprinkled all through the article on Simon Peter. " It is unthinkable " (column 4573). " Passing from these unquestionably unhistorical elements " (column 4571) ; " quite irreconcilable;" " at hopeless variance " (column 4592).

The cock crowing incident is shown to have crept into the text only gradually, and column 4576 states that the cock-crowing incident is called in question because " it was forbidden by law to keep fowls in Jerusalem."

Why, then, was this fictitious person and history introduced into the New Testament?

The old Hebrew religion took no account of heaven, and, as Sayce says in *Higher Criticism*, p. 279 : —" The Mosaic law maintained a resolute silence on the doctrine of a future life. Of the doctrine of a resurrection there is not a whisper. The law of Israel did not look beyond the grave." But wherever the sun was worshipped the idea of a future life was always present. The greater part of the complicated Egyptian ritual dealt with this idea.

Hitherto, therefore, the priests of the Hebrews with their phallic feasts, tents of Venus, breaking of the waters, etc. (see my *Queen of Heaven and her Debasement*), had a supreme command over the conduct and lives of their people, as the voice of the High Priest was the voice of Iové (Joshua xxiv., 26-27), and Iové was the Phallus or Rock. This is clear from Joshua xxiv., where he delivers a long speech to the Israelites, relating their history, beginning as usual with the phrase, " Thus saith the Iové of the Eli-im of Israel," and after setting up a Phallus under an Oak, he says : —" Behold, this stone shall be a witness unto us, for *it hath heard all the words* of the Lord which he spake unto us," while as a matter of fact Iové never spoke a single word. Joshua was the sole speaker, and the stone the " hearer."

With the advent of Sun worship there was a fear that the old predominant phallic worship would take second place, and we feel all through the Gospels the shadow of this hidden struggle—Peter and Jesus having, as it were, a fear of each other. Jesus challenges Peter to declare his divinity, and in return he gives this Peter or Rock the keys of heaven and the power of a god, thus insuring that the worship of the " Rock that begat thee," with its great Kadeshoth revenues, shall flourish unchallenged on earth, and the solar worship of the Saviour will be relegated to another world.

We shall see that the death of Jesus was taught by Paul to have paid all debts incurred in transgression of the law, so that the uncontrolled reign of phallism in all its debased forms would still constitute the great staple of the church's industry and the source of its wealth. After the introduction of Christianity the clergy lapsed into the most licentious body of men known to history. All historians tell the same tale, but we may quote some lines from Lecky, an author accessible to everyone, who in his *History of European Morals* gives a glimpse here and there of the state of the church.

In Volume II., p. 329, Lecky says :—" I can at present, however, only refer to the vast mass of evidence which has been collected on the subject, derived *from the writings of the Catholic divines and from the decrees of Catholic councils* during the space of many centuries " [my italics, to show the unbiassed source of the information]. " It is a popular illusion which is specially common amongst writers who have little direct knowledge of the Middle Ages, that the atrocious immorality of the monasteries in the century before the Reformation was a new fact, and that the ages when the faith of man was undisturbed were ages of great moral purity. In fact, it appears from uniform testimony of the ecclesiastical writers that ecclesiastical immorality in the eighth and following centuries was little if at all less outrageous than in any other period, while the Papacy during almost the whole of the tenth century was held by men of infamous lives."

On p. 330 :—" A tax called Culagium, which was in fact a license to clergymen to keep concubines, was during several centuries systematically levied by Princes."

P. 331 :—" The writers of the middle ages are full of nunneries that were like brothels, of the vast multitude of infanticides within their walls, and of the inveterate presence of incest among the clergy, which rendered it necessary again and again to issue the most stringent enactments that priests should not be permitted to live with their mothers or sisters."

P. 217, Vol. II. :—" The Monks, partly by the wealth they had acquired, sank into gross and general immorality."

P. 219 :—" The outrageous and notorious immorality of the monasteries . . . was chiefly due to their great wealth " (see also my *Christianity*, p. 338; also this volume, p. 154).

The cock crowing incident is quite clear from the symbolical point of view. The cock is, all over the world the solar symbol, not the phallic, as cocks crow to the rising sun. In India the peacock is also the solar representative. So when the cock crew the third time (the number three denotes success and a male god), it was indicative of the final triumph of Solar worship, " and Peter went out and wept bitterly," not in sadness but with chagrin at defeat as far as official religion was concerned. This is symbolically illustrated by the cock on the top of the spire of Christian churches. The spire is the Ish, phallus, or husband of the church, and it rests on the earth, while the cock or sun rules above.

This triumph of the Asiatic sun-saviour idea meant the final defeat of the Jewish " An eye for an eye " or payment for transgression doctrine and brought in the Saviour idea where the private prayers of a man might secure his salvation and forgiveness of sins if he merely believed that his particular Saviour, Jesus, or another, had died to remit all punishment—a belief widely held in Asia thousands of years before Jesus. Before this, every sin had its redemption price payable to the priest in cash or cattle, and every crime was legal if done under priestly sanction. Adultery was a crime having its sacrifice price if done by a man privately, but the Feast of Tabernacles was a feast of adultery and incest, which, so far from being criminal, were meritorious acts because done by priestly sanction, nay even commanded to strangers and enemies by the great Iové, as in Zechariah xiv., 16, where " everyone that is left of all the nations which came against Jerusalem shall even go up from year to year to worship the King, the Lord of

Hosts, and to keep the Feast of Tabernacles."
By the way it was no feast, but primarily a
" dance," and that " dance " or " play " was
adultery under the sanction of religion (see
my *Romance of the Hebrew Tabernacle*.)
When the Israelites " rose up to play " Dr.
Adam Clark and the *Encyclopædia Biblica* tells
us this meant pairing for open sexual intercourse. That the Israelites could invite former
enemies to a dance where incest was rife, is
very indicative of their extremely low moral
status, or even want of manliness. The Feast
of Tabernacles was still held in all its phallic
glory at the time of Jesus. So here we have
another of the semi-gods of the Hebrews,
Peter, living on earth but with the keys of
Heaven in his hand, a position since mono-
polised by the Pope of Rome, with his " indulgencies," or sin licenses.

But Peter was a purely Hebraic character,
and although the worship of the " Rock " was
widespread, it seems to have been the peculiar
Zur of the Israelites which was to rule on earth
under Peter. This word Zur or Tsur was once
widespread, and, as S and T are interchangeable and R and L are identical, we find such
towns as Tyre which should be Tur and our
word tower were identical with Zur. Sur. or

Sul. Tyre is still called Sur on many maps, and Sul was the common name for a holy peak or a sacred pillar all over ancient Germany. Our words " Peel Tower " applied to the round towers of Ireland are simply " Palic or Phallic towers," Pala Tur, and we find the word as Tor in Devonshire and Derbyshire as a peak of rock.

The fructifying part of the male organ, the Orchis or Orchané (Testicles) of the Greeks yields our word Orchard, " the place of fruits," and—as witnessing or swearing an oath was performed by holding the testicles—an oath in Greek is Orkos. The testicles on which Abraham swore his servant are called Eduth or Witnesses, and we continue the parallel by calling witnessing testifying, back to the Latin Testes. Multiply this example by hundreds, and one gets an idea of the phallic ideas which have inter-penetrated the languages of all nations by familiar words from others.

CHAPTER V

PAUL

The compilers of the New Testament, probably under Roman influences, thought it important to have another purely phallic prophet or godlet introduced who would not be strictly Hebraic, but claiming to be a Roman citizen; and they took the bold step of naming him after the ancient and universal Indian name for the phallus, Pala, or Pal, used as Pul in the Old Testament. And we have created for us the Apostle Paul, a purely fictitious personage whose existence and writings have been negatived by modern criticism. Let us look at the great compendium of church criticism, the *Encyclopædia Biblica*, and see what the Professors of Oxford have to say as to the reality of the Pauline story.

The *Encyclopædia Biblica* says the name Paul is difficult to understand or explain, and the writer abandons the attempt, but these writers seem to be, or pretend to be, ignorant of the names and symbols used by the univer-

sal cult of the religious world, phallism. Paul
is Pala, or Phul, or Phulu, or Pul, or Phallu,
or Palu of the Old Testament; the " p " being
sometimes hard (as our " p ") and sometimes
soft as in the " ph " or the open P, our " F."

He is even openly described in language
commonly used to describe the Phallus as
" Bald," or Bald-head, and we remember the
Tonsure of Siddartha (p. 162, Part I.), the
" Rosh Geeza," bald or shaved one, or Korah,
the ribald epithet applied by children to Elisha
(see p. 163, Part I.).   He is further described
as short of stature with a prominent nose, a
common description of the phallus; in fact, he
was the " Adam," the " Red," or " Naked "
one (see p. 143).

Paul is, of course, only known to us from
the " Acts " and the Epistles attributed to
him; and in a very learned analysis of the
researches on this subject the *Encyclopædia
Biblica* says : —

Column 3627—" The principal Epistles cannot be the work of Paul," and A. D. Loman,
of Amsterdam, " upholds the entirely symbolical character of the whole Gospel history."
Column 3624—" We cannot regard the ' Acts '
as a true and credible first-hand narrative of
what had actually occurred. The Book bears

in part a legendary historical and, in part, an edifying and apologetic character." Column 3625—With respect to the Pauline Epistles in the New Testament, " there are none of them by Paul." " Neither fourteen, nor thirteen, nor nine or ten, nor seven or eight, nor yet even the four so long universally regarded as unassailable. They are all, without distinction, pseudepigrapha." So Paul, as a writer, disappears. Column 3630—" The conclusions of criticism on our knowledge of the life and activity of Paul are of a purely negative character." [Not one point of his history or actions has been proved, or even shown to be probable; everything stated has been shown to be false.] Column 3630— " Thus all the representations formerly current regarding the life and work of Paul must be set aside. These representations are very many and various and discrepant in character; far from showing any resemblance to one another, they exhibit the most inconsistent proportions and features. But, however different they were, they all of them have disappeared; they rested upon a foundation, not of solid rock, but of shifting sand. So, too, . . . the ' ideas,' the ' theology,' the ' system ' of Paul " have " irrevocably passed

away, the right foundation being wanting."
We possess no Epistle of Paul."   Column
4145 says that the " Roman Church was *not*
founded by Peter or Paul."

The *Encyclopædia Biblica* concludes that
" it is always better, safer, and more profitable
to know that one does not know [Huxley's
position] than to go on building on a basis
that is imaginary."   A bold conclusion, because the basis of all supernatural religion is
purely imaginary.   Why, then, were all these
" Epistles " written under the name of the
Phallus, the Rod of God of the Old Testament?

The purpose of these competitions amongst
the clergy—for many hands penned Epistles
and many brains were busy to help on the
" good work "—was that of establishing a
Free Church outside the " law," to make the
new religion popular.   There were scores of
Epistles written, most of them, however, too
honest and too nakedly written in their support of Phallism.   The Church requires carefully wrapped-up symbolism and statements
always varied or contradicted elsewhere, or
stated in such obscure language as to give a
fertile field for discussion.   Mystery is the
food on which religion lives, and the more

credulous the person is, the better a church-man will he make (see my *Christianity*, p. 119). We will now glance at the true teaching for the priests' private enlightenment, as told in the " Acts " and the Epistles by Paul's sayings, journeys, acts, and companions. Both Saul of the Old Testament and Saul or Paul of the New Testament were Benjamites or sons of Gemini (see marginal notes, 1st Samuel ix., 1; Judges iii., 15; Judges, xix., 16), and the Gemini were the twin sons of Jupiter with Leda, to whom he appeared as a Swan. They are an extremely phallic pair, and, as the astronomical " twins," they had originally a still more phallic origin. Paul travelled in the ship named Castor and Pollux, the Gemini, and this name is evidently used as another link in the chain of symbolical hints to the clergy, as Castor and Pollux are, of course, the Gemini or Benjamites. Benjamin is Ben, son of, and Gemini or Jemini, the twins, spelt both ways in our Bible. The use of Gemini, quite foreign to Hebrew, shows the Roman control of the composition of the Bible.

We find one Saul, who was busy helping to put down the new Christian or Sun worship by haling men and women to prison. Now,

Sun worship is a masculine religion, whereas
the Hebrews were originally, as Arabians,
worshippers of the night sky, with the moon
as queen of heaven (Goldziher), and very
happy they were under her benign reign (see
Jeremiah xliv.), and their time, feasts, sab-
baths, and years were all regulated by the
female moon. Saul of the Old Testament was
a Benjamite, and there are two phrases repeated in four texts (Judges iii., 15; Judges
xix., 1-30; Judges xx., 15-16; 1st Samuel ix., 1—
and so considered to be of great importance
—wherein the Benjamites are declared to be
sons of Gemini or Jemini and to be left
handed, meaning worshippers of the female.

The first text especially emphasises the Benjamite as being of the left-hand cult; so Saul of
the old Benjamites, and the New Testament
Saul, the new Benjamite or left-hand persecu-
tor of the right-hand cult, are linked together.
The new Saul in the New Testament is a perse-
cutor of the new Sun worshippers, and his
name (now in Greek) means " effeminate," or
simply " feminine "—meaning he is like his
namesake in the Old Testament, a man of the
left-hand cult, an adorer of the Muliebre
Pudendum Yoni, woman, or Queen of Heaven.
When going on his mission to persecute the

Sun worshippers, the sun himself (" a bright light ") shines so strongly on Saul as to blind him, and calls out (in the person of Jesus), " Saul, Saul, why persecutest thou me?" (compare Exodus xxiv., 17 and 10). He is taken blind to Damascus, and a Christian disciple is sent by Kurios, the Sun (disguised by the word Lord in the English version of the New Testament), to cure him in the name of Jesus. There are then several chapters of Acts, x., xi., and xii., devoted to Peter, the Rock, and Saul is apparently forgotten; but suddenly in Acts xiii. it is said :—" Then Saul (who is also called Paul)," and so the left-hand cult and name are finally abandoned, and " Paul," a form of the Indian Pala, the Phallus, became his name. So he, like Jacob, changing Luz to Bethel (Genesis xxviii., 19), changes from the left-hand or feminine cult to that of the right-hand or masculine. Pala has all forms of vowels— Pall, Pale, Pel, Peel, Pile, Poll, Pole, Pul, Pyle, and compounds Pawl and Paul, which is Paol in other languages; so all the vowels, a, e, i, o, u, w, and y, have been used. The Greeks also distinguished masculine from feminine by P and S, as in Philip, male love, and Phillis, female love, or in Sal, Pul, Saul, Paul, male and female cults.

As though to prepare for the New Testament, as in the case of the two Josephs, the Old Testament has men named as the Phallus in Palu, Pallu, or Phallu, with the variation in spelling, as in Pala and Phallus, and has also the left-hand phallic cult in Salu, so Salu and Palu are forerunners of Saul and Paul (see Genesis xlvi., 9; Exodus vi., 14; Numbers xxv., 14; Numbers xxvi., 5-8). There is another direct connection in Sur or Sar, the " Rock that begat thee " (Numbers xxv., 15), which is also written Sul, so we have Sul and Pul, phallic King of Assyria, mentioned in 2nd Kings xv., 19. Sul was largely used in Germany in the time of the Romans, and they used to gather round a great column called the " Irmin " or " Herman Sul," the " God column," or God Rock, Tsur Elohim of the Old Testament, and vow peace or war, make covenants, or take other great decisions, as did the Israelites. The name is still common, as in the picturesque peak or sacred " rock " hill, the Sulberg, the hill of the Holy Rock or Phallic Rock, near Hamburg, and Sulgrave Manor, ancient home of the Washington family, which gave America its President, and Langdon tells of hundreds of Suls (Phalli) in Cornwall alone.

Another interesting point is that, as R and L are the same letters in old languages (both palatals), Pul, the Assyrian King's name, becomes Pur, or in Greek Pyr, fire, the male element, originally the fire of passion. The equivalence of R and L is well illustrated in the Bible name of a god, " Belial," which is also written in the Hebrew Bible, Beliar and Berial, showing both L's separately replaced by R. Others occur, such as Mercurius and Markulis, and Mazzaroth and Mazzaloth. So the man Saul of the left-hand cult becomes Paul, the direct representative of the Phallus, is converted into a strong convert of the right-hand cult, worshipping the sun as Saviour, and carries Christianity under the phallic cross as a solo-phallic cult, to the ends of the earth. Saul or Salu means in Hebrew the " thing which may be erected," and Palu, the " miracle worker," " miraculous one," or that from which the miracle of life arises—the Rod of God which Moses found in " Midian," and with which he performed all his miracles—so both are the phallus; but Salu indicates adherents of the left-hand or feminine cult, like Vishnu in India, while Palu is like Siva or Christna, the Christ of the Hindoos, the right-hand cult, as was Saul after he was called Paul, when he became the worker of miracles, like the Rod of God in the hands of Moses.

Paul is said to be a " Tent-maker." We remember the tents of Venus at the Feast of Tabernacles (or tents), or Succoth, a name so important that towns were named after it, and this is no doubt another cryptic utterance to tell the priests of Paul's true mission, a teacher of free Kadeshism. So we see the two great founders of Christianity are simply priestly creations asserting that the old phallic worship was to be continued by the circumcised Jews, by the old Hebrew method of Tents of Venus, or Succoth Benoth, represented by Peter, and by the more open pagan method of Temple women and uncircumcised men, represented by Paul; or simply by the devotees lying together to increase their religious zeal, as was so often asserted of the Christians, a practice still extant in Sakti worship in Hindoostan, Abyssinia, and other countries.

The second statement in the text referred to on p. 112 links up the two Sauls through the constellation of Gemini. In the margins we are told that the Benjamites are the sons of Gemini or Jemini. and the two Sauls are stated to be Benjamites. The Gemini were the Dioscouri or the " Lads " of God, the same as the two stones, called Eduth or Testimony, which Moses put in the Ark. This is shown by the name of one of the Gemini, Castor, that which was removed when a man was castrated, or from Castor (the Beavor), which with the Turtle has genital organs of extraordinary size, which are eaten to produce fecundity and to cure maladies of the womb. The other twin is Pollux, the same word as Phallus, and used in that sense when Harpocrates placed his "pollex" or fore-finger at his mouth to make the double-sexed symbol of life. The word Lad, Lat, or Lath, Hindu for the phallus, has a phallic colour-ing even to this day. So Saul in the Old Testament is of a very phallic origin, and is of the cult which is opposed to the male sun, like the New Testament Saul. He was re-placed by David or Dudu, the "-cupid " or " love " king of the right-hand cult.

In ancient times, when the worship of the Queen of Heaven was widespread, the devo-tees vowed perpetual virginity to the great mother; and to prevent their breaking their vows they emasculated themselves voluntarily (see *Encyclopædia Biblica,* under Paphos, and my *Christianity* and *Queen of Heaven*). The priesthood was thus at that time composed principally of Eunuchs. Circumcision may have been introduced as symbolical castration to avoid destroying the priests' manhood; and any cult depending on circumcision must theoretically uphold continence as the greatest virtue. As a matter of fact, the effect was contrary. The great attention called to the phallus by circumcision produced a highly erotic nation, or the Jews may have been so intensely erotic as to have discovered circumcision as an aphrodasiac, as many authors assert. The new dispensation changed all this, and instead of the very severe Jewish ritual, the Christians had constant love feasts, and " faith alone " was required to purge away one's sin. What a glorious prospect for phallic worshippers this freedom from the " law " opened out ! Hence Christianity flourished amazingly.

The constant repression of the natural " wildness " of man under the old Hebrew religion was extremely irksome, while here was a religion offered where all man's sin was taken over by another, if one had only faith enough to believe that Jesus died to pay for all our sins in advance. Faith alone could gain for a man the entrance to heaven. Complete emancipation from "law" was promised. Jesus had laid up an infinitely large cash deposit in heaven, and no matter how much we squandered on earth, we could always draw a cheque on the bank of heaven (see Dean Inge in the Preface) to clear off our debts and secure a place in paradise. This was a delightful doctrine, and, as we know, it caught on. Life was hard enough for men in these times, and the affairs of earth demanded much labour and sorrow; so, when a new doctrine requiring no material sacrifices of costly animals, no intervention of any priest, no fees, but solely a matter between the man and this faith in Jesus, was it wonderful that the Christian religion became the religion of the poor? And the poor meant practically the whole population. The desire for the fleshly enjoyments, which were the sole pleasures of the people in these days, was still as strong, and here was a religion which carried a free pardon for all excesses, and no priestly indulgence to be paid for. As late as the eighteenth century a Protestant divine thus explains justification by faith. " Even adultery and murder do not hurt the pleasant children [those who have faith], but rather

work for their good.   God sees no sin in
believers, whatever sin they may commit.   My
sins might displease God; my person is always
acceptable to him.   Though I should out-sin
Manasses, I should not the less be a pleasant
child, because God always views me in
Christ."   Here is the new Gospel carried out
to its legitimate conclusion.   Could the degradation of human reason sink to lower
depths?

The "Apostle Paul's" writing is tinted all
through by the doctrine of free love and a
covert objection to marriage.   He says that
no works of the flesh (Sarx, Basar, Phallus)
can be justified by the law, but only by the
new religion, faith.   Even the symbol of continence or male virginity, the circumcision,
was to be abandoned; he comes to teach the
" uncircumcision."   The Epistle of Galatians
is one long jesuitical plea for free sexual intercourse.   In 1st Corinthians x., 4, he tells them
that the " Rock was Christ."   Certainly the
" Rock that begat thee," our Dorset pillar or
phallus (Part I., p. 33), was the anointed one,
the Christ.   It is called to this day the Christ-
in-hand.   Paul speaks of knowing Christ after
the Flesh or Phallus.   He even clearly teaches
the modern cult, to which necessity has driven

the young people of Paris and Berlin, and other towns where rents are high. (1912).

" But if any man think that he behave himself uncomely towards his virgin, if she pass the flower of her age, and need so require, let him do what he will, he sinneth not [" let them marry " is by another hand, as it directly contradicts what he is teaching]. " Nevertheless, he that standeth steadfast in his heart having no necessity, but hath power over his own will, hath so decreed in his heart that he will keep his virgin, *doeth well*. So then he that giveth her in marriage doeth well; but he that giveth her not in marriage doeth better." Free love in cryptic language, or making the girl into a private Kadeshah, on the Cyrenaic idea, is taught; as well as the avoidance of the production of children in case of marriage, " by the power over his own will." The " marrying not " is the cult so much discussed a few years ago, and which has found so many disciples in modern towns that the problem facing statesmen in the near future is the question of how the populations of modern European countries are to be kept up. Everyone wishes to " keep his virgin " now. It is openly stated that the young army officers of Berlin have gone back to patriarchal times, and the popular cult among them is digyny, like Jacob, with his two sister wives, Rachel and Leah, dimly repeated in their maids, Bilhah and Zilpah. (1912).

In Acts xiii., 1, we have a statement about prophets and teachers connected with the Church of Antioch, which throws much light on the teaching.

Barnabus, " son of the prophet," or Nabi, Mercury, also called Joseph (a god), is linked up with Simeon, " that was called Niger " (Black), or the " hearing Rock which was Black," or " the Black hearer of prayers." Now, nearly all the famous phallic temple stones to which devotees prayed were black; the famous Hebrew or Arab stone in the Al Kaba (belly) at Mecca (Makah, womb) is a black stone; and so we have in Simeon Niger the old, old phallic symbol. Then we have Lucius of Cyrene, " the strong one " or " Lion " of Cyrene, where the phallic doctrine that intense ephemeral sexual pleasures were the chief end of man's existence and the only object worth pursuing. The lion was held to be the most salacious of all animals. These phallically named preachers accompanied Manaen and Paul.

The *Encyclopædia Biblica* has shown us

(see pp. 260 and 262 this volume) that the man Paul is a mere pen name, and used by different priests or monks, under which to weave their phallic and mirophilic web, and to create a *double entendre* text for the priests' secret information. This esoteric atmosphere saturates all priestly writing, and they were so full of the joy of deceiving and playing on the intelligence of the laity, that they engaged in all sorts of puns and hidden " unseemly levity " in their writings. They employed another method of parable in these writings which would also make an interesting study, but which I can only touch on here, and that is the journeys the imaginary Paul is supposed to have made, and his " going through " the phallic centres. The inverted commas are from the *Encyclopædia Biblica*. Paul started his round of visits at Antioch, of which the *Encyclopædia Biblica*, column 186, says :— " In no city was pleasure more earnestly pursued. Duplices mores were proverbial; the Orontes was synonymous with superstition and depravity."

Gibbon, in his great classic, tells us in polished periods that the " ancient rites of Greece were imitated by the royal colony of Antioch, and that thirty thousand pounds

were annually applied to public pleasures.
Amidst groves a thousand streams of the
purest water issuing from every hill preserved
the verdure of the earth and the temperature
of the air; the senses were gratified with har-
monious sounds and aromatic odours; and the
peaceful groves were consecrated to health and
joy, to luxury and love.   The vigorous youth
pursued, like Apollo, the object of his desires;
the blushing maid " [or rather unblushing
temple Kadesha] " was warned by the fate of
Daphne to shun the folly of unseasonable coy-
ness." Strabo tells us more bluntly that
" hundreds of sacred prostitutes or Kadesha
were kept at the temples, and that this Antioch
was the focus from which spread the most
violent phallic cults all over Western Syria;"
and it was significantly the focus from which
Paul made all his journeyings.   Leaving
Antioch, he took ship from Seleucia, the sea-
port of Antioch, and equally famous for degraded religious sensuality, to the place most
famous in the whole annals of the world as
being the headquarters of what Paul calls
" freedom from the law "—that is, promiscuous religious prostitution—the famous
Island of Cyprus.   He landed at Salamis, a
celebrated centre of female worship, and

" passing through " the Island, he arrived at the most famous shrine the world has seen, namely, Paphos. Every form of religious vice was carried on here on the most extensive and luxurious scale, a thousand sacred prostitutes being maintained at the principal temples. So great was the fame of Paphos for the practice of the rites of Venus or Aphrodite that the word Paphian is used as synonymous with prostitute in our modern dictionaries, and " Paphos and Paphia " as Lingam and Yoni, or as the male and female prostitutes of the temples.

The *Encyclopædia Biblica* (column 3555) tells us that " Paphos owed its celebrity to the Paphian Queen, the Goddess Paphia, who was identified with Aphrodite and also the Babylonian Istar, and the Phœnician Astarte," and of Diana, a very inclusive Queen of Love. " The characteristic of the worship lay in the strongly organised college of priests and priestesses living, often in thousands, round the Temple (c.p. Strabo, 558, of Comana Pontica ; see Diana), and the sexual excesses of the devotees and their self mutilation (c.p. Alhan. Contra. Graec., 10), constituted the Cyprian cutlus of the deification of lust." or the deification, adoration, and sacramental practice of the sexual act.

" As at other centres of the worship, the goddess was represented only by a conical stone (c.p. Mass. Tyr. and Tac. Hist., 2-3), c.p. *Coins*, and see *Perga*, also at Pessinus in Galatia." Pessinus was the centre of the most voluptuous worship of Cybele, or more correctly Kubele. Kubl is Arabic for the Muliebre Pudendum. Note that Perga and Pessinus were also frequently visited by Paul, but what he did there, other than worshipping like the others, we are not told. He also visited Corinth, inhabited by a population, who, the *Encyclopædia Biblica* tells us in column 3615, " had added to the traditional worship of Aphrodite the still more sensuous cults of the East," and it was famous for its " filthy sensuality." The names of these famous phallic shrines were quite enough cryptic notice to the priests reading this " new gospel " to tell them the sort of worship which writers of the epistles of the imaginary Paul were inculcating.

" Models of the image were sold as charms (Athen., 1518, c.p., ' silver shrines ' at Ephesus, Acts xix., 24, used somewhat differently). The fame of the Paphian shrines attracted costly gifts and distinguished pilgrims (for example Titus visited it before undertaking his campaign against the Jews, *Tac. History*, 2-2f). The apostles appear not to have come into direct conflict with this worship." Quite naturally as the Acts and Epistles show us that they were specially engaged in teaching its holy character and its exemption from control of the priests under the old Hebrew " Law " through the sacrifice of Jesus. But the *Encyclopædia Biblica* goes on to say, " It should be remembered that an analogous cult must have been familiar to them at Antioch in Syria." In fact their journeys only include famous phallic shrines, so that was their religion. "Although a considerable time must be implied in the expression, ' Go through the isle ' (Acts xiii., 6), this did not bring them into collision with the native priests," because they were not opposed to the old cult but were making its practice universal. The opposition came almost entirely from the Hebrew priests whose income they were destroying. Only at Ephesus did the priests and silversmiths protest, because Paul taught maiden worship *under any or no Goddess*, whereas the Ephesians had established the supremacy of their Diana and it was a source

of wealth to them locally, endangered by
" Paul's " very wide teaching.

Paul made several voyages in his history, but
only in one is the name of the ship mentioned,
and it is given there as being called " Castor
and Pollux," the Gemini or Twins, and Paul
was a son of Gemini or a Ben-jamite. The
Gemini in the Zodiac were frequently represented in the Zodiac as sexual twins, a man and
a woman conjoined, which we see so often in
Greek pottery decorations in the British
Museum, and they are still represented as male
and female " in coitu," as shown by Edgar
Thurston in his book on *Omens and Superstitions in Southern India,*" p. 114, where he
tells of such pairs being worshipped. They
were similarly depicted on the old bronze
doors of St. Peter's at Rome, signifying eternal
life, or creation of life. Castor and Pollux
were held in special veneration in Cyrene.
This town was the birthplace of Aristippus and
gave the name to a school of philosophy
" Cyrenaics," which held that intense ephemeral pleasures are to be preferred to more
lasting tranquil enjoyment. This doctrine is
called Hedonism, which means that pleasure is
the chief good, and the only rational aim of
human conduct, a doctrine which Paul is made

to teach secretly, as he journeyed in an exceedingly phallically named ship bearing two god-names, Castor and Pollux, which were the very soul and essence of phallism, and whose cult was the worship of intense ephemeral pleasures of the senses as being the only pursuit worthy of rational men. Paul was preaching that the embargo on this pursuit had been abolished by the death of Jesus, who " had paid the price in full."

Now Paul is supposed by Christians to be engaged in preaching against these practices, but he was really engaged in undermining the power of the Jewish priests to collect fees by announcing the glad tidings that " sacrifices " were no longer necessary to purge away sin, as Jesus had made the universal sacrifice; and so Paul was taking away the only source of income of the priests. In fact he was engaged in a new or modern Rebellion of Korah (Paul and Korah are identical in meaning, see Part I., pp, 138-146), saying that every man was as sacred as the priest, and by the death of Jesus he had only to have private faith in the efficacy of that sacrifice to have direct access to God without the intervention of any priest. Hence he could carry on the practices of the Succoth Benoth without paying any fees to the priests.

In fact the thing which enraged the priesthood most was that male and female " Saints " of the Christian cult lay together all night in the early Christian Churches to increase their " religious " zeal, and thus replaced the costly Succoth Benoth and Kadesha of the Church by quite inexpensive means of enjoying the same luxuries.

That there were some secret " flagitious " crimes committed at the early Christian meetings (Agapae) is clearly proved by the writings of Romans of that era. In discussing the exaggerated statements as to the persecution of the early Christians under the heading of " Christian name of," columns 752-763 in the *Encyclopædia Biblica*, the writer shows that there was the utmost liberty of worship in Rome so long as the adherents were not seditious or aiming at the subversion of the State. Even the ancestral gods included those of all Italy and Greece (col. 755). " Noncitizens were forbidden to proselytise to strange gods, but were not forbidden to worship them, so far as this did not appear to be of danger to the State " (col. 755). There was therefore no crime in holding meetings, but for some reason never clearly stated, their meetings " were never for a moment free from the risk of police interference. Still they did not expose themselves to persecution or to death *merely* by holding unauthorised meetings. For such an offence these [death] penalties were much too severe. When a *sodalitas* of this sort was broken up, unless its object had been in itself criminal, the members were subjected only to a mild punishment. *In fact, they were allowed to divide amongst themselves the funds of the society, which were confiscated in the case of all capital offences* " [my italics] (*Encyclopædia Biblica*, col. 756). So they were not even fined for the religious side of their meetings. " Persecution and capital punishment fell to the lot of the Christians only because their religion was regarded as criminal;" or was accompanied or made attractive by criminal practices. And we see that this was the constant accusation. It was not their religion, but their " practices," which were condemned, and which, according to the historians, had filled their own " City of God," Jerusalem, with " every kind of debauchery and vice."

The correspondence between Pliny and Trajan shows that the charge against the Christians was one of " flagitia," a term which is exceedingly apt when applied to " every

form of sexual debauchery and vice," but
which was not at all applicable to any con-
spiracy against the State.

It is possible that the religious name of
Christian was used to cover irregular houses,
as there was found in Pompeii an " inn " with
the word " Hristiani " inscribed on it along
with an advertisement of " Vina Nervii " and
a " Cella Meritricia," and we know that wine
and women were always linked in extorting
money from the weak and sexual (*Encyclopædia Biblica*, cols. 754-755).   That the repeated charge of flagitia as being the crime of
the Christians had a solid foundation is shown
from Pliny's letter, which lets us know that
the term flagitia meant, when applied to
Christian practices, " Cibum promiscuum et
innoxium," and the crimes indicated included
" Epulae Thyesteae " and the " Concubitus
Oedipodei " (*Encyclopædia Biblica*, col. 156),
which the great Christian, Father Justin,
admits as being specially charged against the
Christians.

We know the horror in which the latter
crime was held by the Greeks, even when committed innocently, from their great tragedy
of Oedipus.

This crime has always been charged specially against Christians, and that the charge had a good foundation is shown by the special laws passed in Europe prohibiting priests from living with their mothers and sisters, owing to the deplorable results which ensued (see p. 305).

It was not to the actual practice of prostitution and unnatural sexual crimes to which the authorities or the Hebrew priests objected. We know all temples at that time had Kadeshoth, or female prostitutes, and even Kadeshim, or male prostitutes, for the exercise of unnatural connection, as may be gathered from the following quotations from the *Encyclopædia Biblica* :—" The holiness of Kadeshim [masculine] and Kadeshoth [feminine], who were certainly found in Israel very early, can have consisted only in separation. Either they were dedicated to foreign gods, or perhaps they were set apart at puberty from the households in which they grew up according to a custom which ranges from the Gold Coast to Tahiti " (see Frazer's *Golden Bough*, II., 225 ff.). Col. 837—" The offer of the body in honour of the deity prevailed widely in north Semitic religions, . . . a special class of temple harlots were maintained. Commerce with them was a religious act accompanied by sacrifice " [not necessarily, as the act itself was called the great sacrifice], *" the hire was sacred and was brought into the treasury of the god "* (col· 2156).   Hence the bitterness of the Hebrew Levites against Paul's free love teaching.   He was cutting away their greatest source of income.   " The licentious intercourse of men and women in which the priests and consecrated women set the example was a rite hallowed by sacrifice " (col. 2066).   This use of the word sacrifice simply means the act was declared sacred or holy. " Religious prostitution was not confined to the temples of Astarte, nor to the worship of female divinities.   Numbers xxv., 1-5, connects it with Baal-peor.   Amos xxvii., Deuteronomy xxiii., 18 (17), etc., show that in Israel similar practices   infected   even   the   worship   of Yahwé "   (col.   338).   Before   these   orgies began " all lights were put out " (col. 756), and the " saints " lay together all night to increase their religious zeal.

It was these Agapic feasts, or what may be called their " free love," or private prostitution, and unnatural practices, which brought no fees to the temples, which so enraged the priests, who instigated their prohibition, as the Romans had nothing to say against religious prostitution conducted under authority in properly constituted temples charging fees. We see Titus visiting Paphos, where Paul went when he set out on his travels, and leaving rich gifts at this, the chief centre of such practices, when he was on his way to put down the very same " religious zeal " practised at Jerusalem by the Christians and without priestly sanction or fees. (See my *Christianity*, pp. 82, 88, 225, 316; my *Queen of Heaven*; also pp. 139-140, Part I.).

Their Agapic feasts scandalised the Romans, and in Jerusalem " the mummeries which disgraced the Christian shrine and filled Jerusalem with every kind of debauchery and vice," so enraged the Emperor Julian that, about 360 A.D., he destroyed the Christian Church and rebuilt the Jewish Temple.

Paul " passed through " and stayed at the great centres of phallic worship, Antioch, Salamis, Paphos, Perga, Pisidia, Lystra, Pamphilia, Iconium, Athens, and Corinth, all great centres of religious prostitution, and travelled about, according to one of the Apocryphal books, with a concubine named Thecla, who is represented as having been much attached to him, thus keeping " his virgin," as he advised all Christians to do (p. 273). This

keeping of concubines was common to priests
from the remotest antiquity; and even to the
present day in India Yogis travel with Yoginis
(see p. 45 in my *Christianity*), their concubines, and in Judges xix., the Levite is
spoken of as travelling with his concubine
quite naturally, and the Levite's concubine
seems to have been of much greater importance than any other woman if we are to
believe the story and its sequel. They exter-
minated the entire Benjamite women and most
of the men to avenge the death of one
Levite's concubine. Then as late as 1560
Lecky tells us a tax was levied on priests'
concubines, and one Abbot had a goodly
harem of 70 concubines, quite a Solomon.
So Paul's preaching that the " Law " was re-
sponsible for the creation of sin, and that Jesus
had "fulfilled," or abolished, or paid off
the law up to an infinite amount (see
Dean Inge in the Preface), led to most
lascivious outbreaks. Paul says, " I had not
known lust except the law had said Thou shalt
not lust," Romans vii., is an ingenious argument that only the law made sin, there was no
real sin, at least in sexual matters. " And the
commandment which was ordained to ' life, I
found to be unto death.' " The whole chapter

is written in the usual Biblical way, every phrase differing from and contradicting every other, so that nothing is quite clearly stated, but the whole drift is that " Ye also are become dead to the law by the body of Christ." " But now we are delivered from the law, that being dead wherein we were held," and so on, the argument teaching that all sin had been paid for in advance, and, if one only had faith in this fact, his sins and their punishment fell off him like " Pilgrim's " burden. Paul's only real antagonists were the established Hebrew priests, whose living he was destroying.

The fact that Paul made no revolutionary change in the modes of worship of his time is commented upon by the *Encyclopædia Biblica,* but the real truth is that Paul and his Epistles and voyages are a purely literary composition of the priests (pp. 260-262).

The *Encyclopædia Biblica* says, at column 3656, that at Perga, a great centre of Cybele, Artemis, or Venus worship, " the preaching of Paul and Barnabus made apparently no impression," and again, at Pisidia, " little success attended the effort " (column 3781), and at Lystra, where the healing of a cripple astonished the natives, " Paul's efforts don't seem to have produced any converts at Lystra."

Again, column 3614, the *Encyclopædia Biblica*, says " his visit to Athens was a comparative failure." This was so because Paul was not founding a new religion, but only giving liberty for phallic practices outside church authority. All the tenets of Christianity were held all over Asia, and even Augustine wrote : " The same thing which is now called the Christian Religion existed among the ancients. They have begun to call Christian the true religion which existed before " (see Justin Martyr, pp. 237-8). The only change was the elimination of the payments to priests and the free and open practice of promiscuous sexual intercourse—involving neither sin nor payment to the priest. Paul was teaching that the idea of the crucified redeemer contained as a concomitant the fact that all sin was atoned for, and the intermediary of a priesthood with its fines, payments, sin offerings, etc., was no longer necessary.

The only great discussion was a purely phallic one, whether or not the great " covenant of Iové," the circumcision of the Phallus, was or was not essential to salvation. The quarrel was entirely about the condition of the phallus.

The Romans had adopted the Hebrew scriptures as the basis of their universal religion, but as a great part of their subjects did not practise circumcision, they required authoritative " epistles " or amendments to the old Hebraic constitution upholding what Paul is made to call the " Uncircumcision," and so rendering the reformed religion applicable to all the subjects of their great Empire.

As Peter held strictly to the great covenant (in Genesis xvii., 10), which was cut on the body of every Hebrew, and without which " Berith," or circumcision ring or mark, he was cut off from the nation, he beheld with horror the old Hebrew phallic rites being joined in by uncircumcised foreigners, and hence arose the bitter quarrel between Peter and Paul. There were thus three different sects basing their religious belief on the old phallic Hebrew scriptures. (1) The orthodox Jews, who held that Jesus was simply a Nabi, or perhaps a false prophet. (2) The Jews, like Peter, who held that Jesus had paid the debt of sin, and yet who held to all the old Hebrew " Law," and especially to the religious practices of circumcision, Jehovah's "covenant." (3) Paulinists who declared that the death of Jesus, having " fulfilled " the law for all time, there was no " law," not even circumcision.

binding on the people, at least as between them and the priests; and especially, as Payne Knight says, in " honouring God by a liberal display and general communication of his bounties " by the free use of " that organ which endowed them with the power of procreation and made them partakers not only of felicity of the deity, but of his great characteristic attribute, that of multiplying his own image."

We find all this set forth in various Epistles, where discussions are held as to the nature of the teaching—for instance, between Paul and his companion, Apollos.

In 1st Corinthians i., 12, we find that there were four sects actively pushing their propaganda. (1) Paul preaching the abrogation of the law as between priest and people, and teaching phallism through the most universal of all phallic emblems, the Cross.

(2) Apollos, who seems to have taught like Paul, but more directly urging phallism and naked phallic feasts without using veiled language (as we shall see), and

(3) Cephas, the rock or stone, Peter, or Simon Peter, inculcating the worship of the phallus, but no doubt with all the old Jewish ritual, and

(4) The Christ, weak echo of the sun god

Christna and the Buddha, Sidartha, but linked
with the phallic cross and upright pillar, yet
really far removed from earth, ruling, in fact,
only in heaven.   Another link between Christ
and Christna is that Christna was often written
Kreshna or Krestna, and Christians were at first
called Krestians.

I have dealt with most of these points, but
must touch on one or two additional texts
which throw more light on the new gospel.

We find Paul and Apollos, two names with
identical meaning and with great personal
attachment, yet forming two schools at
Corinth, a famous phallic centre.   Paul is
charged with " Wisdom " being absent from
his teaching, but replies that " wisdom " is
contained in the " simple teaching of the
Cross " (the oldest phallic symbol), but only
to Christians of mature growth—the initiated.
Now, wisdom invariably bears a sexual meaning.   All through the Old Testament sexual
intercourse is expressed as " knowing."
" And Adam ' knew ' his wife;" and even
Sodomy, in Judges xix., 22, where the sons of
Belial wanted to " know " the Levite, is expressed in the same way, and we have the
"tree of knowledge," equal to the " tree of
life," in the garden of Eden, and, lastly,

Solomon was the " wisest " man, as he had
700 wives and 300 concubines. The serpent
promised Eve knowledge by an act which
brought sexual shame and made Eve the
" mother of all living," and in all lands and
faiths the serpent is he who gives knowledge
or wisdom. So the quarrel between Paul and
Apollos was that while Paul veiled his teaching by calling the Phallus the Cross, Apollos
no doubt openly taught Phallism and the
Christian agapy or sexual intercourse without
professional women, instead of the Hebrew
" hag " with temple women ; of course saying
that by Christ's death all sin connected with
this god-like act had been wiped out.

That the Cross is the Phallus has been recognised from the very earliest times, and thousands of carvings on temples, tombs, and rocks
have given us every modification, from the
most realistic sculpture and painting of the
triple male organ in Hindu temples (see my
Christianity, p. 30, and pp. 32, 44, 45, and 46
this volume), through Thor's hammer, and the
Greek Tau, to the most elaborate multiple
crosses, daggers, and " piercers," with triple
cross handles. The Egyptian handled cross or
crux ansata contained both the male and
female idea, as shown in my *Christianity*, pp.

75-77, illustrating its evolution, but the Christian cross was strictly male. Wherever crosses are found in the ruins of prehistoric towns, sculptured phalli are also found; and coins or medals have frequently been found with the cross on one side and the phallus on the other. Bishop Colenso has very fully stated the ubiquity of the Cross symbolism, and it had its origin in phallism and flourished where no other religion was known. Colenso wrote :—" From the dawn of organised paganism in the Eastern world to the final establishment of Christianity in the Western, the cross was undoubtedly one of the commonest and most sacred of symbolical monuments. It appears to have been the aboriginal possession of every people of antiquity. Delineated on temples, palaces, natural rocks, sepulchral galleries, on the heaviest monoliths and the rudest statuary, on coins, medals, and vases of every description, and preserved in the architectural proportions of subterranean as well as superterranean structures of tumuli and temples. Populations of essentially different culture, tastes, and pursuits—the highly civilised, the demi-civilised, the settled, and the nomadic—vied with each other in their superstitious adoration of it, and in their efforts to extend the knowledge of its exceptional import and virtue amongst their latest posterities. Of the several varieties of Cross, St. George, St. Andrew, Maltese, Greek, Latin, etc., etc., there is not one amongst them the existence of which may not be traced to the remotest antiquity." (Colenso, *The Pentateuch Examined*, Vol. VI., p. 113.) (See p. 242.)

Another proof of the identity of Cross and Phallus is illustrated by the words used by scholars showing their identity. For instance, the word Phallobates is used by Lucian (Dea Syr., 29) to express the ascent of the Cross (Cruci Ascendere), and it means " one who mounts a Phallic shaped column," or simply " a phallic priest," and modern writers protest against the " Adoration of the Cross," as being a revival of " Phallo-proskunesis "—that is, prostrating oneself before the phallus, as the Pope and Cardinals do—approaching the Cross on their knees and kissing it.

So scholars of all ages treat the Cross and the Phallus as being identical, and presume that their readers tacitly accept the fact as beyond dispute.

In Hebrew the same word Iada is used for wisdom of knowing and the sexual act. We have Jeho iada, the Lord knows; and knowledge is Adach, from the root Iada; and when Adam " knew " his wife it is still Iada—in fact, all sexual intercourse is " know " or knowledge—so the quarrel between Paul and Apollos was simply one about the intensity and openness of their phallic teaching. The same root Iada is used by the Hindoos in exactly the same way for knowledge and the sexual act.

We find Paul and Barnabus (whose name is probably Latinised Bar, son of, and Nabi or Nebo, the Babylonian, Mercury or Hermes, so he was son of Mercury, *i.e.*, the phallus), travelling together at Lystra and healing a lame man, which so astonished the natives that they called Paul Mercurius or Hermes, the Phallus, his true name, and his perhaps more dignified priestly companion, Barnabus, they called Jupiter or Iové, also symbolised by the phallus, thus indicating the true teaching. Barnabus was also called Joseph, and here IO is identical with IhOh or Jehovah, and seph the serpent of passion or creative organ; so he was a true phallic god. (See p. 156, Part I.)

At the end of Acts there is the incident of the viper which hung on Paul's hand, yet he suffered no harm, and this is another symbolical statement that Paul is the phallic teacher in chief, as he was the only apostle personally friendly with the serpent, the universal symbol of the phallus. Here they also proclaimed him a god.

Lastly, Paul had a secret affliction, or " stake in the flesh," an infirmity of the flesh, and flesh is a word always phallic; no doubt a secret indication to the priests that as sacred prostitution was still rampant so were its consequences—sexual diseases, emerods, ophalim, the botch of Egypt—of which so much is made in the Old Testament, when the Israelites trafficked with strange women. Passach, the Passover, means a phallic dance or " hag," and also " lame," the frequent result of such " dancing " (see my *Passover and Crucifixion*)

Yet Paul in Romans xii., urges the brethren to " present your bodies in living sacrifice " [a thing dedicated], holy acceptable to the Lord, " which is your spiritual service," no doubt a cryptic invitation to the agapic feasts where the " Saints," male and female, lay together all night in the temples to increase their religious zeal.

CHAPTER VI

THE TWO GODS

While all the great nations from China and India through the Euphrates valley and Persia to Egypt and Rome had adopted sun worship, or the worship of a personified Sun Saviour, as the official basis of their religion, the little Hebrew clan held firmly to their phallic celebrations and the fear of their bloodthirsty Iové. When, therefore, the Romans adopted the Hebrew scriptures as being the only pos sible basis of an authoritative religion with a monotheistic tendency—their god having no father and being self-existent " in the middle of things," and perhaps the only revelation claiming to have been written by the direct command of the god—they found that the Hebrew religion scarcely existed as a " future-life " religion, the Hebrews having no clear idea of a soul, and their " law " did not look beyond the grave. Their religion was devoted to priestly ritual and to its phallic observances and feasts, and to the sin offerings and seasonable dedication of lambs and fat beasts for the sustenance of the priests. As such observances were common to all religions, it made the adoption of the Hebrew scriptures as a basis of the universal religion all the easier. The conclusion is gaining ground that the New Testament is entirely an artificial compilation and has no relation to historical occurrences. It was evidently composed for a purpose, and as its authority had to rest on the assertion in the Hebrew scriptures of the god's personal dictation of his will to Moses, Joshua, and Ezra, it had to found largely on the Old Testament writings. It thus embodied fragments of popular legends and references to the older Hebrew fables, history, proverbs, and beliefs, so as to carry the authority of the older scriptures, and even recapitulating the whole story of the Jews as in Acts vii. and elsewhere.

But the Hebrews would have none of the new humble sun god Jesus, as they were waiting for a personal King who would make their race predominant, as had been promised by Iové or his priests. It seems to have been decided by the state ecclesiastics to incorporate the new sun cult with the old phallic worship; and Simon, son of Jonah, was conceived to argue out the position and to show that although the sun in heaven was to be in future the chief god, yet phallism was to rule all the earthly arrangements.

Simon was afterwards called Peter, so here we have a name, Simon Peter, half Hebrew and half Greek. Jesus is portrayed as being uneasy about Peter. He asks, for instance, " Simon, son of Jonas, lovest thou me?" " What thinkest thou, Simon?" " Blessed art thou, Simon Bar Jona," and so on, in a tone quite different from that otherwise used. Simon is called by the Hebrew name alone at first, and afterwards the Greek name Peter is added, and the complete personification of the " Hearing Stone " is set up in Simon Peter, the great Phallic representative of the faith of the common people.

This is the Tsur, Sur, Sul, Tur, Tyr, or Tor, the Scandinavian god, and our own " Rocks " of Derbyshire, Dorsetshire, or Devonshire, representing the earthly saviour idea, while Hesus the Christos represented the solar or scientific saviour idea, of Europe and Asia.

Thus a double hierarchy was set up, as, although Hesus was to judge souls in heaven at the Judgment Day, Peter was to have the power to say who was worthy to enter heaven. Thus was a double judgeship set up, still

retained by the Catholic Church, as the Roman
Pope gives indulgencies and absolution in
spite of the Judgment Day. This is why the
phallic practices were much more flagrant and
shameless under Christianity than before. We
find the same accusations of debauchery and
vice following Christian religious centres for
fifteen hundred years after Christ, especially
amongst the Knight Templars and Rosicrucians
(a grossly phallic name), but indeed in all
monasteries and religious institutions. But
except for this incident maintaining phallism
as the ruling religion on earth, the retention
of the phallic cross as the basis of Christianity,
and the fact that the highly phallic feast
of Tabernacles was still a religious practice of
the nation, there is no direct injunction to
phallism in the Gospels. There is a vague
protest against the sale of doves in the temple,
which may have been a protest against the
religious prostitution rampant at that time, as
the Feast of the Tabernacles was still celebrated by the Hebrews at the time of Jesus,
and it, with its " pouring out of the waters,"
was a very phallic feast with promiscuous intercourse. (See my *Queen of Heaven and her
Debasement*.) But the sun god Jesus seemed
to see none of it. He stands a figure of stain-

less white in a world of scarlet sin, on which the priest lives, and which must continue. All this symbolical teaching was for the ear of the priest alone. The most rigid morality was no doubt inculcated from the pulpit. Jové thundered out the ten commandments, and was himself the most flagrant in breaking every one of them.

Now when the gospels had fully established Sun worship, with Hesus Krestos as the Sun Saviour, and the Romans, who were always Sun worshippers, had adopted the Hebrew basis and made it the official religion, it was time to let the world know that, although the sun ruled in heaven, the phallic cult was to have full rein on earth, so we find that the ideas taught in the Epistles are not always those of the Gospels, which were derived from the teaching of Siddartha.

The Jews held that only those who kept up the practice of circumcision could enter into the temple, because when circumcision was declared in Genesis xvii. to be the special covenant between the Hebrew clan and Iové, Al Shadai, or the Elohim (for all these are mentioned), " it was commanded, and the uncircumcised man-child whose flesh of his foreskin is not circumcised, that soul shall be cut

off from his people; he hath broken my covenant." But such doctrine could never be
acceptable to the Roman Empire, as they had
great populations where circumcision was
unknown, so while Peter, the " Rock that
begat thee," upheld circumcision, Paul was
created by the ecclesiastical story-tellers to
declare that it was unnecessary for salvation,
and he preached the Uncircumcision. Jesus,
as the sun-god, having ascended to heaven,
the road was now clear for the spread of
Christianity by Phallism. So the old phallic
god Iové was replaced by new conceptions.

One is struck with the absence of grossness
in the Gospels, due no doubt to their being
derived from the gentle and sensible teaching
of Siddartha and Confucius. Their only
phallic feature is the promise that the Petros,
Tsur, or Rock-saviour shall rule on earth,
while the solar Saviour rules in heaven, a
double Saviourship emphasised by the Vatican
Bronze mentioned on p. 249. After the purity
of the Gospels the Epistles are shocking in
their naked teaching of Priapianism. This
history of the morality, or rather immorality,
of the Christian Church is one of crass phallic
worship on the part of the clergy, while hypocritically teaching continence to the laity.

We have only to read such books as Lecky's *History of European Morals*, and especially most of the authorities mentioned in his footnotes, to realise the depths of iniquity to which the indolent and licentious clergy sunk. For instance, amongst many similar passages, Lecky tells us (p. 419, vol. I., *History of Morals*) :—" Wives in multitudes deserted their homes to frequent nocturnal meetings," and quotes Tertullian, who quotes a friend, saying of the conversion of his wife, ' I would rather have her a prostitute than a Christian.' The pagans would not permit their women to attend any such nightly conclaves.   At p. 440 Lecky says that accusations of incestuous impurity became frequent; and we know that it was so common with the priests that special laws were passed to prohibit them from living with their mothers or sisters, and many nunneries were simply brothels.

That it was equally bad in earlier times is dimly set forth by Gibbon, who, however, hesitated to attack Christian morals; but at the end of his monumental work, regretting the setting in of the " dark ages," he sorrowfully says :—" I have described the triumph of barbarism *and religion* " little to chose between their power for the degradation of mankind.

" These be thy gods, oh Israel !" of Phallic Birth every one. The sun god was neither created nor accepted by the children of the Phallus god, Israel. Originally they were "deification of natural desire," as Dr. Oman tells us is still the case in India ; and the symbolical expression by man of such worship in terms of the reproductive organs of his own body is the secret basis of the Christian Creed, although its direct meaning has long been lost, and is now never taught. It is coupled, as in all other religions, "however vile," with many good and pious injunctions always with a " Fear God " basis, " God " being the Church and its Clergy, or monarchs like the German War Lord or God. These are the gods of the Hebrew Bible, repeated and emphasised in the New (Greek) Testament. They were " born in hot-beds of savage sorcery," as the *Times* writer declares that Frazer's books have demonstrated.

When the old phallic gods of Greece and Rome were understood in all their nakedness they ceased to control the rising intelligence of the people, so a more hidden form of the same worship was devised, coupled with the characteristic Hebrew god idea—half god, half man—and founded on the Sun Saviour ideas

of Asia, and fixed as a new yoke on the mind
of man.

The " Faith alone " shibboleth of the
" Paul " group of writers, coupled with the
freedom from " Law " granted to all converts,
and the utter rejection of the irksome and
expensive control of the Levitical body, constituted the great attraction of Christianity.

But the new religion so constructed made
one great forward step. The old solo-phallic
double-sexed IhOh or IoVé was split into the
solar Hesus Christos and the phallic Peter,
and there seems much evidence of an attempt
to produce a very pure religion, free from
phallism, founded on the solar myth with the
teaching of Siddartha and Confucius, when
the spiritual character of Jesus was sketched by
the writers of the Gospels. It may even have
been the original idea for Peter to play the
part of the betrayer of Jesus, as he appears
as an enemy when he denies the Christ, and
to have abolished official phallism by his
suicide in place of Judas. But no doubt the
church would see financial ruin by any such
reformation, so the course followed was to
relegate the non-phallic religion to heaven,
leaving the popular phallic cult with its

308   GODS OF HEBREW BIBLE

Kadeshah revenues to sustain the earthly body of the Church.

The Sun Father, or Sky Father, Kurios, was thus transformed into the true friend of man, making the necessary transit or crucifixion of his son for man's salvation, exactly as did the sons of the Roman Jove (*Christianity*, pp. 115, 135, 136), copied into the Bible at Genesis vi., 2-4. While the pure heavenly or solar religion was to be represented all over the world by one Son of God, Jesus Christos, the earthly sensual cult was to be represented by as many gods as there were cults or nations—Peter for the Hebrews, with circumcision; Paul for the Romans and other Europeans, with " uncircumcision;" Apollos where Greek thought predominated; Barnabus possibly for the Middle East, where Nabis flourished; and so on, creating as many Apostles of phallism as there were differentiated sects. In this they followed the Hindu practice, where sects are divided and subdivided into hundreds (see *Christianity*, pp. 34-36). The principle followed is quite clear. The chief actor was purified from Phallism, which was relegated to a lower sphere, or, roughly speaking, the old Iové was split into two.

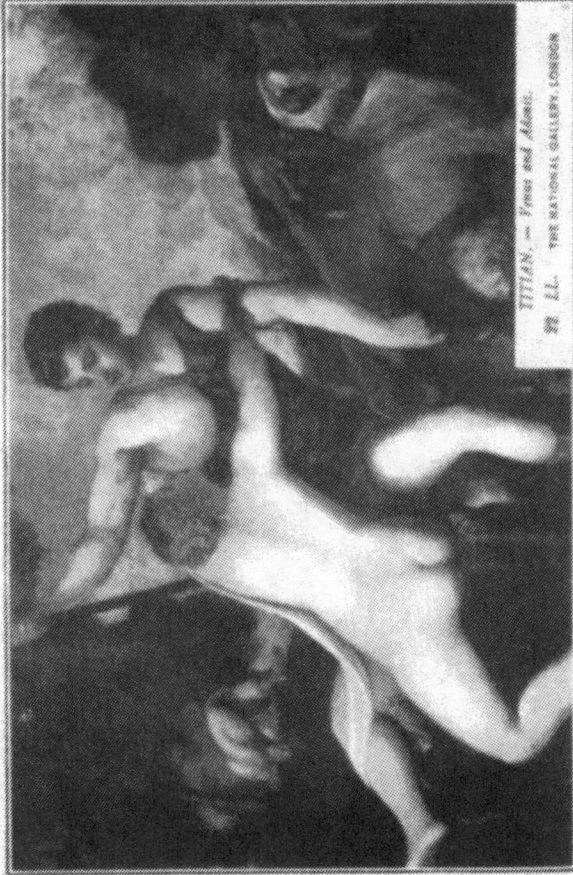

TITIAN. — *Venus and Adonis.*
37 LL. THE NATIONAL GALLERY, LONDON

Fig. 14.

Even this was not new, but had been a growing cult long before the Hesus Christna creation. We find Adonis, the sun god, represented by the greatest artists and poets as freeing himself from the embraces of Venus, the Magdalene of the Near East and Europe (Fig. 14). But early Christianity retained the profitable religious prostitution as demonstrated so fully by Lecky. The prevalence of incest among the clergy gave rise to special laws prohibiting priests from living with their mothers or sisters, while they were closely associated with temple prostitutes (p. 255). This position is defined in the New Testament by Jesus repelling his mother—" Woman, what have I to do with thee?" and yet closely associated with the temple prostitute, Mary Magdalene.

But we have seen that IhOh, like all creative gods, was double sexed, the fundamental idea of all creative gods (see Ardhanara-Ishwara, p. 47, my *Christianity*), so the female parts of the name IO could also be split up into a heavenly and an earthly part, and we find IO formed a very important Tetrad or Tetragrammaton in the Christian religion of a kind quite different from the Three and One of the Iovic religion (see pp· 78-84, Part I.).

The ecclesiastical story tellers split up the female member of the creative god into the Virgin Mary, the sinless woman, as Jesus was the sinless man, and another woman, sinful, in fact they put seven devils into her to emphasise her sinfulness—Mary Magdalene, Mary of the Almond, as Magdala is Greek for Almond.

We find the ground partially prepared in the Old Testament by a scene indicating a change of worship on the part of Jacob from female, Luz, or almond worship, to that of the rod, pillar, or male El.   Jacob in journeying toward Haran " lighted upon a certain place " (Luz), and dreamed of a ladder to heaven, a Babylonian symbol of the Virgo Intacta, and on awaking he was afraid of being caught adoring the Yoni or female, so he immediately set up a stone phallus " and poured oil on the top of it."   The " Matzebah " he set up is a " statue," " image of an idol," or " stem," like our Dorset pillar (p. 33).   "And he called the name of that place Beth El," the house of the god represented by the idol, the phallic pillar El, as he tells us in Genesis xxxiii., 20, that the altar he erected was " El, the strong thing," or " Ram " or " god " or " Israel."   He therefore changed the name of the place where he had dreamed from Luz, the "Almond" or Queen of Heaven or female place, to BethEl the phallus god or male house. This change is so important that it is related three times—Genesis xxviii., 19; xxxv., 6; and Judges i., 23. His own name was changed from Jacob, a feminine noun, to Israel, masculine. "Almond" is again used as the female, under the name Shaked, in miracles with the rod of god in the Ark (Numbers xvii., 8), in the temple furniture, lamps, etc. (Exodus xxv., 33, etc.), and as Ezekiel's prophetic password in Ezekiel i., 10. Even the pistachio nut, a kind of "myrtle almond," is called Baten in Hebrew (Genesis xliii·., 11), a word which means "womb," "pistachio nut," or "almond," and in Greek mythology we have Phyllis mercifully turned into an almond tree when heart-broken by the desertion of her lover, the Almond being ever after called Phylla, the feminine of Phulus, Phallos. We thus see the universal application of the almond as sexual woman (see also pp. 61, 62, 63, and 215 of my *Christianity*, or pp. 10, 85, 128, 135, 197, 198, 203, 310, 316, this volume). So the Hindu Maya, the old Queen of Heaven, who was also

Queen of Love, as were all ancient queens of heaven, the female side of the creative god, is split up into the two Marys, the principal, the Virgin, immaculate Queen of Heaven (with seven stars, like Isis), free from all sin, who ascended into heaven (see my *Queen of Heaven*), and the other Mary, she of the " Almond " (Magdala) " who had much loved," the Kadeshah or temple harlot, with the holy number of seven devils instead of stars, who, like Peter, remained on earth; and so the female half of the double-sexed creative god was purified, or split into pure and impure.

As in the case of the phallic gods, there are produced a number of female phallic sub-goddesses, " the other Maries," always present in the important death or resurrection groups of the New Testament, and ready to take up the varied rôles of Mother Superior, Kadeshah, Oracle, Nun, etc., in the various sects in the Roman Empire. These " other Maries," whose mention has puzzled many scholars, among them the learned writers of the *Encyclopædia Biblica*, are complementary to the Peters, Pauls, Barnabi, etc., of the male phallic side of the god. Following nearly all tales or incidents in the Bible, there is generally a weak echo of the main tale by a second person, as we see Adam in Genesis v., after the gods had created man " in their image," begetting a son " in his own likeness after his image," or Ezra a weak echo of Moses, or Isaac a weak echo of Abraham, even to prostituting his wife. Abraham's wife was twice taken, once by Pharaoh and once by Abimeleck in Gerar, while Isaac has his wife also commandeered by the same Abimeleck of Gerar, and so on in numerous instances. This principle is applied to the disinherited Iové in the New Testament. He is the great Tetragrammaton, the most holy name in the Bible, the ubiquitous, incomprehensible mystery, which Hyppolytus told us was always the Pudendum, to pronounce which was visited with the death penalty, just as was the case for looking into the Monstrance and Pyx, which are the same tetrad; and, when he is split up, the two elements, male and female, again form Tetrads, " the four Maries," and the four doctrinaires, Peter, Paul, Barnabus, and Apollos, each group a dim echo of the almighty Tetragrammaton.

In the " dark ages " the ecclesiastics made a retrograde movement by decreeing, in 692 A.D., at the great Constantinople conference, "in trullo," that in future the figure of Christ was to be nailed to the Cross, the oldest and most universal phallic symbol, so they again soiled the pure solar god with phallism. The crucifix, however, was a very old pagan religious symbol, so the Christians retrograded to a purely pagan symbol as their standard.

That the Cross is the essence of phallism is also told in symbolical language in the Crucifixion scene· When Jesus was led out to be crucified "they compelled one Simon, a Cyrenian, to bear his cross" (Mark xv., 21), repeated in Matthew xxvii., 32, "a man of Cyrene, Simon by name," and in Luke, "Simon a Cyrenian," "on him they laid the cross." Simon was the original name of Peter, "the rock that begat thee." Cyrene was the home of Hedonism, as I have shown at p. 280, and what was more natural than that the cross, the special phallic symbol, should be laid on the shoulders of one given over to intense ephemeral pleasures, and so relieve the Christos from this stain.

The deep hold which phallism had on religion is vividly shown by the fact, that after creating a special incident—that of Simon of Cyrene having the Cross of Jesus transferred to him to finally rid the new sun god of this taint

Fig. 15.

of phallism, the Church, as late as the end of
the seventh century actually reversed this
decision and placed the sun god again on the
prime phallic symbol, the Cross, and definitely
adopted the very ancient pagan life symbol,
" the cross with a man on it."

Simon was said to be the father of Alexander
and Rufus, the Strength of man and the Red
one, both phallic, so as to enforce the phallic
nature of Simon of Cyrenaica.   This is told by
Mark, the earliest gospel.

I have shown in my *Queen of Heaven*, p.
499, that artists must put in their sacred pictures only such details as were ordered by the
Holy Fathers, and I give here two pictures
which well illustrate the division of the
Jehovah or the IO, and the position of the
two sects, Sun and Phallic worship.

I give one of Dürer's vigorous engravings
with the four Maries at the Cross.   Mary
Magdalene as queen of love kisses the Christ's
feet, and has at her side the skull—Death
caused by her calling—and her hand stretched
out to the book, " liber," sign of her sexual
Freedom—Freia is the more direct Saxon
name for an " Almond " woman, Freia, the
" Free One," Friday, or German Freitag,
" free day," on which fish were eaten, fish

Fig. 16.

being the emblem of fertility or of Venus.
In this and all other crucifixion Jesus has his
head towards heaven, and the cross has its two
arms at the upper end, the contrary of the triple
emblem in stone, shown in Fig. 11, Part I.,
and most other complete stone triple phallic
emblems; whereas St. Peter is represented
being crucified, that is combined with the
phallic cross, with his head to the earth, and
the cross in the position faithfully portrayed
in the Stone ages. Lastly, there are the four
men in the Peter picture, representing the
Pillar, or I, or male element in the Tetragrammaton, and four women (Maries) in the
other picture, representing the female or O
side of the Tetragrammaton, each telling of
the quadruple composition of the " Three in
One," IO or IhOh complete life symbol.

We see the meticulous accuracy with which
the " holy fathers " carried out their secret
symbolism, as compared with what the *Encyclopædia Biblica* describes as the constant
" inaccurate," " contradictory," " wholly
irreconcilable," "untrustworthy," "childish,"
" legendary," and " unhistorical character of
the New Testament narratives," as told by
these same holy fathers in Greek or Hebrew.

In Fig. 17 we have a very full expression of

the Tetradic construction of the Creative
Deity, in a little Hindoo altar in the British
Museum. In the centre is the supreme
creative combination of the male and female
organs, and it is placed in a square shaped
yoni, with the four principal god-ideas adoring it. Bram is represented with four heads,
as he is the supreme creative god from whom
the "four quarters," or the whole universe
sprung. The square area is decorated with
Lotus, as being symbolical of both sexes (Part
I., pp. 81, 82). All the gods wear the Pileus
or conical cap, which converts the heads into
phalli.

Thus we have four Tetrads, the Lotus, the
Square, Four gods, and a four headed god; so
the most holy Tetrad or four-some Creator is
expressed four times. The yoni was often
made into the square of Pythogoras, especially
when it was represented as marked with the
imprint of the " foot " of Buddha.

The only official declaration on the question of the basis of the creative God idea is
that of the Chinese Government, whose
censors,—men who had deeply studied all the
great religions,—examined this wide subject
when our missionaries applied for official permission to publish our Bible in Chinese. The

Fig. 17.

only words in Chinese suitable for the Christian God were those denoting double sex, such as Yang-Yin, identical with Lingam-Yoni, and they declared that there was no religion whose god was not founded on this sexual basis, and that the " Yang-Yin operation " represented by all Tetrads—or the Three-in-One—was the universal conception of the creative act (see my *Christianity*, p. 99).

Do not let us forget the truth of Mr. King's conclusion, " In religion there is no new thing," and this is nowhere better illustrated than in the Christian hierarchy. The only change is that the ancients had chief gods and minor gods, while we have chief gods, or a multiple god-head and " saints." But saints are true gods, performing miracles and living for ever. Our Jehovah or Kurios is simply the Brahm, Priapati, Saturn, Ouranos, Zeus, Jupiter, or father of the gods of all countries, the Virgin and Mary Magdalene are the universally worshipped Queen of Heaven, Mother of the God, and Queen of Love; Juno and Venus in Latin; Kubele, Astarte, Istar, Vesta, Pallas, etc., in other countries; and the patriarchs and apostles who seem to have gone direct to heaven on their earthly demise, such as Elijah, Peter, Paul, etc., are the Mercuris, Vulcans, etc., who served under the Father of the Gods.

The Christian gods are passing away, like those of Greece and Rome, into the dead past, for in truth they were all the same. Will the world suffer the creation of a new bogey to be used for its enslavement by a cunning clergy, or shall the church, as Bishop Carpenter long ago promised, turn and make good the promise—" In the future not the kingdom of God, but that of man, will be the great theme and care of the race?" Let us have no new Moses, Joshua, Ezra, Paul, or Joe Smith enslave us once more. The world has now a chance of starting fair to gain a true knowledge of the marvellous interaction of matter and motion as constituting life.

Let us join mercy, peace, and justice with a true knowledge of the universe, the nature of its energy and of the mechanism of life, and shake off for ever the shackles of the priesthood and its ever-changing but always pernicious " revelations," which ought never again be allowed to rise to clog the wheels of true brotherly love and progress.

THE QUEEN OF HEAVEN

CHAPTER I

INTRODUCTION

The Queen of Heaven dwells in the heart of every man in whom the divine influence of youthful love has begotten visions of the most holy realm of the heart's desire. Under the elemental awakening which first impels his thoughts along the rosy path, man clothes the common clay of some woman with all the childish innocence and wondering delight of the wide-eyed Psyche, invests her with the glowing perfection of Venus—that Paradesa or summer garden of all beauty, and veils her with the maidenly reserve and silvery virginity of the divine Astarte.

After the first great flame of Cupid and Psyche has become the more prosaic fire of the domestic hearth, and he has come face to face with the grim realities of the struggle for existence—into the meshes of which his great passion has driven him—is it to be wondered that man has endeavoured to enthrone in some far-off heaven, a picture of that beautiful Queen of Heaven glimpsed for a brief moment through the pearly gates of that fleeting paradise which every man visits during his pilgrimage in the enchanted land of love?

So was born the Queen of Heaven.

In his awakening civilisation all mankind has at some stage enthroned this Queen of Heaven.

" She was worshipped," says Johannes Clericus, " by the Persians, the Syrians, and all " the kings of Europe and Asia with the most " profound veneration;" and Herodotus tells us that the Queen of Heaven was the most worshipped of all divinities, while Tacitus found her worship universal all over Germania and Europe; Tacitus having travelled with the conquering Romans throughout Europe. So every nation had yielded to the realisation of the universal love impulse, and enthroned a beautiful symbol of its young dream in the heaven beyond the skies, to dwell for ever there.

All tribes or nations worshipped different gods, who were supposed to aid them in their battles with hostile tribes, each god aiding his own side, but the peaceful image of the mother and babe was supreme and common to them all.

The Babylonians had their Marduk; Nineveh, its Ninus, Nimrod, or great hunter; Persia, its Ahura Mazda, Ahriman, or Rimon of the Bible; and even the tiny Clans of Palestine had all their tribal gods, or Als, or Ale-ims, be it Milcom, Chemosh, Molech, Astoreth, the Baals of the Ammonites, Moabites, Zidonians, or Perizzites; or the Iah, Shaddai, or band of Ale-im of the Hebrews—fierce masculine gods —each fighting for his own clan, and each the sworn or " covenanted " enemy of the " false gods " of all other tribes.

Quite other was their Queen of Heaven, and we shall see that the Hebrews, who were brought under a most severe, almost malevolent masculine cult which despised woman, yet yearned to worship under the more benign influence of the Mother and her Babe.

Jeremiah tells us, xiv., 15-19, that " the men " with their wives and all the women, a great " multitude," would continue to burn incense and to pour out drink offerings to the Queen of Heaven as " we and our fathers, our kings " and our princes, did in the cities of Judah " and in the streets of Jerusalem, for then we " had plenty of victuals, and were well, and

" saw no evil. But since we left off to burn
" incense to the Queen of Heaven and to pour
" out drink offerings unto her, we have wanted
" all things, and have been consumed by the
" sword and by the famine."

But, for reasons we will examine later, the Hebrew priests continued to impose on the clan a fierce masculine god, who breathed out fire, and whose very name was Jealousy, and to incessantly condemn any worship of the Queen of Heaven.

So the Levites, one family of an insignificant clan (for the Hebrews were only one amongst many clans inhabiting the small country called Palestine), have by the intensity of their prejudice, and perhaps more by the poetical fervour of their language, imposed on Europe and much of Asia a cult whose principal tenet is the snake-like innate wickedness of woman, whose influence on man is the cause of all evil.

This tiny band left a terrible legacy to Europe, and we find the beautiful Queen of Heaven of the ancients banished from her throne beyond the skies, and her prototype woman, with her loving gaze, caressing the sweet babe in her protecting arms—the most beautiful picture of pure love in this hard world—is turned into the author of all evil.

and is stigmatised as the " Gate-way of Hell."
(See Lecky, *History of Morals*.)

The gentle influence of the mother was
sternly banned from the Hebrew heaven.

Unfortunately, Christendom adopted the
Hebrew Scripture as the basis of their religion,
as all religion must have a miraculously
revealed source, and so its heaven has never
been officially graced by the ameliorating
influence of a Queen. The Hebrew Nabis
went too far in the direction of severity, and
the only glimpses of a heaven presented to us
are rather terrifying ones of a place and a god
belching smoke and fire, with terrible animals,
really demons with horns, claws, four wings,
double and quadruple faces, " crying with loud
voices;" seven vials of wrath, seven plagues,
and a general devastating terrifying atmosphere, like German frightfulness.

We can see the Catholic Church gradually
elevating the earthly Virgin Mary to the position of the divine Queen of Heaven, but she
does not yet fill the position held by the
ancient Queens of Heaven in the past. The
statement is made that the ancestors of the
Virgin Mary were without sin and that she did
not " see corruption," but ascended directly
into heaven. So the ancient Queen of Heaven

is nearly reconstituted. And this is the basis of the intense quarrel between the Protestants and Roman Catholics in Ireland. The Protestants following the Hebrew tradition, described so well by Milton, in whose heaven no female exists, look upon the admission of any female to the Heavenly Hierarchy as rank blasphemy, because woman, through Eve being the author of all evil, is the same as a devil, and one might as well admit Satan to Heaven as a daughter of Eve.

To this unlovely conclusion have the doctrines of the infallibility of scripture and of the "fall" in Eden driven the ultra-Protestants, and so strong was the Hebrew prejudice against woman in religion that they never evolved any word for goddess.

But there was a time when men all the world over worshipped the Queen of Heaven with the most profound veneration, and we will attempt to trace the causes which led to her dethronement.

The earliest cult of which we have definite written evidence was the cult of the Mother, and it is quite possible that it was the excess of devotion to this cult that led to its ultimate downfall.

There is no doubt that there was a time when

all the family centred in the mother, and the descent of name and property was by the female side. Frazer writes of a time when the duties of priesthood were centred in women, and there was a time when the dead returned to the " Great Mother," and when the Great Mother was the Judge of the Dead, and no doubt she would judge more leniently of the errant footsteps of her little children than the irate Jové with his thunderings and lust for slaughter till his arrows were drunk with blood and his sword devoured flesh (Deuteronomy xxxii., 42).

The Old Testament Iové had no pity for little children, but constantly revelled in their brutal slaughter, however much such ideas are modified in the New Testament (see Deuteronomy xxxii., 25 ; 1st Samuel xv., 3).

But here, in order that the story may be clearly understood, we must turn aside for a moment and deal with the names and symbols of the gods and of the Queen of Heaven.

I was much struck when young with the fact that, up till the time of the great religious artists, Michael Angelo, Titian, and Raphael, and even after their epoch, two sets of miracle plays were acted alternately in the Roman churches, one founded on the Christian tradi-

tions, and the other on those of the ancient
Romans, and that Bulls were still sacrificed to
Jupiter or Jové, and the great cistern to collect
rain water at St. Peter's was dedicated with
purely pagan rites to Jupiter Pluvius, and
Cybélé, with a globe in her lap (see Figs. 38
and 39 in my *Christianity*), was still worshipped
(*Rome and its Story*, p. 358.)   Nor did it
escape my youthful ear that Jehovah and
Jové were identical names, taking out the h's
and remembering that the initial J (or I, as it
was) may always be written Ie, or Je, or He,
or Ihe, as, for instance, in the case of Jerusalem, which in various documents is written
Jerusalem, Herusalem, Ierusalem, Hierusalem,
Iherusalem, and so on; so that Jehovah is
really Jová, the vocative of Jupiter.   But even
the " a " in Jehovah is not right, and should
be " é," as modern scholars write Jehovah as
Yahweh or Yavé, the last letter being " é "
instead of " a."   We must never forget that
the English translators made a fatal blunder
in adopting the German J, which is our I or Y,
in rendering so many Hebrew proper names,
as the English J or soft G in place of I is
unknown in any other language.

In comparing the English and German
Bibles, I find much evidence that our trans-

lators were rather timid of their Hebrew
knowledge, and often copied Luther's German
rendering, when a little study would have
shown them that it was, when rendered into
English, by no means the equivalent of the
Hebrew text.

As Jupiter is of Babylonian derivation,
meaning Iu, sky; piter or pittar or pater, father
and as u is v, and also o or w, as in Greek, so
Iu is the same as Io or Iv, we see why the
vocative of Iu piter was at one time Iové, when
the nominative was Iovis or Iovos, and identical
with (I(eh)ové(h) of the Hebrews.   Modern
scholars favour greatly the use of "a" where the
vowel is not quite strongly defined, but o and a
are everywhere interchangeable, as witness in
the prophet's name, Mahommet, Mohammed,
Mahamad, and so on, showing the equivalence
of " a " and " o " and of " a " and " e."
Again, when modern scholars write Yahweh
for Jehovah, we must remember that our
English " a " may be equally well pronounced
as " ai " or " eh," or as " ah," or as " o," in
such words, " apron," " rat," and " war;"
so that we may write Iawé or Iové and still
have the same sound, as even in English " v "
and " w " are interchangeable, as Dickens

showed us in the vocabulary of Sam Weller,
or as in German and English.

I notice even in modern times a tendency in
the Higher Critics, who are mostly divinity
professors, while quite honestly telling us the
truth about the Hebrew scriptures, and showing us that many parts are quite untrue, yet
when it comes to the Holy Name they fight
shy of writing the name in such letters as would
show its identity with the " heathen " Jové.
There is no valid reason for writing Yahweh,
when Yové, or the Roman Iové, or in English
(erroneously) Jové, will represent the sound
equally well.   The   real   reason   is   that
J(eh)ova(h) is itself far too near Jové for
safety, so the Oxford scholars make it more
innocuous by extending it to Yahweh,
although some come dangerously near to the
Roman Iové by writing Yavé or Javé. The
traditional pronunciation Jehovah shows that
the sound was Iové, not Iavé. Another point
we must bear in mind is that in Hebrew there
were no vowels and all words were simply
composed of consonants and the actual pronunciation was handed down from mouth to
mouth by tradition.   About 500 A.D. some
monks called Masoretes at Tiberias on the Sea
of Galilee reduced the then accepted pro-

nunciation to script by putting in dots or
points at various positions to represent the
vowels just as is done in " shorthand " to-day.
These Masoretes did not use the Hebrew Bible
but that of their enemies the Samaritans, and
they created our Bible by collating the old
documents, editing them, and dividing them
into chapters and verses, and of fixing the
pronunciation. We must not forget also that
the holy name Jehovah was originally a name
given to the Hebrews no doubt after one of
their numerous captivities by the Babylonians,
and was, according to Sayce, Ya Ava (as detailed in p. 156 of my book on *Christianity*),
and Ya is rendered Iah in our Bible,
and forms the termination of hundreds of
names in the Old Testament, as Hesekiah,
Jeremiah, Isaiah, Ahaziah, and so on, which
should be pronounced at Hesek-yah, Yerem-
yah, Isa-yah (Eesa-yah), and Ahaz-yah, meaning " strength of," " servant of," " friend of,"
" supporter of," Iah, just as Messiah is
Mess yah, son of Iah or son of Javé. This Iah
is the first and the two last letters of the sacred
name I(ehov)ah, and symbolises the double
sex necessary to all creative gods—I being the
Rod or Pillar (masculine) and AH being the
regular feminine determinative in Hebrew.

**All ancient nations believed that creation
could not be accomplished without the co-
operation of both sexes, hence their god-names
included male and female particles.**

QUEEN OF HEAVEN

CHAPTER II

RUACH

Although the first chapter of Genesis is one of the very latest parts of the Hebrew Scriptures yet it contains a reference in one-half of verse 2 to the very oldest idea of the Queen of Heaven as creator.

The English translation gives it as the "Spirit of God moved on the face of the waters," but that is an entirely arbitrary rendering. The translators knew very well that Ruach, which they translate "spirit," is a feminine word, RKh or RCh, the source of our words Ark and Arch, as meaning primarily "high" or highest, as Arch angel, and is only the spirit of god in so far as it represents the superior force or life of the god which sets him into action. Now the cause of all activity in man according to the ancients was the female element which excites him to action, and hence when the old matriarchy became extinct, and male rule, or patriarchy, took its place, the writers were still imbued with the idea of the female being the impelling force.

I must here digress to say that all ideas of
creation were founded on what men saw
happening in nature, and to produce life or to
create, required the two sexes, and all ideas of
creation were based on the mother bringing
forth her young by the intervention of the
father. This led to a universally employed
symbolism relating to religion which employed
the two organs of reproduction of man and
woman to symbolise creation, and also, as these
same organs insured the continuance of life on
earth, or life without end, the combination of
the models of these organs were adopted by all
nations as the symbol of Eternal life. The
necessity for the two sexes in creation is stated
by the Hindus thus : —" Ishwara the supreme
" god felt not delight being alone. He wished
" another, and instantly became such.   He
" caused his own self to fall in twain and thus
" became male and female. He approached
" her, and thus were human beings produced."
Even Shelley sarcastically says—" From an
eternity of idleness, I, God awoke," having
no cause for the awakening. The masculine
worshipping Hebrews even implied the female
in their gods as they say, " so the Gods
" (Ale-im, plural) created man in their own
" images male and female created they them."

So the female was always necessary to creation. In early times it was held that the female alone was involved in the act, and the Queen of Heaven created whatever she desired and was the Great Mother. Ruach, translated as the spirit of God, conveys a totally false rendering. The word might have been honestly translated as the wife or consort of God, but here she is really alone and engaged in the creation of life out of the waters of fertility. I have already said that the ancient myths followed very closely the facts of nature, and as the old observers saw that in actual birth life came out of the waters, water was employed as the symbol of female creative power.

Whenever the translators came across a word casting a strong light on the ancient pagan beliefs and showing them to be the basis of the Hebrew conceptions, they always adopted a quite meaningless translation, which might, however, bear a very distant connection to the real idea. Besides these modern alterations of holy writ the Rabbis constantly altered the text, and issued a rule to all scribes or copyists who were engaged in multiplying the manuscript Hebrew Bible, " That all words " which are in the law written obscenely must " be changed to more civil words," and this was especially applied to the bodily parts of their god and to all the phallic references with which the writ was freely sprinkled. They were finally toned down so much as to render the passage quite unintelligible. Such was their action in the case of this word Ruach, and this opens up a very interesting land of myth or story.

Proclus tells us that the region of air, breath, or spirit, was allotted to Juno the Queen of Heaven with her symbol the dove, so Juno is D'Iune " of the dove," a symbol common to all Queens of Heaven, and Juno imparted the soul or life to the infant, in fact she was the creator of the soul of the child as its mother was the creator of its body. Now Ruach was the very first Queen of Heaven, so one can see the dim connection between her and " breathed " by which the translators dishonestly escaped from the first Generator of life the Ark or Ruach mother or wife of the Gods.

Although the Hebrew composers changed the name of the author of life to Eve, the meaning remained the same, as the name Eve means " Breath," to " Breathe," or " Life," and, as Breath is always soul or spirit, we see that Eve was identical with Juno. Kubélé.

Semiramis, or with Ruach, the Queens of Heaven of the ancients.

The Hebrew spelling of Eve, HVH, may be rendered in Hebrew Eve, as the Hebrew H was like the Greek Eta, capable of being rendered E or H, or both. So HVH may be Eve, Eva, Evah, or Hevah (as in Persian), or Chevah (ch as in Loch), or, lastly, in Genesis, Chavah or Chavach. When this Eve was coupled with the rod or pillar I, meaning man, we have the most holy Tetragrammaton, IHVH or IHOH (vav represents O, U, or V), the unpronounceable name of Jehovah, but only unpronounceable because the priest did not wish their devotees to know that it was simply a name for the double-sex necessary to a creative god. The degradation of the female begins early in Genesis, as it is not the man but the woman who discusses the " fruit " with the " serpent," and plucks it ; and man is only condemned because he listened to the advice of his wife. Iové puts enmity between the woman (not Adam) and the serpent, and wills that each should " bruise," " wound," or " cover with evil," the " head " of the one and the " heel " of the other. " Head " means the phallus, as shown in Fig. 115, p 257, of my *Christianity*, and this is further proved

by the Greek use of " Phalakra " (phallus top)
for " Bald-head." " Heel " is the female
organ, as shown in Fig. 42, where the Queen
of Heaven is seated with her heel in the middle
position. So this is the first curse, and it was
that of syphilis, or " Love disease " (Exodus
xx., 5), which I treat at greater length on pp.
435-440. As in all other religions, it is woman
who urges the man to the act which brings
about the creation of life. In India, Bram, the
supreme god, was too much immersed in contemplation to create, but the Queen of
Heaven urged the god to action, and creation
resulted. She was called " She who urges
the god to action," and if we look up Mary
or Mari in any Hebrew lexicon we will see it
means " She who urges to action;" and so it
is not the name of a real person, but a symbolical corner stone in a fictitious edifice.

In speaking of the Queen of Heaven, I say
mother or wife, because in all mythologies
one female impersonated both, and the
Christian dogma does not escape from this. If
the Son is part of the Trinity which acted the
part of husband to Mary, then Jesus is his own
father and is suckled by his wife, or Mary
becomes both his wife and his mother. The
Roman Catholic Church calls her the Mother

of God, and yet the god-head was her husband.

Rkh, or in the " pointed " (p. 334) Hebrew Ruach, was the Ark, which, as with Noah, brought forth all life, or with Moses brought forth individual life, and here we must enter upon another symbolism.   The ark is the habitation of God and is used to symbolise the womb, as, in fact, do all hollow things.   As we must be able to follow these ancient conceptions we must have words to express the things meant and as native familiar words used for the reproductive organs have an indecent sound we cloak our ideas in foreign words, as all nations do, and for the female organ the word yoni, from India, which also means Dove, has been most extensively used, although Latin equivalents are also common, such as Muliebre-pudendum or Membrum Feminum.   Now this yoni or the Ruach is symbolised by all lenticular shaped things or openings, such as the form of the fishes' bladder, or " vesica piscis," *especially almonds or anything almond shaped*, and all wells, boats, arks on the water or arghas, chests or arks in the church, altars, nave (navis ship), dolphin (delphys womb), whale, derketos, all round mammelated mountains or even heaps of stones called Omphs, clefts, caves, cups, vases, bowls, *especially with almond shaped openings*, basins or crescents, ring, cradle, shoe, window, door, arch, asses or horses shoe, etc.; in fact, everything hollow or open, but especially by the Lotus flower and seed vessel and the triangle and circle derived from the seed vessel.

Another word in the same sentence is also dishonestly translated. The word " moved " does not mean moved in any sense of the term. It means brooded as a hen does upon her eggs, and is really not at all a movement, but generally the opposite, a stillness. Here again, however, the translators found a faint connection, for the word also means brooding by spreading out the feathers, and this is sometimes accompanied by a movement of twitching of the feathers or a " movement " or fluttering. Lady novelists sometimes use this word in the above sense, as when they say of ladies when excited about anything, they " fluttered " over the diamond necklace or the new baby in excited admiration.

So much was this brooding idea adopted by ancient nations that even with a male god, as in this Persian God he was always seen in the act of creation with turned up feathers (Fig. 1),

Fig. 1.   Fig 2.

and here in the Babylonian with his Bow and Arrow (Fig. 2). Bow is feminine, arrow masculine, but the arrow in this case is a Trident, the same symbol as the Fleur-de-Lys, Prince of Wales' feathers, or Broad Arrow, which are all symbolical of the male trinity or triple organ.

So here we have the earliest account of creation, and this part of the second verse of the first chapter of Genesis should read, " The " Great Mother brooded on the fertile waters " and brought forth Life."

The first Queen of Heaven of which we have definite myths is Semiramis of Babylon, and here we will see that not only was she the creator of Life but her influence was so strong that when she was chased by " the Adversary," Typhon, she changed herself into a dove and plunged into the waters of Babylon, and so

consecrated them as to fit them to give new
life or regeneration by baptism. This name
Semiramis is probably a symbolical or terri-
torial name, as nearly all the Queens of
Heaven were derived from the Indian Maya,
and India is well called the Mother of
Religions, as we can trace nearly every idea in
the religions of Asia and Europe to India.

The Indian religion, when we get to know
it, was Solar, having Christna as the hero, but
before that it was Cosmic with the most distant
planet then known, Saturn, as Father of the
Gods or Ancient of Days. Maya was the rosy
dawn, mother of the sun; yet also called illusion, because the lovely rosy dawn so soon
melts into day when the sun rises. From this
Maya, arose a whole series of mothers of
heaven, all with the letter M as their initial.
Ma of Cappadocia may have been of local
origin, as Ma is the word for mother all over
the world, as the child forms that word on first
opening its mouth to cry for food, so that it
indicates both the mother and the child's food-
source, as in our word mammal. But beside
that there is a whole series such as Myrrha,
Mylltta, Mary, Miriam, Morwen, Myrinna,
and we find the Myrtle sacred to the Queen
of Heaven, while Mother and Matter are

words meaning the source of things. Even in religious symbolism we have the Monstrance, an almond-shaped vessel for holding the Pyx, the oil font, used in extreme unction, or the Host, and, as the Pyx is, according to the Church, the " Body of Christ Himself," as is the Host, the Monstrance is the Mother of God, her name beginning with M. Chemists, who imitated the " mysteries " of religion very closely, had the mortar and pestle like Monstrance and Pyx, with, as we shall see, an identical symbolic meaning.

India had another, and a more fundamental mother of all than Maya, who, after all, was only Queen of Heaven, in being the mother of the sun. The universal mother was Uma or Ooma, who was the original female half of twin-sexed Ardha-nari-Ishwara. Her name is the original of our word womb, as the Saxons added " w " to many words beginning with " o," as Odin into Woden, Wednesday, so Oom became womb, and the man with the womb was the woman, dropping the b and making its plural like man,—women. Ooma also gave rise to the word Om or Omph, p. 136, signifying, like the pomegranate, the fertile belly of the woman. We must now look at the male symbolism for a moment, so that we may find the complement of the female symbolism, given on p. 340. In the first place the name of the god which was nigh universal all over Western Asia was simply the letter l, but written Al, El, Il, or Ol; Il by the Babylonians, as in Bab-il (or ilu), the gate of God; the Phœnicians' Ol, and the Hebrews' Al in Ale-im (the god or gods of the Old Testament), and El on whom Jesus called as Eli when deserted on the Cross.

Fig. 3.   Fig. 4.   Fig. 5.

We know that El, the God of Israel, was a stone pillar, which Jacob erected and made into a living, hearing god by pouring oil upon it. This was represented in all countries by Fig. 3, in writing, or by Fig. 22, in sculpture— the Pala, pole, pale, pillar, or phallos; and in its active condition it was represented as in Fig. 4, which was worshipped all over Asia, and was identical with the Egyptian ithyphallic Osiris, or creative male. In China the symbol for man was crossed by an inverted phallus, as in Fig. 5; and then a " more-than-man " or a god was created by crossing the " man " symbol by two phalli, as in Fig. 6. The Chinese also had an Ark or Queen of Heaven, so they finally symbolised the double-sexed god or the Three-in-One, as in Fig. 7, where the Ark, or the Ruach of Genesis, is associated with the " More-than-Man."

Fig. 6.   Fig. 7.

The reproductive organ of man has a very old Aryan root, Pal or Pala, also written (as vowels are of little consequence) Pol, and even Pul, Pallus, and Phulus, used by Rodriguez, which are the original of our words Pole, pillar, pale, as in impale or paling or ecclesiastically within the pale, or a sacredly marked-off place. The Greeks adopted the phi spelling and called it Phallos, Latin Phallus, and from this we use both the noun and especially the adjective Phallic, as in " Phallic cult," to indicate the use of symbols of the sexual organs in religious emblems. This cult was at one time universal and in one sense may still be considered so, because the greater part of our church architecture, dress, and ritual is entirely phallic. In India the cult is the living religion of the Hindus, and is actively taught and practised by three hundred millions of our fellow subjects, and if we count the Japanese, Chinese, Malays, and Africans, who practise this cult we will find that it is still the cult of more than half the human race. In India the Altar at which all Hindus worship is a combination of the male and female organs, thus representing everlasting life or the Eternal, and is called the Maha Deva or Great God (see Figs. 11, 12, and 29; also other forms in my *Christianity* and *Gods of the Hebrew Bible*). The Hindu peasant simply calls it the Maha Deva, and does not seem to know what it physically represents; but all educated Hindus openly acknowledge that it is a representation of the creation of life by the conjunction of the male and female organs.

So the phallus, or Lingam as it is called in India, is represented by all upright things, such as pillars, gate posts, upright stones (which Jacob anointed), tree stems, especially Oak and Cedar, peaked mountains (Ararat and

Adam's Peak in Ceylon), rods, trees, serpents, sceptres, tortoises, fingers, hands, feet, toes (St. Peter's toe was originally the phallus), goats, rams, bulls, and other male animals, especially lions, sword (which is a cross), dagger, spear, trident, or other " piercer," the Cross, the Stauros, the pyx, the spire, the tongue of the bell (the bell is bi-sexual like the Indian lingam-yoni altar), the bell tower, the balance (zodiac), and the Lotus bud, but especially the serpent. We are now in a position to go into the complete symbolism connected with the Queen of Heaven and her debasement. Without a knowledge of this symbolism, which was common to all the world, and is by no means secret or esoteric, but openly known to everyone who cares to read, we could not understand a great deal of the ancient literature. I mention that this symbolism is nothing new or secret in order to prevent anyone from thinking that it is any supposed discovery of my own or that I pretend to have found a key to literature otherwise obscure. The key has been known and fully understood by all writers since the most ancient times, and is explained by many classical writers, as well as by many modern authors in such books as Payne Knight's " Worship of Priapus " (Phallism), Westropp's " Phalicism," Major - General Forlong's " Rivers of Life," and many anonymous books, such as " Bible Myths," and others with the title " Phallism." I have dealt with it as fully as an open publication will allow in my work on " Christianity : The Origin of its Teaching and Symbolism." I mention this, as one evidently enlightened and well-read reviewer, writing in a review intended for Eastern people where such symbolism is an every-day affair, actually expressed surprise that I should consider the serpent as a symbol of the Phallus. Now the serpent is *the universal symbol* for the phallus or for sexual passion, and the reason why it became the universal symbol is closely connected with our present study.

The Tortoise or Turtle is a complete phallic or creative symbol—" the world rests on a Tortoise "—its head when protruded being a model of the phallus, while its oval shell or carapace represents the female, as the O of the IO of Hebrew names or the Ring of the creative " Ring and dart " of Persia. By its rounded form it represents the Dome or D'Om (place of the womb) of our churches, like Minerva's shield with its serpents. The serpent was introduced because religious prostitution caused syphilis to be rampant and the Cobra not only erects itself, but its bite is fatal like syphilis, so the Cobra represented the " evil " side of " Adam's first transgression " better than the tortoise. In fact, the two incurable things were the serpent's bite and syphilis; and that the latter was rampant where temple women were kept will be amply proved in the following pages.

I have therefore felt it necessary to make this statement in order that critics who are not conversant with the subject will refer to one or other of the authors I mention before expressing surprise at such information. But in an open publication such as this it is quite impossible to give a statement of the absolutely naked symbolism which was employed in India, Babylonia, Palestine, Egypt, and Europe, and which is still employed in India, but some little idea can be obtained if anyone can peruse a copy of Payne Knight's book, privately printed, and so available to few, or in my book on *Christianity: The Sources of its Teaching and Symbolism*. I have in my possession photographs of temples, and finely coloured drawings done by our officers in India, in which there was no concealment but naked Ithyphallic gods, representing the act of creation, were minutely portrayed in beautiful colouring and with intense realism, so realistic as to be unpublishable. As I have said, it is a living cult and the mode of worship of more than half the people in the world at the present day.

Our own scientific conchologists are not above using phallic symbols to describe shells. I have pointed out on page 337 that Juno was derived from D'Iuné, " she of the Yoni " or muliebre pudendum.   In Latin that became D'Ioné, pronounced D'Yoni, " she of the Yoni," Hindu for the female organ. Here is a very beautiful shell from Nicaragua and Trinidad, called popularly the " Venus " shell, but the conchologists have made plain what this means by calling it Dioné Dioni, " Yoni of Yonis," an appellation of the

Queen of Heaven, and emphasising the great beauty of the Australian form as " D'ioni Veneris," the Yoni of Venus, and doctors write of " venereal " diseases, so we know what Venus signifies.

Fig. 6A.

Botanists also use purely phallic names when the plant has a Priapic appearance, as witness a very phallic form of the Stinkhorns (also called Phalloids), named Ithyphallus Impudens—the " Shameless Erect Phallus "—belonging to the Class of Mutinus, a form of the god Priapus— too realistic for illustration here.

CHAPTER III

EPOCHS IN THE HISTORY OF THE QUEEN OF HEAVEN

We can now consider the three epochs which will tell the history of the Queen of Heaven. First her universal reign, second her widespread worship in temple women or palakis or " serpent maidens," and thirdly the cause of her fall and her utter banishment from the heaven of austere religions.

Austerity seems to characterise all religions which are of such a character as to excite the devotees to a high pitch of religious excitement, and the earlier religions seem to have driven their worshippers to great extremes. It is recorded that extraordinary acts ensued on the conviction of the devotees of the Queen of Heaven that they had found salvation, and wished to prevent any lapse from Grace. We know that some devout women contemplate the subject of the crucifixion, and exaggerate its horror in their minds till it fills all their thoughts and so affects their nervous system that it disturbs their natural functions and at certain periods red spots of extravased blood appear on their hands and feet and even on their sides, where Jesus was said to have been pierced. From this hysteria we have the phenomenon of the " Bleeding Nun." So the devotees of the Queen of Heaven vowing themselves to perpetual celibacy that their vows to love no other might not be broken, worked themselves into such a state of ecstatic frenzy that they actually mutilated themselves in such a way as to destroy their manhood, and so render their vow inviolable, and at the same time assumed women's clothing, as priests do in all religions.

We thus see that these religious frenzies are a distortion of the sex sentiment as has been so often pointed out by serious writers, even by the Registrar-General for Scotland, who blamed the erotic effect of the intensity of the Scottish devotion to the Jewish Sabbath, for the high rate of illegitimacy in Scotland.

All the deepest rites of the Church embody the idea of sexual intercourse, as when a nun " takes the veil " becomes the " Bride of the Church " really the " Bride of Jesus," or the young priest becomes the " Bridegroom of the Church," and vows to take no other Bride. It must be remembered that all churches are

founded on the double sex idea, and embody
that most fully in their architecture, dress,
altar furniture, and ritual, so that either sex
may become the spouse of the Church, as we
see by the Nun " taking the veil " and the
Bishop on his appointment wedding the
church, " mea sposa," my wife, with his
ecclesiastical ring. We thus see that the very
intimate basis of the Church is sexual, and we
shall see that this was the case in all ages; in
fact, as has been said so often, no religion can
exist except on a basis of sexual emotion, dis-
torted and repressed it may be, but still sexual
emotion is the perennial fount of religious
emotion.

To return to the religion of the Queen of
Heaven, we find that all records of early
religions are records of the worship of the
Queen of Heaven in one form or another;
and that at one time the functions of the
priesthood were dispensed by women. Their
oracles and witches, or raisers of spirits, were
invariably women, as witness the Witch of
Endor, and every temple, tabernacle, or
church had its oracle, even down to the
austere Jové-worshipping Hebrews (see 1st
Kings, viii., 6).

Although the commandment went forth,

" Thou shalt not suffer a witch to live," and this edict has caused tens of thousands of innocent women to be tortured, burnt, and drowned, yet the very people who evolved the superstition were the greatest devotees of the witch cult.

Even now, although looked at askance by the Church, we find the most emotional women who come under the spell of religion are the greatest frequenters of the Bond Street American fortune-tellers, and we are made the laughing stock of more scientific nations by the President of the British Association announcing that he *knew* that there was continuity of life or soul after death by, I suppose, experimental evidence—the result, no doubt, of his earnest consultation with the modern Huldahs with crystal sphere, trance, or table rapping methods, who dishonestly declare that they have found a quick and easy road to knowledge.

These are the last degraded remnants of the Queens of Heaven which our masculine religion have left to us.

To return to the worship of the great Queens of Heaven of the past, the worship took the form afterwards adopted by our knights of vowing eternal devotion to some peerless maiden, and so the devotees vowed eternal devotion to the Queen of Heaven; but so strong was their determination to keep the vow and to prevent lapse in the future that they took means to put it out of their power to yield to any future weakness, and so they rendered themselves unable to exercise the sexual function by making themselves Eunuchs for the " Kingdom of Heaven's sake," as Jesus said (Matthew xix., 12).

Herodotus and many other historians give us graphic accounts of these sacrifices made in public during some of the great religious meetings or " revivals," which were even more common in the ancient world than they are to-day amongst the poetic, mystic, and erotic Celtic people of Wales and Scotland.

Lucian in his " Syrian Goddess " gives a graphic account of the manufacture of Eunuchs by the devotees of Mylitta in their erotic frenzy, caused by their constant contemplation of her divine virtues, just as our Nuns do in the case of Jesus.

At the town of Hieropolis, says Lucian, there were feasts and sacrifices of the most extravagant description at the Spring equinox, and everything was conducted on a scale of the greatest magnificence. These Spring feasts are in celebration of the marriage of the Sun and the Earth. Terra is the fruitful earth arriving at womanhood ready for motherhood, bringing forth all fruit, grain, and increase of flocks by the young spring sun's influence; so the marriage of the Sun and Earth by the crossing of the sun over the equator to bring renewed life to the earth was a very emotional, erotic, or phallic celebration of all northern nations, and as continued winter would mean death to these countries, the sun was hailed as the " Bridegroom " and " Saviour," as was Jesus.

Now, in this great spring feast at Hieropolis in celebration of the Great Mother, Ma, the young men vowed themselves as her perpetual lovers, and those of especially religious tendencies made this vow absolutely unbreakable by a very terrible sacrifice. Lucian tells us that so important was this festival that people came from great distances and brought their gods, " phalli," " Urim and Thummim," " Lares and penates," so that they might worship properly.

Then those who in their religious frenzy became obsessed with the idea of renouncing the pleasures of this world so that they might be united to Ma, as Nuns give themselves to

Christ, committed the great act told by Lucian as follows :—

In their religious frenzy they sacrificed to their protectress not the symbol but their real reproductive power. Seized with sudden religious fury, a devotee would snatch up a sharp knife left on the altar for the purpose, castrate himself publicly, rush off, and throw what he had cut off into any house he fancied, when the occupier must give him a complete suit of women's clothing. Then he was qualified to become a priest of Ma, or Kubele, or Mellitta, or the Queen of Heaven, by so retaining perpetual virginity or celibacy. How old are our modern practices. When a young priest takes the vows of celibacy—the same as castration, if not so irretrievable—he is given a woman's frock to wear, just as was the case four or five thousand years ago. In the modern case it has a double significance, as it also represents the priest as double-sexed, like the god he serves. " In " his own image male and female created he " them," so the god was double-sexed and we symbolise this by putting women's gowns on all church servants, even down to the choir boys' surplices (girls' chemises).

In important cases like the Pope they make

an actual examination to make sure he is a man (there was one woman Pope), and then clothe him in silk and lace garments, the very essence of femininity. Also when the priests officiate at the altar, in presence of the deity, everyone must have noticed the richness of the apparel, and especially the use of women's capes, gowns, or frocks, rich with the finest lace. From these indications we see the respect paid to the female in early religions.

Whether it arose from the temples having been administered by female priests, or whether from the worship of the female in the form of the Great Mother, even after men superseded women priests, or simply from the inborn impulse of human nature, the fact remains that, as far back as we have records, there have been women connected with every temple, devoted to sexual intercourse with men. Payne Knight writes of this tendency as described by the ancients in their sacrifice to Bacchus :—" Their acts of devotion were " indeed attended with such rites as most " naturally shock the prejudices of a chaste " and temperate mind, not liable to be " warmed by that ecstatic enthusiasm which is " peculiar to devout persons when their atten-" tion is absorbed in the contemplation of the

" beneficent powers of the Creator, and all
" these faculties directed to imitate him in the
" exertion of his great characteristic attribute
" [creation]. To heighten this enthusiasm
" the male and female saints of antiquity used
"to lie promiscuously together in the temples
" and honour God by a liberal display and
" general communication of his bounties."

So Knight thinks it was a natural outbreak
of the erotic emotion with which all religion
is charged. Whatever may have been its
origin, it was universal, and towns like Corinth
and Eryx had each a thousand sacred prostitutes attached to their temples, while Paphos,
where the apostle Paul went, was so famous
that the word Paphian is used in our dictionaries as synonymous with temple prostitute, and Paphos and Paphia are used as
Lingam and Yoni, or as male and female prostitutes.

CHAPTER IV

QUEEN OF HEAVEN AS PRINCIPAL MEMBER OF THE GODHEAD.

We must now consider the position of the Queen of Heaven as being the Great Mother or maker of all and her position in the Trinity as the Unity in which the three are united. The " mysteries " of all religions were entirely phallic, as we learn in hundreds of expressions in classical authors; so there are good grounds for looking into this side of the origin of the " incomprehensible mystery " of the Christian churches, both Catholic and Protestant, which forms their central point of dogma. The Christian religion, say the Christian fathers, was exactly the same religion which existed before the time of Jesus.

St. Augustine wrote :—" The same thing " which is now called the Christian religion " existed among the ancients. They have " begun to call ' Christian ' the true religion " which existed before." Justin Martyr gives more elaborate proof of the parallelism of the new Christianity with the old paganism (see my *Christianity*).

We find, then, that Rch was the mother of
all, and is expressed in two different senses as
Ark, the dwelling place of the god, and as
Arch, meaning highest, as Arch angel or Arch
fiend. From this we see that the Ruach was
at that time the highest, and that the Ruach
was the dwelling place of the god represented
by a rod, pillar, or post, the two forming our
broad-arrow, the mark of king-godship.   In
the Trinity in Unity, or Dreieinigkeit, " Three
in oneishness," of the Germans, the female
was the unity or uniting power in making
one god.   Not only so but amongst many
others there was one complete symbol of the
creative power produced in enormous numbers, and to be seen in many drawing-rooms
to-day, namely, Una on the Lion.   I have
already said that one of the most special
symbols of the male or the male reproductive
organ was the Lion as it stood for male force,
strength, and salaciousness.   Now in this
case, the female member of the creative combination is given her ecclesiastical name Una,
" The One," so that not only was the female
the chief or highest but she was " the One "
in which the complete creative force dwelt.
Now this was the case with the most sacred
arcanum of the Hebrews. their Ark of the

Testimony, which represented Rkh, the Queen of Heaven, or The One. Anyone looking into the ark was condemned to death, and we know that it contained at one time the Rod of God and his two stones. Here we have the Trinity or Triple full creative organ of the god inclosed in the Ark, Ruach, Uma, womb of the Queen of Heaven, and so we have the " incomprehensible mystery " of the Church of England prayer-book.

The Ruach was the Kunti or Well of Love (now Kunthos or Cynthia) " Spouse," " Dove," " Love of God," " Kun," " Kiun " (Queen), " She Kunah," rose on a prolific stem, Zoroaster's " Divine Wisdom " (Palas Athené), " Altrix Nostra," nurse of man and all existence " Eros " (creating love) " Ceres Mamosa," and " Diana Multimamæ," the many-breasted Diana of the Ephesians. We thus see that the Queen of Heaven reigned supreme until the Hebrews dethroned her and made her the author of Evil; because Eve was the Eva or Heva of the Persians and Queen of Heaven turned into the first woman. The Roman Catholic Church has always seen the powerful attraction of the Family idea, Father, Mother, and Son, especially the mother, as the Protestant or Theistic heaven

Fig. 8.

with no Queen is a cold conception and will
never attract warm-blooded humanity, so the
Catholic Church has gone back to the Queen
of Heaven idea. To do this they declare that
all Mary's female ancestors were "without
sin," and therefore without death, and were
therefore goddesses, and Mary is Queen of
Heaven, the habitation of God, as here shown
in an engraving of the fifteenth century, showing the death, ascension, and coronation of the
Virgin. By the kind permission of Bernard
Quaritch, I am enabled to illustrate this legend
by a very valuable and rare specimen of engraving in " La Maniere Criblée," a curious
style of which few European specimens sur-
vive (Fig. 8). It had its home in India, and
specimens may be seen in the India Office
Library (Photos 4750-4753, etc.).

Cardinal Newman tried to renew this idea,
and pointed out that in the Christianity of
Egypt there were three persons in the Trinity,
the Father, the Virgin, and the Messiah their
son (or Osiris, Isis, and Horus in Egyptian)
All the early statues of Mary and Jesus introduced into Europe were actual statues of Isis
and her babe Horus, the Saviour.

Thus wrote Newman :—" The controversy
" opened a question it did not settle. It dis-

" covered a new sphere, if we may so speak,
" in the realms of light to which the Church
" had not yet assigned its inhabitants." [Note
the Church's position not to record facts but to
create them as it pleased.] " Thus there was
" a wonder in heaven ; a throne was seen far
" above all created powers mediatorial inter-
" cessory " [Melitta, the name of the Queen
of the Syrian Heaven, means the mediatrix],
" a title Archetypal, a crown bright as
" Heaven, was the mediatrix " [as her name
means], " a title Archetypal, a crown bright as
" the morning star, a glory issuing from the
" eternal throne, robes pure as the heavens,
" and a sceptre over all. And who was the
" predestined heir of that mystery? Who was
" that wisdom, and what was her name? The
" mother of fair love, and fear, and holy hope,
" exalted like a palm tree in Engadi, and a
" rose plant in Jericho, created from the
" beginning, before the world in God's Coun-
" sels and in Jerusalem was her power " [the
last place for a Queen of Heaven].   " The
" vision is found in the Apocalypse, a woman
" clothed with the sun, and the moon under
" her feet, and upon her head a crown with
" twelve stars " [Isis's insignia centuries
before Mary].

" This," says Hislop, the Arch Protestant, in his *Two Babylons*, " is the very poetry of Blasphemy," but the Catholic Church is right from a purely human point of view, a companionless god is a lifeless conception.

We have seen that all Queens of Heaven have the dove as their symbol, and are Queens of fair love, as Newman said, although their symbolism was very varied, pp. 39-40, including the universal group of Arch or Dome of Heaven, Dove, Boat, or Crescent, and finally

Fig. 9.

water, as shown in Fig. 9. Now, in all the early pictures of the Trinity of the early Christian ages, and even of the middle ages, when woman was the " door of hell," represented the Trinity as shown here, as two men united

in their breaths [or souls, they were the same
then] by the wings of the dove. Now, what is
the link that can join the souls of Father and

Fig. 10.

Son but the mother? In Fig. 10 she shows her
unity or uniting power, and although the
Eden story barred woman from the godhead,
the Church admitted first of all her symbol,
and now begins to instal Mary as the most
sacred and powerful member, because he who
blasphemes Ruach or the " Holy Ghost " will
not be forgiven, this being a deadly offence—
the blasphemy of the Father or Son being a

trivial offence in comparison. So we see that even with the supremacy of the Eden story man ever and anon became conscious that a heaven without a Queen was not complete, and that she should occupy not only a place but the highest place, centre of the Trinity, as her " Arch " name indicates.

The gods, being creators, were often named from the words, signs, or symbols of male and female, or the organs for the production of life, as I have shown in the case of Jehovah on p. 37. Another example is Pharaoh, which should be pronounced Phara-O, and as R and L are expressed by the same letter or hiero-glyphic in Egyptian, it should be written Phala-O, that is the phallus, and the widely-used feminine symbol, the ring or circle, or door of life, the muliebre pudendum or yoni.

In the creative act the male and female are called the " three-in-one," that is, the triple male in the yoni or unifying female, or, as Moses phrased it, the rod and two stones of Iové, or Yové, in the ark. This combination was, and is, the great " incomprehensible mystery " of all religions, and is represented in India by the Lingam-yoni altar (Figs. 11, 12, or 29), and this became a very sacred sign, like our Cross or the Royal arms, and was

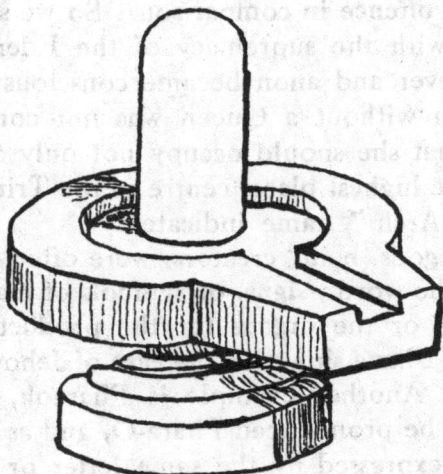

Fig. 11.

Fig. 12.

Fig. 13.

carved at the top of proclamation and boundary stones. Its double sex was emphasised by the sun and moon, carved on the same stone, as in Fig. 12, as can still be seen all over India. The three-in-one made a foursome creative-god combination called the Tetrad or Tetracht of Pythagoras, the Pyr-Om or Pyramid, the Arba El or Arbil, god of the " four quarters," meaning the universe, the monstrance and pyx, the mortar and pestle, and so on (see my *Gods of the Hebrew Bible*, pp. 64-66).

The Hindoo form of the monstrance and pyx is that of a silver dove, hung round the priests' neck by a chain, and it contains the triple male organ modelled in thin silver, so that it may be compressed, and when this phial (a modification of the word phallus) is pressed by the priest in administration of extreme unction it causes the oil to drop on the dying, to give life to the departing soul. One of the wings, or a lid, opens so as to allow of its being used as a box or ark for the pyx. It is not so long ago since our church used the same phylacteries. Fig. 13 is a rough sketch of a " Pyx " (it should be called a monstrance—that which holds the pyx—a mistake often made), modelled by Leonondi da Vinci in the sixteenth century.

The dove (Queen of Heaven) has an opening
in the back, exactly as in the Indian phylactery,
or the monstrance and pyx of to-day. It was
made of copper, gilt, and was sold in London
for £3255 (see *Illustrated London News*, July
6th, 1912, p. 4).   From this we see the truth
of describing the Virgin as the " habitation of
God," " Tabernacle of God," in whom dwells
all the " fullness of the God-head bodily," a
description admirably materialised by putting
the Trinity bodily inside the Yoni, Iona, dove,
womb, or Queen of Heaven.   The castellated
turrets on Fig. 13 are indicative of virginity,
as being unbroken, while the round stand is
modelled on the lotus top, or Ring of Persia,—
symbol of woman.

Just as man has made his gods after his own
image, and thinking him lonely has given him
a wife and offspring, so in later times the
Queen of Heaven was given a husband. But
as the male was of little consequence at that
time he had no personal name, but was called
simply El, the word or sign for man or god,
the upright column l, and he became as husband of the Ark, Arkel, then Arkelaus,
Heracles, Hercules, the " H " having no significance. Now, Hercules was a sun-god all
radiance, and he performed twelve labours or

miracles, and he pursues a beautiful goddess
called Iolé, the " dove," who must have been
a Queen of Heaven by her name.   But he
never attained success in his wooing, and the
elusive dovelet always escaped his embraces,
and he then returned to his next miracle.
Now, in the pantomimes we have a harle-
quinade at the end, with the harlequin, or in
French little Hercules, or Arquelin, little
Ark, without the H, who has a lath
sword in his hand and is dressed out in
spangles to imitate the radiant sun.   With
this lath or " lat," which word has a purely
phallic meaning, and means exactly the same
as the club of Hercules, he causes demons to
spring up and scenes to change; in fact, it is
the same as Moses's Rod of God, which he
found in Midian.   But between his labours he
is joined by the Columbine—Latin for " little
dove "—and they dance together a dance,
which, when performed by professionals who
have the proper traditions, always make the
Columbine elude the arm of the harlequin,
and so becomes elusive.   At the end the
elusive Columbine, Iolé, or dovelet disappears, and he, Arquelin, with his " lat "
resumes his labours and performs his miracles.
Here we have one of the oldest characters in

the world, a sun god, enacted at the birth of the sun, Christmas, in our theatres.

The very earliest Queens of Heaven had the dove as their symbol, and we find that symbol universally used for the Virgin Mary, so she is the direct descendant of the universal Queen of Heaven. All the other Queens of Heaven were likewise immaculate virgins, and yet were the mothers of the sun god as was Mary. We find later that there were two goddesses nearly allied, one moral and austere, such as Juno, wife of the father or chief of the gods, and she still had the dove as her symbol; but although she ought to have been Queen of Love also, she was so no longer, as the new Queen of Love, Venus, had taken up the rôle of the Dove. And all such goddesses of love were considered to be a little loose in their loves. Dove and Love have henceforth two separate rôles. Juno is D'Iuné—she of the Dove.

We have the same curious duplication in the New Testament. We have the Virgin Mary pure in her love, austere, and without blemish, and we have that other Mary of Magdala, " quia multum amavit," the close friend of Jesus, who was considered of loose life, but was undoubtedly the Venus of the New Testament drama. Then, as is nearly always the case, the favourite is used as a type, and we have four Maries created to symbolise a female Tetrad. Our last Queen of Heaven in Mallory's *Morte d'Arthur* was the loose-living Guinevere, and again the good Maries are multiplied in Elaine and other peerless virgins, who abound in the tale. The tale of Arthur is purely a sun myth with its round table and twelve knights—the year with its twelve months, Hercules and his twelve labours. The death of Arthur in Mallory's work has the same weary sombre tone as the end of John's gospel, and in the dying scene he is surrounded by " Maries."

We find the dove idea is used in the little word-pictures spun by these monks in their cells, which are so common, and we have a sample in Scotland, which no doubt had its long tale of miracles, martyrdoms, and conversions in early times, but lost, like much more religious folk-lore, since the reformation.

We have the small island of Iona, which was the centre of Roman religion in the West of Scotland. Iona is Greek for Dove, so we see the dove religion settling in Scotland, just as the spirit of God descended on Jesus as a dove on baptism in the Jordan. But this dove

was brought by Saint Columba—Latin for
Dove—and was conveyed across the narrow
strait to the Morven shore. Now, Morven is
the early Gaelic for Mary, whose symbol is
the dove; so we see the philological ground-
work for a dove story now entirely forgotten.

CHAPTER V

QUEEN OF HEAVEN AND PHALLISM

We have seen the universal rule of the Queen of Heaven with her dove symbol and her little babe, the sweetest symbol of love man could set up.

But in mankind we have few Saint Anthonys, the type of Dr. Faust is naturally most frequent, since the favourite command of Iové in the Bible, " Be fruitful and multiply," was not only an ecclesiastical commandment constantly repeated, but was the very core and essence of life—every impulse in the young ripening human being tends towards the union of sexes, who are driven to pair as inevitably as are two atoms set free from combination.

The fundamental scheme of active matter is pairing, and the higher the scale in the living world, the more complex the animal produced, the stronger and more absorbing is the pairing instinct.

But in the difference of the sexes comes the eternal struggle between the different inclinations of man and woman. The consequences of sexual union to man are very slight, except as a source of pleasure; while the consequences to woman are fundamental. Hence man's primary instinct as that of many of the higher animals is towards the pleasure side of the union of the sexes, and as we are taught in Holy Writ polygamy is his natural bent, and the patriarchal state was that of the animals best known to man, the deer, the goat, the sheep, ram, etc., where the male appropriated as many of the females as he could. The patriarchs were constantly adding to their lists of wives and the glory of man as a stag-like animal culminates in Solomon's 700 wives and 300 concubines, and Solomon was the " wisest " man.

Further, he showed his wisdom in one striking case of the quarrel between two women about a newly-born baby, again phallism associated with wisdom. And we must not forget that the most outspoken love song allowed in English, where the parts of the nude female are openly praised, was a song attributed to the " wisest man."

The constant association of phallism with wisdom in the Bible and other ancient writings is very striking. First, in Eden, everyone

now admits that the Tree of Knowledge was
the phallus, as indulgence in its fruit causes
shame and makes the pair cover their nakedness; whereas before the enjoyment of what
the *Encyclopædia Biblica* calls the " erotic
fruit," they were " naked and not ashamed."
Then the eating of the Tree of Knowledge
made Eve the " mother of all living," and
through that act she was apparently cursed
with child-birth.   Then " the serpent was
wise."   " Be ye wise as serpents and kindly
as doves."   Adam " knew " Eve, and she conceived and bare Cain, and David " knew
not " the young maiden placed beside him
when dying, and so on.   If one has any doubt
let him turn to Judges xix., 22-25, where the
meaning of " know " is not doubtful when
applied to either sex.   In heathen nations it
was the same; " Palas Athene " means the
" phallus, the serpent," and was the great goddess of wisdom of the Greeks.   Here we have
the double symbolism explained, that in the
use of the serpent symbol, the phallus was
meant, or sexual enjoyment.   All temples,
from China, Tibet, India, Greece, Rome, to
Mexico, had the constant association of naked
maidens with serpents.   Fergusson tells us
that such serpent shrines were everywhere,

and that all temples were originally serpent shrines. Two well-known classical examples from contemporary writers must suffice for proof here. In the grove of the Dodona Jove, the virgins had to approach the sacred serpent with its food in a state of absolute nudity, thus creating the bisexual symbol of immortality; and the manner of the serpent in taking the food was the oracle on which they judged of the prosperity of the coming year.

Again, Roman maidens proved their chastity by offering food when in an unrobed condition to the sacred serpent of the Argonian Juno in the grove of the Temple of Argiva, about sixteen miles from Rome. If the food were accepted they were considered pure and certain to be fertile. Argonian and Argiva are derived from Argo (ship); itself the ark or womb.

In the Old Testament the more uxorious the man the greater his wisdom. Wisdom and phallic power were the same; and the " wisdom " was in no way connected with marriage, as Paul says that he that giveth his virgin in marriage doeth well; but he who giveth her not doeth better. It referred purely to the enjoyment of intact virgins, who were enjoyed even by Jehovah or Iové, as is shown by the Midianite story. Nor is this view repudiated in the New Testament, nor was any continence in this matter taught by the ecclesiastical authorities or practised by them up till the time of the Reformation. Priests and prelates alike practised polygamy, or perhaps we should say extensive promiscuity; in fact, so amatory were these well-fed ecclesiastics that the villagers refused them admission to their precincts unless accompanied by their concubines, as they invariably seduced the wives and daughters of the people. Gibbon, Lecky, Green, and many other historians have given us similar pictures of the clergy up till quite recent times, and as a contemporary traveller Poggia, in about 1400, says :—" I found them " [about twenty years after Chaucer's time] " given up to sensuality in abundance."

So universal was the custom of priests keeping a harem that the governments levied a tax upon this luxury, and we learn this from the German section at the Council of Trent in 1560, complaining this tax was levied on poor priests who could not afford even one concubine. An abbot mentioned had seventeen illegitimate children in one village; another had seventy concubines; and the Bishop of

Liege had over seventy children. We know that this was the moral tone at the time of Cæsar Borgia, and courtesans, " meretrices honestae," concubines, and plural wives were honoured and protected not only by kings, statesmen, and humanists, but by princes of the Church. It was always so, as we read in Judges xix. of a Levite priest travelling with his concubine, and when Paul V. proposed the suppression of licensed brothels in the Holy City the Roman Senators petitioned against any change and in favour of maintaining brothels for the priests, on the ground that their existence was necessary to prevent the priests seducing their wives and daughters. It was not very different lately, as we see from an article by A. F. Whyte, Esq., M.P., in the *Daily Chronicle* of 2nd June, 1914, in which he states that in the eighteenth century " irreligion and immorality were rampant among the clergy."

Whenever a man has more than sufficient money to keep his legalised household, we find him keeping the company of other women under one excuse or another, secretly or openly, hypocritically or honestly facing the results of the impulse of nature. It is much the same yet where the Church rules. In

Rome, while under the full control of the
Church in 1836, out of 4373 births, 3160 were
illegitimate, or three-quarters of the total
births were from unmarried girls. Rome in
the Bible sense was then very " wise."

I touch upon this side of man's nature in
order that we may consider the curious phase
of religion, which seems to be as old as religion itself—that of attaching women for sexual
pleasure to all temples or churches. Man is
a gregarious animal, and hence when a common impulse is supreme in a herd there is
bound to be much promiscuity. We have
considered the impulse in man. Nature has
placed no bonds upon him in order that all
females shall produce young. The tendency
of the female to seek the male and to delight
in his presence is equally strong, but the
results are very different. As soon as the
young is produced, unless there were absolute
communism in the herd the woman claims the
man for the purpose of finding food, shelter,
and protection for her and her young. Man,
not the church, purely civil man saw the
justice of her claim, and made marriage laws
even against his own fundamental inclinations.
The Church only adopted this idea as it did
baptism at birth, extreme unction at death.

the burial service, and prayers for the dead, in order that it might attach men more forcibly to the Church by making him pay its taxes at the solemn and important epochs of his life. Money was what the Church was always after, and we find that a true blood tax was levied on the Hebrews by those who were authorised to make levies—the Levites. Every first-born child of every Hebrew was dedicated as a sacrifice to Jove; that it was to be killed by the shedding of its blood—in crude parlance, have its throat cut like a lamb—unless it was ransomed or redeemed by a payment *in cash* of five shekels, each shekel to be 20 gerahs paid to the Levite (Numbers iii., 45-51). [Note the financial exactitude of the Hebrew even in the price of blood.]

These Levites or Levyers of temple tribute were entirely dependent for their living on the sacrificial offerings made by the devotees, as the Levites had " no portion in Israel;" and we shall see that the character of the god they evolved was greatly influenced by the constant tendency of the Israelites to abandon the worship of the irate Jové and go " a-whoring " after other gods whom they thought for the moment superior to Jové, as we see in their longing for the worship of the

Queen of Heaven.   The Levites, therefore, said their god's name was Jealousy with a capital J, and poured out curses by the chapter on anyone who would dare to worship other gods, *and so cease to pay the leviers of the temple their tribute*. If a large number abandoned Jové, the Levites would starve.

We shall see that this was one active cause of the debasement of the Queen of Heaven, and with her of all womanhood.

But the great cause of the change from the worship of the Great Mother to an entirely masculine religion, with woman as the enemy, was, I believe, the terrible results which ensued through making the temple the great centre of prostitution.

I can find no records to show when that was instituted. Of course, private prostitution is as old as mankind; there were always women who preferred free love to the marriage tie— a slavery introduced by man to secure his property, as early man had the power of life and death over his wife as he virtually yet has among the rich in Mohamadan countries.

The Bible gives an example of common or private prostitution in Judah with his son's widow in Genesis xxxviii., but the institution of temple nuns or Palaki is older than Judah;

in fact, has apparently always existed. The worship of the Queen of Heaven seems to have given rise to Eunuch priests, which points to the cult being a very severely moral one; but, on the other hand, extremely ascetic sects, such as the Sacti worshippers in India, have the most lascivious rites when they do break out. It may be that the Queen of Heaven, being an immaculate virgin, as she always was, and it being quite impossible for her devotees to expect any phallic favours from her, the temple maidens were provided as her substitutes, so that the male devotees might carry out the " great sacrifice " with her by deputy. Or it may be that when man seized the offices and emoluments of the temple and ousted the women priests, and substituted circumcision for castration, he found the necessity of a concubine system, and, for a price, allowed devotees to share in his harem. In any case we are not so much interested in its origin as in the deplorable results which were the great cause of the degradation of woman in the Church's eyes. It is very difficult to trace different diseases in ancient times, as they were considered as visitations of God, as they are still by the Church, and no one ever suspected that they were the result of dirt and insanitary practices. But one nation was, even in very early times, very practical, and China collected in a medical work descriptions of the various diseases from which the people suffered, and the description of one of them is identical with syphilis, as we know it to-day. Unfortunately, the Chinese language was largely written in a diagramatic form, so the exact descriptions required for the identification of a disease are not so exact as would be the case in modern text-books, but one point is very clear : they recognised, as did the Hebrews, that the disease visited the sins of the fathers on the children to the third and fourth generation. Many have held that syphilis is a modern disease, but now that it is admitted that the Chinese knew of it and described it, this objection to the mention of its terrible effects in the commandment is no longer valid. But even if the Chinese had not listed it, we would find plenty of proof in classical writing and oriental fable to show that it was well known. However, the Hebrews were so intensely phallic and so interested in all things relating to sex that they have left us unmistakable references to the ravages which syphilis made amongst them, owing to their

promiscuous intercourse with temple women;
and in the great annual festivals where, in the
tents of Venus, the young women exposed
themselves for hire. This was the great
annual feast several times ordained by Iové,
and called euphemistically the Feast of Tabernacles, but the Hebrew words are Succoth
Benoth, which is clearly the Tents of Venus,
Benoth and Venus being identical in Hebrew;
and it was an extremely phallic feast very merry
with wine and good eating. Now, the word
" merry " has only one meaning in old writings, and that meaning is invariably in the
direction of unrestrained sexual intercourse.

The orthodox Dr. Adam Clarke says " there
" is no room for doubt that these Succoth
" were tabernacles wherein young women ex-
" posed themselves to prostitution in honour
" of the Babylonian goddess Melitta."

Dr. Kalisch, a great Jewish Biblical scholar,
has told us that " the unchaste worship of
" Astarte, known also as Beltis (my lady or
" madonna), and Tanais, Ishtar, Mylitta,
" Anaitis, Ashera, and Asteroth, flourished
" amongst the Hebrews at all times, both in
" the kingdom of Judah and Israel; it con-
" sisted in presenting to the goddess, who was
" revered as the female principle of concep-

" tion and birth, the virginity of maidens as
" a first fruit offering, and it was associated
" with the utmost licentiousness. This de-
" grading service took such a deep root that
" in the Assyrian period it was even extended
" by the adoption of new rites borrowed from
" Eastern Asia, and described by the name of
" the tents of the maidens (Succoth Benoth),
" and it left its mark in the Hebrew language
" itself, which ordinarily expressed the notion
" of a courtesan or harlot by the word Kade-
" shah, a consecrated woman and a Sodomite
" by Kadesh, a consecrated man," so that both
prostitution by women and sodomy by men
were consecrated temple practices.

" Consecrated prostitution was a revered
" practice. Judah and Tamar show that,'
says Abbe Loisy, p. 119.

Dr. Adam Clarke writes : —

" Succoth Benoth may be literally translated
" the Tabernacles of the daughters, or young
" women, or nymphs of Venus, or if Benoth
" be taken as the name of a female idol
" (Venus) from BNTh, or its equivalent VNS
" (unpointed Venus), and meaning to build
" up or procreate children, then the words
" will express the tabernacles sacred to the
" productive powers feminine."

Plutarch tells us that the Feast of Tabernacles, the merriest festival of the Jews, was " exactly agreeable to the holy rites of Bacchus," and Bacchanalia were phallic orgies with promiscuous coition when all bonds of marriage or relationship were loosed and incestuous intercourse was considered a merit and indulged in without shame and in the most public manner.

The worship of the " Grove " was simply the worship of the sexual organs arranged as in the Indian Lingam-yoni altar, but sometimes when called Asher (masculine) the phallus alone, and when called Asherah (feminine) the Yoni was worshipped. Ashteroth or Asherim were probably the combined organs, but no very clear description exists. However, the important point is not that they worshipped these " idols," but that they made their worship practical by accompanying the adoration of the god by at the same time accomplishing the sexual act, or " great sacrifice," or " holy kiss," as the Christian saint Augustine called it.

The prophets or Nabis in their rebukes to the Hebrews in falling away from Jové worship told them that they erected the abominable thing (phallus) " upon the hills and

" under every green tree," " upon every high
" hill and under every green tree," " upon
" every high mountain and under every green
" tree, and there played the harlot," " upon
" the hills and in the fields," " by the green
" trees upon the hills," " in every street, " at
" every corner," " at every head of the way,"
" at the head of every way," so that this
worship was universal. But the erection of
an " abomination " or of the Asherah does not
convey much to our ears. But when we consider two different renderings—one, our own
Bible; and the other, the Douai Bible—we get
more light. Ezekiel xvi., 24, says :—" Thou
" hast also built unto thee an eminent place,
" and thou hast made thee a high place in
" every street," which is carefully translated
under the Rabbis' rule to convey nothing; but
the Douai Bible blurts out the truth. " Thou
" didst also build thee a common stew and
" madest thee a brothel house in every street,"
so we see that the erection of the shameful
thing was only a sort of signpost to a house
where the living Asherah, Ashteroth, or
Venus could be enjoyed. The Hebrews were
in about the same stage of civilisation as the
Dahomeyans, as Sir R. Burton wrote in the
Journal of the Anthropological Society, Vol.

I., No. 10 :—" Amongst all barbarians whose
" primal want is progeny " [exactly as with
the Hebrews] " we observe a greater or less
" development of Phallic worship. In
" Dahomey it is uncomfortably prominent,
" *every street* from Wydah to the Capital is
" adorned with the symbol, huge phalli."
This is the condition of all phallic countries,
our own India not excepted.

But not only was it worshipped in private
shrines, but the worship and practice was
carried on in the temple and in cells " by the
" house of the Lord, where women wove
" hangings for the grove." Josiah brought
out these phalli from the house of the Lord
and " stamped them to powder," " made dust
of them," no doubt clay or stone phalli, so
common to-day in India and other phallic
countries. Amos even says that a " son and
" father would go in unto the same maid to
" profane his holy name," as Kadesoth were
servants of Iové.

Yet these temple women were respected,
and Strabo tells us that " women, after being
" prostituted a long period at the temple of
" Anaites, were often disposed of in marriage,
" no one disdaining a connection with such
" persons;" hence it was quite natural that

the Lord should tell Hosea (i., 2) :—" Go take unto thee a wife of whoredoms."

I only mention sufficient here to prove the practice; we are really only interested in the results and their effect in assisting in the debasing of the Queen of Heaven.

We see that the great feast, the Feast of Tabernacles, three times specially commanded Leviticus xxiii., 34; Deuteronomy xvi., 13; and Zechariah xiv., 16), where curses are uttered for any failure to keep it, is continued in the New Testament (John vii., 2), and still rampant at the time of Saint Augustine, who commanded " ladies who attend the feasts of " the Eucharist to wear clean linen, as the " holy kiss was administered." It was the most " Holy " (that is phallic) feast of the Hebrews and was continued for the holy period of seven days, and yet this feast was in honour—as Dr. Adam Clarke and Dr Kalisch tell us—of the " productive powers feminine," and young women exposed themselves in tents for prostitution for seven days in a feast specially commanded three times by the Jové whom we are still invited to worship. Now unless it were recorded by authorities who had no end to serve but simply that of recording, one could scarcely believe the depths of realism

to which the Hebrews descended in their
worship of natural inclinations and processes
as is described to us as being solemnly enacted
at this Feast of Tabernacles. On the other
hand, we know that priests, living lazy lives
and constantly indulging in promiscuous
sexual indulgence—for the priests or monks
were, according to all authorities, " given up
to sensuality," " steeped in every form of
sexual indulgence "—spent their ample leisure
in writing; sometimes composing " Christian
Fathers," as Father Hardouin describes, and
sometimes writing satires on religion, but
always writing with hidden meaning sometimes
in the form of puns, such as " Saint Frumen-
tarius of Wheathampstead from the *Granary* of
his Wisdom," creating a saint out of the name
of a hamlet, and so on with a wink of the eye
to their fellow forgers and their tongue in their
cheek at the simple folks who believed them.

India had sacred prostitutes like the Hebrew
Kadeshoth, called Palaki, female of Pala, just
just as Devaki (goddess) is female of Deva,
and these Palaki or Kadeshoth were the origin
of the custom of keeping Nuns or Holy
Women under church rule.

CHAPTER VI

HEBREW PHALLIC FEASTS

As the great Tabernacle in which the feast of Tabernacles was held and which we are about to describe shortly, has been proved by eminent Biblical critics to be a myth— the work of such a scribe in his moments of inspiration, so the last great ceremony of the terribly phallic feast of tabernacles may be the fabrication of such a priest, but we know that other nations indulged in " mysteries " of a similar nature. And we also know that the Hebrews stooped lower than most nations in their degraded phallic exercises, so much so that special " commandments " had to be issued against having connection with goats and other animals. However that may be the " Pouring out of the water," which was the concluding nightly ceremony of the Hebrews' great Phallic feast, must originally have been in honour of the Queen of Heaven, who " brooded on the waters," as it had water for its subject, the element emblematic of woman's creative force, just as oil was that of man. We must remember that oil and wine were and are still poured on all the stone phalli erected, as by Jacob.   As all these ancient rites were "mysteries," they were always symbolically treated, so that only those initiated might know their true significance, and the ordinary reader has little idea of the infinite ingenuity shown by the priests to symbolise phallic knowledge and to repeat the facts symbolically again and again so that future generations might have many keys to its true significance. As it is manifestly impossible to explain and prove by historical references these symbolisms in all cases I will enter more fully into it here in relation to this feast of Tabernacles and the "pouring out of the waters." That the symbolism I illustrate here is well known to all scholars and not any special application of my own, will easily be proved if any one will consult Dr. Smith's Dictionary of the Bible or his Greek and Roman Antiquities, or Dr. Hastings' compendious work, or lastly the *Encyclopædia Biblica,* he will find all the symbolism I mention fully explained.   I therefore give one sample of complete interpretation, as, in a review of the whole Hebrew Scriptures, it would require many years of not one writer but a committee of scholars to complete the task.

Dr. Isaac Benzinger, a great authority, tells us in the *Encyclopædia Biblica*, that the feast of tabernacles had gradually grown to be *the* feast of the Hebrew year. At first it was a wine and fruit harvest and hence very merry with feasting and drinking, like the Scotch Hallowe'en described by Burns, but it finally became a celebration of the " increase " and thanks for the whole produce of the year.

Now the one idea which was ever uppermost in the Hebrew mind or in the mind of him who at the moment wrote the Hebrew Scriptures, was, " Be fruitful and multiply," the commandment most frequently repeated in the Bible, so increase meant increase of children as well as lambs, kids, or calves, which were in the case of the Hebrews, all classed together. We read in Numbers xviii., 15—" Everything " that openeth the matrix (womb in Exodus " xiii., 2) in all flesh which they bring unto " the Lord whether it be of men or beasts shall " be mine." So this feast, being a general feast of increase, and the visible cause of increase being the female or woman, was a feast, every movement of which, and every article used, was employed to symbolise the conception, begetting, and delivery of young.   But to avoid confusion we must note that we have two periods in the development of this great feast. 1st. That period when it was a Bacchanalia in the vintage fields and orchards and when the participants were those who really dwelt temporarily in tents as our hop-pickers do now, and is still done in Syria; and when the vintage was gathered in, the young maidens performed choral dances (Jud. 21, 19, *et seq.*) These "dances" produced results such as are described in Burns' "Hallowe'en," and we are told that the young men and women of Jerusalem danced in the vineyards with such results, that marriage songs were sung very soon after.

The *Encyclopædia Biblica* says that this form of feast was taken over by the Israelites from the Canaanites and that these rites were all the same, but were differently named when taken over by another tribe. Of course, the Priests, when really acquiescing in what the people were already doing, always wrote—for rites were always practised before they were "written"—that Jové commanded them. No one now believes that Jové breathing fire out of his mouth and sparks which set fire to coals out of his nostrils, actually spoke to Moses. It is clear from the Bible narrative that Moses wrote his commandments by the advice

of Jethro of Midian, his father-in-law, and
said or wrote that they were written by Jové.
So the great feast, commanded three times by
Jové, was adopted from the Canaanites and
commanded by Jové when already an ancient
custom (see *Encyclopædia Biblica*). So much
for the natural beginning of the Feast. But its
serious and second form was no longer a joyous
country feast of eating, drinking, and dancing,
but became a Bacchanalia or Sakti orgie under
the Priests in the Sanctuary in Jerusalem, and
anyone, whether or not connected with the
vintage, could attend and in fact everyone was
commanded to attend from year to year at
Jerusalem under punishment of plagues, and
" with the punishment of Egypt " (Zech.
14, 16-19), which we may remember was
" the botch of Egypt " (probably leprosy),
" emerods " (which was syphilis), " scab and
itch whereof thou can'st not be healed "
(Deut. 28, 27), diseases they were much more
likely to acquire in the Tents of Venus at
Jerusalem, than by staying quietly at home.
Of course these objurgations and commands
are mere rhodomontade as applied to this
most intimate feast, where all bonds were
loosed and promiscuous intercourse the rule.
Zechariah commands all the enemies of the

Hebrews, " everyone that is left of all the
" nations which came against Jerusalem shall
" go up to worship the King, the Jové
" Sebaoth." It seems a curious thing to command your enemies to join in such an intimate
celebration where the men entered the
women's precincts at night and performed the
" great sacrifice " or " Holy Kiss." We must
remember that it was *the* feast of the Jews, the
only one mentioned in detail in the old historical books. Its high importance is shown
by the fact that Solomon dedicated his temple
at the date of the Feast of Tabernacles, and that
it was a very old phallic celebration at that
time is shown by the fact that long before, at
the same date the Israelites worshipped the
" golden calf " (phallic), and danced round it,
like David, before the ark, " For Aaron had
made them naked to their shame," so this
was an early form of the Feast of Tabernacles. Its great solemnity was further
shown by the employment of the holy
number seven in connection with it. Seven
occurs hundreds of times in the Old Testament, and always when something important
or symbolical is mentioned, so here we have
this feast on the seventh month, and it lasted
seven days, and every day of the seven days

seven bulls and seven rams—both symbolic of male fertility—were sacrificed and the Lulabs (Thyrsi, p. 85 of *Christianity*), symbolic phalli, were carried round and waved over the Altar (female) for seven days and on the seventh day seven times.

The feast of the tabernacles was independently instituted by Jeroboam in an identical form in the Northern Kingdom, so it was considered of vital national importance. The people carried fruit of goodly trees, stems of thick trees, and willows of the Brook.

Now the thick stem of a tree is used as a symbol of the phallus throughout the world, as shown in Fig. 14, caressed by a serpent to show its passion, and the " fruit of goodly trees " was no doubt the erotic apple, and the willows of the Brook were the shadiest trees growing near " water," thick enough and low enough to hide one ; so here was the Eden symbolism, fruit, cedar stem (phallus), and thick shrubby trees, thick enough for " Adam and his wife " hid themselves from the presence of Jové " of the Ale-im amongst the trees of the " garden." We have the same symbolism in Job, where, after creation by the Phallic Behemoth he hides himself by lying under the shady trees, " the willows of the brook com-

pass him about," Job, 40, 22 (see my " Seven
Stories of Creation " in this series).   Dr.
Benzinger asks what could be the application
of " fruit of goodly trees," and he thinks that
the fruit formed part of the Rod wreathed with
myrtle, and which was a Thyrsus, which each
participant carried in his hand.   The thyrsus
was a wand, lath, spear, or sceptre, decorated
preferably with vine leaves and ending in a
pine cone or, in this case, erotic fruit (for the
pine cone is also a phallus; see Bag and Cone
Deities in the British Museum or my *Christianity*, Fig, 89, p. 86), whose point excites to
madness with sexual frenzy; and the pine cone
was called the Pomum Kubele, Apple of
Cybele.   Dr. Benzinger tells us that in the
Tabernacle the fruit of goodly trees was the
" ethrog," apple of paradise, or Adam's
apple, erotic fruit of Genesis.   " The woman
" saw that the tree was good for food
" and pleasant to the eyes, and a tree to
" be desired to make one wise."   Observe it
was the tree itself—the phallus—not its fruit,
or results, which she desired at the last
moment.   The palm tree is the symbol for
man as the conch shell is that for woman, as
we see in the medal, Fig. 14, very common in
early times, of man and woman forming eter-

Fig. 14. Fig. 15.

nal life through the phallus excited by passion.

The palm tree was a symbol having two separate phallic meanings. Its stem had the same meaning as that of the oak or the cedar, while its new leaves issuing from the centre as a firm upright rod of sceptre form coupled with its seed vessels hanging from the lower part of the leafy head could not escape the eye of these early peoples who sought eagerly for every phallic similitude in nature.

Later the Greek Alpha and Omega were put on this tree to indicate that the sexual organs were the beginning and end of life, and repre-

sent creation as in Fig. 15. The Alpha was,
as shown in the Hebrew Aleph (Fig. 16),
originally the Rod and Serpent, as in Fig. 14
or 17, representing the phallus or pillar and
sexual passion, the Serpent.

Fig. 16.   Fig. 17.   Fig. 19.   Fig. 20.

The Omega, the ineffable or great O, is the
universal female symbol identical with our
" lucky " horseshoe, and finds its most vigorous expression in the very holy Indian combination much used in Hindoo architecture
sketched roughly in Fig. 18, where the Lingam
is seen through the Yoni, Omega, or great O.
The Hindoo arch is here seen to be clearly
the Greek Omega, and they both mean the
same thing, as will be seen on comparing Figs.
18 and 19. Egypt had a similar combination
in the symbol of eternal life, which Egypto-
logists veil under the false description of the

Fig. 18.

buckle or tie, shown in Fig. 20, which is a very
realistic or anatomical representation of the
bi-sexual combination of phallus, vagina, and
womb in the act of creation.   I have only indicated the Hindoo sculpture roughly, as it is
executed with a wealth of intricate and beautiful sculpture bewildering to the eye, and marvellous in extent and fineness of execution.
It is impossible to describe it adequately, and
we can only echo the words of the " Ancient
Mariner "—

" .   .   .   .   .   no tongue
Their beauty might declare."

We must note the cross on the phallus of
Fig. 18, put there to emphasise the fact so
often asserted by the early Christian Fathers
that the cross is a conventional representation
of the phallus, like the fleur-de-lys, broad
arrow, etc.   The Omega is also repeated below
in Fig. 18 in a row on the base of the great
arch (ark or Ruach).   The conventionalisa-
tion of the phallus proceeds to such extremes
in all lands as to render the symbolic form
unrecognisable, unless we trace the chain of
changes as I have done in my *Christianity*,
p. 31.   One form is shown on the platform at
the foot of Fig. 18, where the stem is almost
entirely suppressed.

The Babylonian idea of the palm tree symbolism is shown in a well-known Babylonian seal, which is crowded with phallic symbolism

Fig. 21.

(Fig. 21). The Priest with the Piercer, masculine, while his robes are feminine, then the male cherub faces the yoni, while the female on the other side faces the Triple male organ, the fleur-de-lys or Prince of Wales feathers, leaving the phallic tree of life or of knowledge (that is, of sexual action) alone with the best known symbol of pure feminine, Diana or the crescent moon.

The Hebrew Tabernacle practice was as full of symbolism as the Babylonian seal. The sceptre-like unexpanded branch of the palm was called the lulab, which name has a very phallic sound, and was placed between twigs of myrtle and willow. The myrtle is easily understood as it was the special tree of the Queens of Heaven and no doubt took its name from Myrrha the Syrian Queen of Heaven, so the palm and myrtle made the usual pair. The willow is a little more obscure, but it often appears in phallic symbolism and probably because it has almond-shaped leaves and erect " catkins " yielding a bi-sexual significance, and perhaps also from salix, its Latin name owing to its slippery qualities, which has a connection with " salacious " and perhaps " saliva," used by Jesus for curing blindness. It is always found near water, and all water is feminine. So here we have the devotees armed with a Thyrsus charged, super-charged with phallic symbolism, waving this potent emblem over the Altar—which is a feminine article. They held the fruit of goodly trees in the left hand as representing female pleasure and the Lulabs in the right thus carrying out the right and left handed cults like Ardhanari Ishwara of India, and they perambulated the altar on each of the seven days and on the seventh day seven times, singing hosannas and so performed an incantation or prayer for increase, that they and their flocks might be

" fruitful and multiply." Plutarch says that this feast was a Dionysiac festival, and exactly conformable to the feasts of Bacchus. This feast, which was in honour of the productive powers of the female and included the worship of her representatives, the maidens in the tents of Venus, would not have been complete without a reference to water, the representative female element, just as wine was the male. But there was a physical reason for the saying, " all life comes out of water" in the conditions under which the young, especially human children, are brought from the mother. So in this other sense water is female, while oil (semen in Hebrew), poured on stones, is male. The intention of the writer was to represent the ceremony as being of great sanctity as nothing but vessels of pure gold and silver were used, and silver trumpets were blown at every important part of the ceremony. So amidst the blare of trumpets water was drawn by a priest from the pool of Siloam in a golden pitcher which held exactly three logs. [When these all too symbolic writers stoop to accurate measurements to give an appearance of reality to their story as they did in the dream construction of an impossible tabernacle I always begin to think here again is pure invention.]

The priest brings the golden pitcher up into the temple through a special gate called the water-gate from its use in the great female water ceremony. And now ensues the most curious " mystery " I have ever encountered in over fifty years of omnivorous reading. Just as the phrase oil and wine meant a sort of symbol of life or healing—the Samaritan poured in " oil and wine " when binding up the wounds of the man who fell among thieves —the oil representing the male soma—in fact, anointing oil is called " semen " in Hebrew, Latin for seed—and the wine, spirit or passion ; so water as a symbol of the female was not a symbol of the woman in action without the addition of " spirit," so the writer made a " water and wine " parable. Now inasmuch as water is feminine and therefore belongs to the left hand cult while passion or spirit belongs to male as well as female the priest did not lose sight of this point and arranged to include it. So when the golden vessel was brought up by the priest he handed it to other priests in the outer court of the temple amidst a second trumpet blast. They received it probably with the words " You will draw water with joy from the fountains of salvation," from Isaiah xii., 3, says the *Encyclopædia Biblica*, but I think any remarks made would be of a more phallic nature. In any case they took it into the temple and poured it into a silver vessel placed at the *left* hand side of the altar. A similar vessel of wine (spirit or passion) was placed at the *right* of the altar. The idea was that water being quite passive, could only become active when coupled with passion. So by means of small holes or stop cocks the two liquids were allowed to mix and run into another vessel standing at the south-west corner of the altar, and, when mingled, the mixture ran away by a pipe which conveyed it by an underground passage into the brook Kedron. Now considering the blood and mess which is supposed to have been caused daily by sacrifices, and the further fact that nearly all temples had a floor constructed round the altar which was in certain circumstances flooded with water (1st Kings, 33-35), this running off of the water and wine without its being allowed to touch the temple is very striking, and it must have had a very grave reason; because this was the culminating ceremony of the one great feast of the Hebrews, Jové's special feast. Although, like the tabernacle mystery play, no explanation is given in the text, I think it is very easily found. This feast being in honour of the " productive powers feminine," as Dr. Adam Clarke says, we know that when the female by reason of her constitution and passion carries out her natural mission there is an outflow of waters. In every Eastern country this period of a woman is considered especially unclean, and at the present day the common Indian woman is driven out of the house before there is any chance of the house being defiled by water, and allowed to lie in all her agony in a backyard or a field; in fact, it is no unusual thing for our soldiers on the march to see a poor woman deliver herself all alone in the open fields and carry the infant back to her home.

So that is the reason of all this subterranean arrangement. This was all done amid the chanting of Psalms by the Levites. Then amidst further blasts on the silver trumpets, rejoicing that the woman had fulfilled her mission, the whole precincts were brilliantly lit up, there being four specially lofty lamps signifying the four seasons. The male devotees penetrated into the court of the women, and all held Lulabs in the right hand and

Citrons in the left. Here we have the right and left hand cult again carried out, and the citron is simply a fruit like the apple (which does not grow in Palestine) to afford erotic suggestion. The *Encyclopædia Biblica* says under " apple," discussing the citron, quince, etc. :—" The whole classical history " of the fruit is saturated with erotic sugges- " tion, and this falls in with the repeated " mention of it in the Canticles " (Song of Solomon).

After the female had symbolically fulfilled her reproductive function, the two sexes entered on a saturnalia to prepare for the same condition to ensue another year, as the men sought the women in the " court of women."

Serious readers often wonder how the Song of Solomon, a purely erotic song, or rather portions of several erotic songs, came to be included in the Holy Bible. But from the above one can only conclude that they were songs well fitted to be sung at this famous feast of the " Tents of Venus," or at its saturnalia in the court of women after the symbolical representation of woman's supreme function, and they may have been the veritable Psalms chanted by the Levites for this celebration.

Savage races continue these practices to the present day in India, Africa, Polynena, and South America. The Vapes in the Amazon basin hold feasts to Jurupari, the chief member of their Trinity with cruel initiatory rites for youths. The women are then invited to a " great sacrifice," which, like the Hebrew Hag, consists in a wild orgy of sexual promiscuity and drunkenness with dances of unspeakable immodesty.—*Times'* Literary Supplement, 20th November, 1910.

The use of myrtle as one of the symbols is significant of the remark of the Rabbis that " He who has never seen the " rejoicing at the pouring out of the water of " Siloam has never seen rejoicing in his life," as myrtle, although a symbol of Myrrha or any other Queen of Heaven, refers to a Queen like Venus, not Juno, and no one professing to be a true virgin could use myrtle in any wreath or garland, so the feast was one where virginity was out of place.

And yet this Hag is called a solemn Feast and the great Sacrifice but here again the Hebrews fall into line with similar savages, as the Polynesians call the promiscuous sexual intercourse under religious guidance their Great Sacrifice.

CHAPTER VII

WHY THE NAZERITES OR NABIS PORTRAYED SUCH A SAVAGE GOD

We have now traced the worship of the feminine from that of the Queen of Heaven, under which the Hebrews seem to have prospered and been happy, down to its degraded form in the Succoth Benoth and to its orgy of sex, under male priests, culminating in the pouring out or breaking of the waters.

The Hebrews' happiness under the Queen of Heaven may have been due to the ideas engendered by the mother and babe being entirely peaceful, and, being common to all nations, giving rise to no jealousies as to whose god was most powerful; although to-day ignorant villages are at feuds to decide whose Virgin Mary is the most potent, as by giving the name of a church of quite local fame, say, " Notre Dame de Lorette," or other to our lady, the ignorant hold she was born there, or came there to die, or to ascend to heaven, and they resent any other church making a similar claim. However, the female is ever more peaceful than the male, and even when the quarrel is on account of the female the male names are employed, as a " banner," to fight under. We see this in Ireland, where the quarrel is between the Protestants, who adhere to the degradation of woman, and will admit none to their heaven, at least as a member of the Heavenly Hierarchy, whereas the Catholics elevate the mother and her babe to the highest position, yet they pretend to fight over " Billy and his orange lily," whom the Catholics consign to hell, while the Protestants earnestly desire a like fate for the Pope; and they can only decide who is right by breaking each others' heads with blackthorns or paving stones, as I have seen them do even in Glasgow.

However that may be, the Israelites " saw no evil," but " had plenty " under the Queen of Heaven, whereas under Iové they " wanted " for all things and were consumed by the " sword and by the famine."   Why, then, was the worship of the Queen of Heaven so bitterly condemned by the official priests and by the Nabis or prophets, of course speaking in the name of Iové? I think the reason is not far to seek, and it has much to do with the remarkable figure that Iové has played in

religion.   In the first place, we have a picture
of this god built up for us by the preaching
of the priests and Nabis of the Hebrew nation.
These Nabis were the half-mad ascetic
preachers, who were the counterpart of the
Indian Yogis of the present day.   They were
not the temple priests, but were men sworn to
abstinence, and generally in opposition to the
well-fed comfort or even luxury of the priests
in office.   Their name most probably arose
from the Babylonian Nebo, who was the
Messenger of Marduk.   Now, the messenger
of the gods was always he who had brought
life to the earth—that was the great " message " known to the ancients.   Therefore, his
symbol was the serpent or phallus, and he was
the " nimble one."   So completely was this
recognised in Greece that Hermes, the Greek
Mercury or Messenger, was represented by
two serpents intertwined round a " rod "
(Rod of God), with the brooding wings of
Ruach, and this intertwining is the mode of
reproduction of the Indian cobra, the emblem
of the phallus most universally used (see my
Christianity).   So phalli and phallic columns
were called " Hermae."   The intertwined
serpents make the most phallic symbol possible, being both the agent and the act, while

the whole Caduceus is a triple symbol of reproduction—the serpent, the pole, and the brooding wings. It was called the healer, and was
the insignia of Æsculapius, because the great
healer from all the ravages of war (which is
always constant with savages) is the birth of
children.

" Increase " is the constant prayer of all
nations, as all their prosperity and wealth
depend upon it, and the Feast of Tabernacles
was a feast of increase.

Now to return to the Nabis. Such ignorant
men always preach a much more severe religion than do the official priesthood : witness
our own " revivalists," who are constantly
girding at the laxity of the clergy and preaching an emotional " Blood and Fire " religion
of the most curious mixture of infinite cruelty
and infinite love ; the cruelty being self-evident
to all, and is the utterly immoral driving
power of religious " Fear," while the love is
far to seek. The early character of the god
Jové, as stated by the Mosaic and Deutero-
nomic writers, was one of cruel and unmiti-
gated ferocity, and that was improved upon
and made more terrible by the Nabis, such as
Elijah, Elisha, Isaiah, Jeremiah, and Ezekiel,
which last is a typical Yogi or Nabi.   Isaiah

walked three years naked, and so violent did
Jeremiah become that he had to be confined
in the stocks, which were provided in the precincts of the temple when their zeal drove
the Nabis to utterances subversive of order.

The fact that the Nabis were, or claimed to
be, the messengers of Iové, led them to the use
of highly phallic language, as is still to be found
in Ezekiel, much of which book is still unreadable in public, notwithstanding all the bowd-
lerising practised by the Rabbis during the
long descent of the Hebrew scriptures.   The
Hindoos use the same indecent language, but
coupled, as was perhaps Ezekiel's, with much
more indecent actions.   Here, then, we have
two sets of men—one the officials, gathering
their livelihood from the freewill offerings and
official sacrifices at the temple, and dependent for their living entirely upon the enforce-
ment of the Jové cult, and so threatening
terrible things for any defection from that
worship; and, second, another set of excitable
ranters, only too glad to emphasise these
threats and invent the most terrible pictures
of the wrath of the insulted god and of the
punishments he would inflict upon back-
sliders—exactly as we hear at revival meetings
to-day—as all religion is based upon fear.

" He that feareth not is without religion."
" The fear of Jové is the beginning of wisdom."

As I have said, the priests or Levites were entirely dependent on the continuance of the worship of Jové for their daily bread, and any defection by a large part of the population would have led to their starvation.

Again and again the people are reminded that " Moses had given the inheritance " to the other tribes, " but unto the Levites he gave none inheritance among them " (Joshua xiv., 3). " But the Levites have no part among you " (Joshua xviii., 7); and although later on they have land, it seems that in early times they were dependent on the beasts slaughtered at the temple. Also, as they did not go to war or engage in trades which always took their toll of life, they would increase more rapidly than the lay population, so the pinch of poverty would always be felt.

From the history of these tribes, so far as it may be real history, we see one thing very clearly, that while the Levites or preachers were always urging the people to adhere to their own tribal god, the leader of their heavenly host of Ale-im, called Jové, Yové, or Iové, yet the people

when they mingled or intermarried with
other tribes, at once adopted the Ale-im and
leader of that tribe, and we find Solomon
building temples to Ashtoreth, Milcom,
Chemosh, Molech, and other gods for all his
strange wives, and he had " many " among
his seven hundred (1st Kings, xi.).   There
must have been constant inter-communication
between the Hebrews and the host of tribes
who, according to the Old Testament, inhabited Palestine.   There was the usual list of
countries first promised, as Canaan, and then
in a large phrase " from the river of Egypt,
unto the great river, the river Euphrates,"
but then particularised as the land of Kenites,
Kenizzites, Kadmonites, Hittites, Perizzites,
Rephaims, Amorites, Canaanites, Girgashites,
and Jebusites in Genesis xv., 19-21; but cut
down from ten to seven, then to six, and frequently repeated, as in Exodus iv., both at
verses 8 and 17, as the Canaanites, Hittites,
Amorites, Perizzites, Hivites, and Jebusites.
This is repeated like a song all through the
earlier part of the Old Testament, and hence
is simply copied from place to place, as independent writers always give a slightly different
rendering when repeating the same fact.

As we go on in the various wars the number

of tribes and kings becomes quite bewildering—
one list gives 31 kings, and yet the greater part
of Palestine still seems occupied by the people
they were sent to slaughter, as in Joshua xiii.—
" Thou shalt smite them and utterly destroy
them " is a phrase employed more frequently
than any expression of love.   But after studying the history of Israel, written by a dozen
of the great ecclesiastical writers, one is bound
to say that it is mostly a work of the imagination, and by taking this and rejecting that, one
may make any story one pleases.   One thing
is very clear : a great deal of what is pro-
phesied by Jové, or really written down as said
by him hundreds of years after the supposed
events happened, is directly contradicted by
another writer ; so a large part of Holy Writ
cancels itself out.   For instance, the terrible
story of the cruel extermination of the
Midianites, Moses's own family connections,
where they slew every man, woman, and child,
" except the women children who had not
" known man by lying with him," which they
kept for their own and Jové's sexual pleasure,
So determined were they to prevent any
single male heir to arise, they even slew the
" women-children who had known man by
" lying with him," so that no male child could

be born; yet a few years afterwards we find the Midianites enslaving the children of Israel for the usual holy number of seven years, and coming down with the Amalekites, leaving the Hebrews " neither sheep, nor ox, nor ass." " They came as grasshoppers for multitude, " for both they and their camels were without " number as the sand of the sea-side for mul- " titude." And the great number was not of the Amalekites, for they are not again mentioned; it is always the Midianites. So it is plain that these two stories cancel each other. If we treat Hebrew history in this manner, there is very little left that will support any real history, or religion.

They are again and again told to " utterly destroy " the six nations (or in other passages seven nations) " greater and mightier than thou," and promised their land; yet we find them, in Judges iii., 5-6, dwelling amongst these nations, inter-marrying, and serving their gods, all of which was especially forbidden in Exodus xxxiv., 11-16.

Modern scholars have told us that their god Yahweh, or Iové, or Yové, was given to them by the Babylonians, probably after a period of enslavement, and such changes are probable, if we are to believe

Joshua, where he tells them as a sort of dying injunction to " put away the gods which your " fathers served on the other side of the flood " and in Egypt;" so they did not serve Iové in Egypt, and they had various sets of gods from Egypt, from the other side of the flood, from the Babylonians, the Canaanites, the Hittites, the Amorites, the Perizzites, the Hivites, and Jebusites, and the memory becomes bewildered with how many more. All these tribes had Bas, Milcoms, Chemoshes, or Jovés of their Ale-im, nearly identical with the Hebrew Jové, so the change was practically one of name only.   They went over to the lucky name of the moment (Joshua xxiv., 2-14).

Here we see Joshua speaks quite pleasantly of these past gods, as he would of any other natural habit that was quite right at the time, but which had been abandoned as they developed, like a form of clothing or the manner of dressing the hair.   There is no fierce denunciation of these past gods, no jealousy. They were similar to Jové—perhaps an earlier phase of the Jové idea—and certainly they must have been phallic.

No doubt, as the critics now say, all this part of their history is almost entirely mythical, and we only snatch a glimpse of reality when under their kings, although even then they were generally subject to either Babylon or Egypt, and, in fact, received their Iové or Ia Va from their Babylonian conquerors.

Now, my purpose of this glimpse at the people's myths and ways is in order to show what a very slight security the Levites had for gaining a livelihood, and how much it was to their interest to preach a frightfully jealous god who would punish any defection from service in his temple in the most terrible manner. It was the same with the medicine-men of these nomadic Arabs as it is with those of other African tribes to-day : they constantly fulminated against anyone not believing in their god, and gave the god a terrible char-acter, so as to fill their coffers. The Abbè Loisy tells us that the Hebrew Nabis fre-quently became rich by the fear of their devotees of the terrible vengeance their Jové would take on any " back-sliders." So the awful monster in the shape of a god portrayed for us in the writings of the Levites in the Hebrew scriptures was only a bogey created to enrich the priests through playing on the fears of the people. This is the one important thing in the Bible which does not cancel out— the character of Iové drawn for us by the priests and Nabis. His promises all cancel out. He does *not* make " great nations " of all the people to whom he makes this promise in the scriptures, nor does he give everyone descendants " without number," " as the sand " of the sea-shore for multitude," " as the " dust of the earth, so that if a man can num- " ber the dust of the earth then shall thy seed " also be numbered," " multiply thy seed as " the stars of heaven, as the sand of the sea- " shore for multitude," " who can count the " dust of Jacob?" and so on. Nor does he lead the Hebrews to a land flowing with milk and honey, but to a rather barren land, of which all the rivers must have run red with blood, if even a fraction of the frightful slaughter entered upon with devilish gloating had been carried out. Of course, no one believes those constant tales of from sixty thousand to five hundred thousand " men of valour " being slaughtered in one day; but we are tacitly asked by the Christian Churches to serve under the banner of those who set up this god as " infinite " in goodness and wisdom.

As I deal with every side of the character of this god in another volume on the *Gods of the Hebrew Bible*, I only mention enough here to illustrate my point that a heaven containing a god who set fire to coals by the flames out of his mouth, and whose lust was slaughtering man, woman, and babe and suckling, and all enciente women or women girls, was a place absolutely impossible to a Queen of Heaven who had any womanly nature left; so the Hebrews never took the trouble to compose a word for goddess, as such a word could have no counterpart in the minds of men brought up to serve under Jové.

So the Levites in their desire to keep their priesthood a " goodly inheritance " drove out the kindly influence of woman from religion and from the heaven which could never exist under such heartless rule.

The Israelites stole not only women and children, but gods also (Judges xviii.). It has been shown on page 191 that the Hebrews in Old Testament times were always despised, even in their (supposed) own land, and that they lived there practically on sufferance, as they have always done in Europe. In Palestine it is the same to-day, as witness a report on 11th March, 1919, during our recovery of Palestine from the Turks :—" Even in the " home of their birth the Jews have always " been despised by their neighbours, and " herein lies the difficulty of a repatriation " scheme."

CHAPTER VIII

TERRIBLE RESULTS OF PHALLIC FEASTS

We now come to a consideration of the results of the phallic feasts of the Hebrews, from which the priests gained much wealth, and which gave rise to a state of affairs which in their eyes rendered it quite impossible to admit anything feminine, and more especially a Queen of Love, into the hierarchy of their heaven, and which gave rise to the doctrine so intensely held in the middle ages and at the Reformation, that woman was the active cause of all evil.

This was, I have no doubt, due to the terrible ravages caused by the wide dissemination of sexual diseases by the very intensity of the worship of the Queen of Heaven, Melitta, Astarte or Ashteroth, Venus, Freia—a worship at one time universal—and as it gave free vent to the most powerful and joyful instinct in man, it required no spur from the priest, like the bitter worship of the vengeful Jové, to urge all and sundry to join in its practice. There has been much discussion as to whether such diseases are not of modern origin, but one has only to note the prevalence of diseases of all organs with tender mucous membranes to know that the most tender of all could not be exempt.   Besides, it has been described thousands of years B.C. by the Chinese, and mentioned by many historians as the cause of the greatest incident in Jewish history, the exodus of the Hebrews from Egypt.

The Bible gives a very curious picture of the mental trait of the Hebrews in wishing to be considered a race apart from all the world, neither seeking nor accepting aid or favours from any other race, and living absolutely alone in close communion with their god Jové, the phallus.   Every nation is their enemy, and if the nation has played any part in their history, even in a friendly way, it must be "blotted out," and when they were enemies their fury knew no bounds.

But let us take one example.   The Hebrew history is intimately bound up with the land of Midian and the Midianites themselves.   In this word we have a good example of the symbolism used in building up all sacred books.   In the first place, the name Midian has a very ancient and deeply-rooted phallic meaning, and in ancient times "phallic" and

" holy " have identical meanings, as phallism
was the religion of all men. Midian simply
means " the land between," like that blessed
Greek word, Mesopotamia, and may have
been the land between the Gulf of Akab and
the Gulf of Suez. All lands between two
rivers or seas was especially holy, and we find
this land of Midian contained all that was
most holy to the Hebrews, Mounts Sinai and
Horeb, where the tenets of their race were
first enunciated, and they were, as it were,
beaten into shape by Moses. There they
came face to face personally with their god,
and were miraculously fed and watered by his
own hand for forty years, in a foodless and
waterless desert. All their miraculous period
was spent in the fairy " land between the
waters." For the whole story see Numbers
xxxi.

We have in England a Midian in Dorsetshire, whence the two embracing seas, the
Bristol and English Channels, are visible,
and where a very realistic Rod of God,
shown in Fig. 2, was erected in bygone ages,
and no doubt circumambulated and anointed
and prayed to as illustrated in the tale of
Jacob. Tacitus tells us that such columns were
erected in great numbers in Britain, and hun-

Fig. 22.

dreds still exist. This is a good specimen.
Compare with Indian Lingah, Fig. 18. p. 404.

The Midianites were the root and cause of
all the Hebrews' history. First, according to
their history, which of course is mythical, they
never would have seen Egypt but for the
Midianite merchants, who sold Joseph to
Potiphar in Egypt, and Moses would probably
have had his career cut short by hanging for
murder had he not been sheltered by Jethro
in Midian. Here, again, in this land of
mirage he was given the Rod of God, with
which he did all his miracles in Egypt and
divided the sea, a feat saturating nearly every
tale, incantation, song, psalm, or exhortation
in the Hebrew writings. The Rod of God
came out of Midian (the middle position),
just as " the tree of life in the midst of the
garden " of Genesis ii., both purely phallic
conceptions. Then after they were beyond
Pharoah's power Jethro came and told Moses
how he must govern these exiles, and that he
was wasting himself trying to judge each case
individually, but must take a position with
the people as " God-ward " (keeper of the
God) or go-between as explained in Deuteronomy v., 5, " that thou mayest bring the
causes unto God." He learnt this lesson so

well that he pretended like Mahomet, or Joseph Smith, to have constant conversations with Jové. Then Jethro told him he must teach them " ordinances and laws," " and " show them the way wherein they must walk " and the work they must do," and appoint judges over them, and attend personally only to difficult or great matters. " So Moses " hearkened to the voice of his father-in-law, " and did all that he had said." Here is the true explanation of the production of the commandments and the contradictory Horeb and Sinai tales.

But the point is that Jethro treated Moses well, gave him a daughter in marriage, and kept Zipporah and his two sons while he was in Egypt; in fact, Moses owed all his success in life to Jethro and the land of Midian. Then there is a tale of the people committing adultery with the daughters of Moab, and sacrificing to their gods, " bowing down to them." And Israel joined himself to Baal-peor. We are not told what Baal-peor was. But we can find out. In my book on *Christianity*, etc., I show that on a change of religion all the " Baals " became " Bosheths " (phalli) in joint names, such as Jerub-Baal, changed to Jerub Bosheth; and the prophets

of Baal are called " prophets of that shame
Bosheth." Hence Baal or his symbol was the
phallus, while the *Encyclopædia Biblica* tells
us that Peor is the " Cleft," so we know that
joining himself to Baal-Peor meant " joined in
adultery;" and Moses ordered the judges to
" slay ye every one his men that were joined
unto Baal-peor." Meanwhile, apropos of
nothing, a Hebrew brought a Midianite
woman into his tent and Phinehas thrust them
through—the woman through her belly
(another word in the original)—and " so the
" plague was stayed from the Children of
" Israel." Yet there " died of the plague
twenty and four thousand." What plague?
how caused? Not by the Midianite woman,
as we are told her death stayed the plague. By
the daughters of Moab then? The slaying of
those who joined unto Baal-peor was apparently stayed, as Jové " turned away his wrath
from them " owing to the zeal of Phinehas.
Then Jové says to Moses:—"Vex the
" Midianites and smite them, . . . they
" have beguiled you in the matter of Peor."
[We see how accurate the writer is when he
touches symbolical writing; the Midianite was
a woman, and had only a Peor; while the crime
was joining unto Baal-Peor, so the Israelite

supplied the Baal!] But we had just been told that the "whoredom" was committed with the daughters of Moab, and that a Midianitish woman stayed the plague by her death. One would think that again a Midianite had been very useful to the Hebrews. Now, for all these benefits how are the Midianites repaid? By total extinction; man, woman, and child were slain, and some women-children "who had not known man by lying with him," which were specially reserved for Jové's own enjoyment, but were finally given to Eleazer the high priest; so we see what was supposed to be done by Jové was only the high priest's action, and what Jové was supposed to enjoy went to satisfy the lust of the high priest. So determined were they that no even unborn child should exist to recreate the race, the Hebrews apparently examined the women, of whom there were thirty-two thousand "of women who had not known men," etc., so the whole must have been many more, *and slew all those who might possibly have become mothers.* It was a cold-blooded slaughter, as they first of all "took all the women of Midian captives and their little ones." This was the return Moses made for all the kindness he had received in

Midian. His father-in-law and his other six daughters must have been slaughtered, and any virgin nieces used for the Hebrews' lust and that of their god. How could the heaven of such a god allow of the " sweet influences " of any goddess? In order to magnify the greatness of Jové and to create great fear of him, the scribes created a most terrible history, in which Jové was constantly revelling in slaughter till his sword was " drunk with blood."

I suppose that there was no Midian (as the name is Latin, not Hebrew), and the tale entirely mythical. The slaughter was introduced to account for the subsequent non-existence of the tribe which was supposed to have given Moses his religion, laws, and ordinances (commandments), which were later ascribed to Iové. Joshua says that Iové was unknown to the Hebrews in these early times. It was perhaps also used to indicate one method of obtaining a supply of Kadeshoth, whose prostitution formed the principal source of revenue of the priests of Iové.

But my point is that here we have a plague of which twenty-four thousand people died, which was caused by the children of Israel " committing whoredoms with the daughters

of Moab," and it is called the Baal-peor,
" Phallus-cleft," or man-woman disease.

Now, if civil history is to be believed, this
was not the first time the Hebrews made the
acquaintance of this disease, because a very
strong body of independent historians, including Lysimachus, Diodorus Siculus, Tacitus,
and Manetho, who wrote the special history
of Egypt, and also in a special work on the
history of the Jews, Justin in his *Historium
Judaeorum*, five great historians, agree in telling us that the truth about the exodus, painted
in such marvellous colours of conjuring with
the Rod of God by Moses, was that " a band of
" leprous and *sexually diseased* Jewish slaves
" were driven out of the Delta of Egypt into
" the desert, as the oracle of the god Amen
" had declared these insanitary slaves to have
" been the cause of a pestilential disease which
" had spread all over Egypt." This is fully
corroborated by the unconscious evidence of
the scribes, who show that the Hebrews never
forgot these diseases which afflicted them in
Egypt, as Moses threatens that " Jové will
" smite thee with the Botch of Egypt and with
" Emerods (ophalim, syphilis) and with scab,
" and with the itch, whereof thou canst not
" be healed " (Deuteronomy xxviii., 27), and

at verse 60—" He will bring upon thee all the
" diseases of Egypt which thou wast afraid of,"
and at Deuteronomy vii., 15—" The evil
" diseases of Egypt which thou knowest;" or
Psalm xxxviii., 7—" For my loins are filled
" with a loathsome disease;" or Ezekiel xxx.,
9—" And great pain shall come upon thee as
" in the day of Egypt."

That the lay historians were right is also
shown by the admission of the Hebrew writers
in Exodus xii., 39, amongst all their boasting
of punishing Pharoah—" And they baked un-
" leavened cakes of the dough which they
" brought forth out of Egypt, for it was not
" leavened, *because they were thrust out of*
" *Egypt;*" or Exodus vi., 1, it is said of
Pharoah—" shall he drive them out his land;"
or Exodus xi., 1—" he shall surely thrust you
out hence altogether," not " allow them to
depart," as the Nabis would have us believe.

Now we come to the disease of " Emerods,"
a word which seems to be a puzzle to all
scholars, even in the *Encyclopædia Biblica*.
But that splendid work gives us the original
word as Ofalim, while others render it
Ophelim, the same word differently spelt, as
" f " and " ph " are the same, and vowels
vary anyhow; and I would think that the like-

ness of the word to Omphalé, the same word, but with the "im," Hebrew plural, would have enabled anyone with a knowledge of Eastern tongues to translate it. As I have elsewhere explained, O, or Om, or Ooma was the universal sign of the female, which Yogis still make in India with their forefinger and thumb, as in Fig. 23, and is the " ring " of the Persian " ring and dagger." The Ooma is our word womb; while phalim is the Hebrew plural of phalé (Phallus or Pala), as Ale-im is plural of the Alé, so that Ophalim simply means woman-man diseases, like Baal-peor, man-woman, reversed.

We see further that the so-called Emerods (Ophallim) were sexual diseases from 1st Samuel v., 9—" He smote the men of the city, " both small and great, and they had emerods " (ophalim) in their secret parts." That it was not always fatal but extremely painful is shown in verse 12—" And the men that died " not were [likewise] smitten with emerods "(ophallim), and the cry of the city went up " to heaven."

Of this disease there died " fifty thousand three score and ten," as verse 19 truly says, " a great slaughter," " very great destruction," "deadly destruction."

Now, all this great slaughter was because of
the Ark, or female god, or mother of god,
being amongst the Philistines, inhabitants of

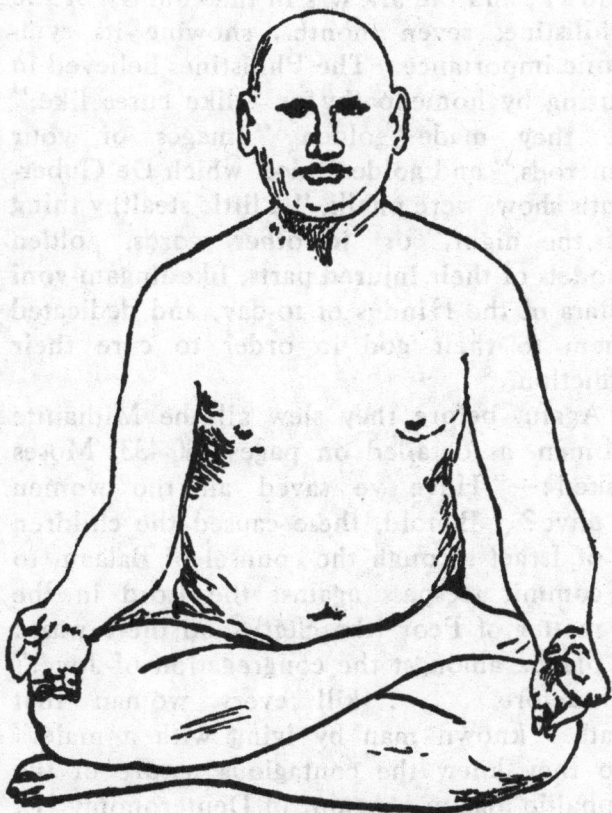

Fig. 23.

" Pala," " Phallus," " Philis," or love "stan"
or land, like Palestine; and the name is mentioned the holy seven times in 1st Samuel, v.
and vi., and the ark was in the country of the
Philistines seven months, showing its symbolic importance. The Philistines believed in
curing by homeopathy or " like cures like,"
so they made golden " images of your
emerods," and golden mice, which De Guber-
natis shows were phalli, " a little stealthy thing
of the night," or, in other words, golden
models of their injured parts, like lingam-yoni
altars of the Hindus of to-day, and dedicated
them to their god in order to cure their
affliction.

Again, before they slew all the Midianite
women, as detailed on pages 430-433, Moses
asked :—" Have ye saved all the women
" alive?   Behold, these caused the children
" of Israel through the counsel of Balaam to
" commit trespass against the Lord in the
" matter of Peor (the cleft), and there was a
" plague amongst the congregation of Jové."
Therefore . . . kill every woman that
hath " known man by lying with a male."
So they knew the contagious nature of the
ophallic plague. Again, in Deuteronomy iv.,
3, Moses in his dying exhortation to his people

said :—" Your eyes have seen what the Lord
" did, because of Baal-Peor; for all the men
" that followed Baal-Peor, the Jové of the
" Elohim hath destroyed them from among
" you." As Baal was Bosheth or Basar, the
shameful thing, the phallus, and peor the
cleft, we know that Baal-peor was sexual conjunction leading to ophalim, woman-man
disease, so well described by its results. That
the disease was known to them in Egypt
appears from Ezekiel xxiii., 8—" Neither left
she her whoredoms brought from Egypt;"
and Isaiah calls them (xxvii., 13) " the outcasts
in the land of Egypt;" and in 1st Samuel, vi.,
6—" Wherefore do ye harden your hearts as
" the Egyptians and Pharoah hardened their
" hearts," always coupling up Egypt with
sexual diseases.

Here, then, was the second great bar to any
female being admitted into the heavenly hierarchy, and at the same time a sort of insult
to their old enemies the Egyptians.

CHAPTER IX

EGYPTIAN ORIGIN OF HEBRAIC PHALLIC EMBLEM

Egypt was the land of Arks, Osiris as well as other gods being often represented in an ark, and the arks were sometimes real boats with or without a box, ark, or house on them, or simply boxes or frames with curtains. There is no doubt that Moses's first religious creation, after finding the Rod of God in Midian, was an ark commanded by Jové, but copied from those with which he had been so familiar in Egypt (Exodus xxv., 10). But as Forlong points out, there was a " thing " for which the ark was made, and that was variously called the Eduth or, in English, the testimony or stones, or even the Jové, and at one time the " Rod of God," which blossomed into " Almonds," was in the Ark. Now, the nature of this " Rod of God " is quite clear when one knows anything of the early basis of Egyptian religion or, we might say, mythology. It was this : There were two brother gods, like Cain and Abel, one good Osiris, and one bad Typhon. Typhon slew Osiris

Fig. 24.

and cut his body in pieces, and dispersed the
pieces all over Egypt. Isis sorrowfully collected all the pieces, and found every part
except the phallus, or " Rod of Osiris," the
god. She then had a model of the phallus
made, and placed it in an ark, in the most
sacred temple, and commanded this to be
everywhere worshipped, like Jacob's anointed
stone, or the daily erection and anointing of
such stones in India at the present time.
The Hebrews lived in Palestine, the land of
the Pala or phallus, as also did the Philistines,
which is the same word in the Greek form.
Egypt had the first call on this name, as it was

truly the land of the phallus, the phallus of
Osiris. Other countries were similarly named,
for instance, Assyria, which is the land of
Assur, which is the Asher or Phallus, which
the Hebrews worshipped, and the name of
their king, Asher-Bani-pal, called Pul in the
Old Testament, means the " Phallus son of
the Phallus."

The name Pharaoh has been a puzzle to
scholars, the derivation commonly given, as
from a word meaning Great Hall, being very
far from convincing. But in Egyptian R and
L are identical, and as Pharaoh has for its
initial letter the Greek phallic letter Phi, Φ,
the ring and piercer, I incline to the opinion
that Phara-oh, which should be pronounced
Far-ah-o, is really Phala-O (as R is L in
Egyptian) ; in other words, it expresses the
double-sex organs of India, Pala and O ; in
Greek, Omphalé, double-sexed amazon ; and
in Hebrew, Ophalim, double-sexed disease (see
pp. 436-7), with the order of the sexes reversed,
Phalla-o and O-phallim. Thus the Egyptian
king's name falls into line with the names
mostly used by monarchs to indicate king-
godship, and is the double-sexed symbol of
eternal life.

Britain has several very realistic phalli still

erect, especially one in Dorsetshire, which shows the sort of Rod of God which was universally worshipped (Fig. 2, p. 35. See my *Passover and Crucifixion*).

Iové was identified with the Eduth, called " Testimony " in our Bible, which stood between the Cherubim, exactly as that of Osiris did in Egypt. That the Eduth or testimony was the same as Jové is shown by Exodus xvi., 33-34—" And " Moses said unto Aaron, Take a pot and put " an omer full of manna therein, and lay it " up before the Jové to be kept for your " generations. As Jové commanded Moses, " so Aaron laid it up before the Testimony " [Eduth] to be kept." Here Testimony is spelt with a capital T, to create holiness and make it the equivalent of Lord (or Jové) with a capital L; so the two were the same.

But I have treated this subject fully in my book on the *Gods of the Hebrew Bible* and in my *Christianity*, and only touch on it here to show the masculine character of the Hebrew symbolism and religion.

I have shown on p. 338, and at greater length in my *Gods of the Hebrew Bible*, that Jehovah or Iové is a symbolic name meaning the two sexes. In Fig. 25 I show an Egyptian repre-

sentation of the worship of the Lingam-yoni—
pillar and bowl combination—which was probably the original, from which the worship of
Iové was copied.

Fig. 25.

CHAPTER X

THE TABERNACLE AS QUEEN OF HEAVEN OR THE SUN'S MOTHER

Up till this time the religious symbolism of the Hebrews had been entirely phallic, as had been the case with all other religions—in fact, there is no other way in which primitive man can symbolise the continuity of life or the cause of the succession of life in the world. But other nations with more observant thinkers had obtained wider ideas of the universe through that great broadener of the mind, Astronomy, and they saw that there was another and a greater upholder of life on this earth, and that was the life-giving sun.

Babylon and Egypt, so well known to the Hebrews by their captivities there, had almost ceased to employ phallism in their official religion, and worshipped the sun as the life-giver, and in the case of Northern nations as the " Saviour." This was natural, because they saw the sun grow weak in winter and everything in the deadly grip of the cold, and if the sun failed to come north again universal death must ensue. So the Sun was the Saviour, who " passed over," crossed over, or was "crossified," or made to cross over the equator from the South, and produced the paradise or garden half of the year to the salvation of mankind. Then the sun was the keeper of times and seasons; the earlier method of Moon-time or months leading to endless confusion, and having no connection with the seasons on which man's food depends.

But sun worship needs a higher state of mental development than the Hebrews reached, and, in fact, it never became in any country the real religion of the people : that was, and still is, partly phallism and partly witchcraft, and the vague superstitions of fortune-telling, crystal-gazing, spiritualism, lucky and unlucky days, and signs, astrology, mascots, and the hundred and one beliefs detailed by Frazer in his great museum, the *Golden Bough*, and which constitute the religion of Bond Street to-day. Even with the Christian religion as established by law in England, the central point of their faith is officially declared to be an " incomprehensible mystery," the " Three in One;" and, were it not so, the religion would not have the attraction for women and men of weak reasoning power (or, stated otherwise, people of emotional nature), whom such things as " mysteries " attract with an irresistible power.

Although we officially worship on Sunday a development of the sun god idea, all our insignia, church architecture, dress, and altar furniture are phallic (as I have shown in my larger work on *Christianity*), so difficult is it to make any changes in the beliefs or symbols of any of the so-called miraculously revealed religions.

But although the Hebrew people clung to their old phallic practices, their worship in the Tents of Venus once a year, and of the Ashteroth, Baal and Ashera, their Ark and Eduth, their Baal-peor all the year round " in every street," " under every green tree," there came to them priests from the conquering over-lords of Babylonia and Egypt (Ezra and Nehemiah were such), who, having been brought up under a more advanced civilisation, wished to introduce the more advanced ideas into the official religion of the Hebrews. Surprise may be expressed that a stubborn people like the Hebrews would allow their old Jové religion to be tampered with, but their stubbornness was only the expression of the Levites threatening fire and slaughter to back-sliders, to keep their sheep in the fold, as any defection meant poverty to the portionless Levites. But they were constantly " bowing down and serving other gods," and for a very good reason. The enormous number of small tribes in the land of the Phallus (Palestine)—for nearly every village had a name, such as " Peleth," and its inhabitants were " ites," in this case " Pelethites "—had practically the same god; that is, they all had " gods " or Ale-im (Elohim in English), led by a chief Al or Ba, and so called Ba Ale-im or Baalim, as was certainly the case with the Hebrews who had Iové of the Ale-im, dishonestly translated as Lord God in the English Bible. They expected and believed that this god or his " Rod " would help them to gain their battles, as shown in Exodus xvii. by Moses defeating the Amalekites by holding up the " Rod of God in his hand," while if he lowered it the children of Israel were defeated.

Now, when they were defeated they thought that their Al was not as strong as the enemy's Al, so they promptly went over to the worship of the stronger Al.   No doubt these tribes spoke dialects of the same language, and were really one race; so that new allies and combinations were easily made.   But all these tribes lived in Palestine, the land of the Pala or Phallus, and so they all worshipped the same symbol; so when some more enlightened priest tried to introduce a totally new idea—Sun worship—he found that his great effort fell upon deaf ears.

We have seen in the early chapters of this book, that the first head of the family we hear of was the mother, and the mother of the gods was Ruach or the Ark. When the sun became the Saviour or god—or was at least his great manifestation, as the Egyptians held Ra as the sun (and a god), but behind Ra was Amen, the inscrutable hidden god, still apostrophised in Christian prayers — the sex changed and the God became masculine.

Now, as Ma or the Ark was the mother of all the gods, she was the mother of the sun. She was believed by many nations to be a great fish, whale or dragon, and called Ked or Ced, out of whose womb came all things, amongst them, the sun. Some priest with a literary turn constructed in imagination a glorified Ark or Tabernacle made of such materials as symbolised the womb of Ked or Ruach; and with the high priest as the sun, enacted the annual death and re-birth of the Saviour. This was really an attempt to reinstate the Queen of Heaven, under whom the Hebrews had been so happy, on her ancient throne (Jeremiah xliv.), and to introduce the worship of her son, the sun, as the life-giver, Redeemer, or Saviour of mankind from the dread grip of winter.

I have dealt with this phase of the Hebrew mythology in my book on the *Romance of the Hebrew Tabernacle*, and I shall only deal with it here at sufficient length to make my argument clear.

The critical literature in connection with the Tabernacle is very voluminous, and I have read over one hundred books and articles by great authorities dealing with every phase of the building, its material, and its purpose. They include historians, ecclesiastical writers of many religions, architects, lawyers, travellers, and medical doctors, besides University professors; and the result of all their work is very well summed up in a few phrases by Dr. Benzinger in the *Encyclopædia Biblica*. The difficulties were pointed out centuries ago, yet our parsons go on making eloquent word-pictures of a thing which never existed.

Dr. Benzinger says the difficulties were pointed out by Voltaire amongst others, and were : —

(1) The imaginative character of the account itself.
(2) The physical impossibility of such a structure in the wilderness.
(3) The inconsistency with the older Penta teuch sources.
(4) The want of evidence for any such tabernacle during historical times.

"Finally, there is the fundamental question : Is a structure of this kind capable of " standing at all? Simply as a technical question of architecture this must be pronounced " utterly impossible." Then he gives the reasons.

It was impossible for another reason. The richest empire would have been bankrupt in importing the gold, silver, copper, precious stones, and fine timber employed in building such a tabernacle in a bare wilderness. But to my mind the fact that these fine timber slabs, weighing half-a-ton each, and all the gold, silver, copper, fine linen, dolphins' skins, etc., were the freewill offering of penniless wanderers in a desert (Exodus xxv., 2) is clear proof that this was a creation of the pen, and must have been written for a purpose. Being entirely mythical, it did not cost anything to do it well, and show lavish expenditure. Precious metals show great holiness, so everything in the holy of holies is of fine gold, and the huge logs weighing half-a-ton are covered with plates of gold and shod in solid silver shoes—not for ornament or beauty, as they are entirely buried in the ground—perhaps to avoid the unclean touch of the " soil."

It is useless going further into this matter of practical construction, as the whole thing is pure myth; and the only tabernacle the Hebrews had was a tent.

But if it was good to boast about this house of silver and gold in the wilderness, what must we think of the ecclesiastical fervour of the man who could say of Solomon's temple (ordered by King David to replace the tent tabernacle) that Solomon employed one hundred thousand talents of gold in its ornamentation (1st Chronicles, xxii., 14). That is nearly sixteen million pounds weight, and at the present value of gold would be worth over a thousand million pounds sterling. He had also golden cups and vessels for service in the temple, three hundred and fifty *tons* in weight, worth about fifty-four million pounds. So does this writer of the Word of God exaggerate.

They are urged to be " fruitful and multiply." Well, they do so in Egypt with a
vengeance—sixty-six (another account seventy)
persons go down to Egypt and they increase
in four generations to three millions, with
610,000 fighting men, instead of 1377 as there
should be. Every woman must have had 42
sons, not to speak of daughters and those who
died young.

But all through the Bible there is this ridiculous boasting; so we need not look too
closely at the description of the impossible
tabernacle.

Our purpose is to know why such a tale
was written, and we know it was not written
from the knowledge of any existing structure,
for the structure was " impossible from every
point of view;" yet the scribe, who must have
been quite ignorant of either carpentry or
architecture, wrote with such cunning as to
convey the idea that such minute instructions
must be real. Even with the chance of being
a little tedious, I must quote Dr. Benzinger
and Wellhausen on this, as they are two of our
greatest authorities, and are both critics without any anti-religious bias. Dr. Benzinger
says :—" The whole description leaves, at first
" sight, such an impression of painstaking pre-

" cision that the reader might be tempted
" forthwith to take for granted its historical
" truth. As soon, however, as he begins to
" examine more closely, and, on the basis of
" this description, proceeds to attempt to
" form for himself a definite picture of what
" the tabernacle was, he finds that in spite of
" the multitude of data supplied, or rather
" precisely because of their multitude, it is
" impossible to arrive at any clearness on the
" subject. As Wellhausen very truly remarks,
" ' without repeating the description of the
" tabernacle word for word, it is difficult to
" give an idea how circumstantial it is ; we
" must go to the source to satisfy ourselves
" what the " narrator " can do in this line.
" One would imagine that he was giving speci-
" fications to measurers for estimates, or that
" he was writing for weavers and cabinet-
" makers ; but they could not proceed upon
" his information, for the incredibly matter-
" of-fact statements *are fancy all the same.*' "

I quote this at length, as it represents my
feeling on reading other parts of Scripture
and trying to visualise or construct the supposed reality from the description. It is the
same with the symbolic parts of Solomon's
Temple, and many other parts of Holy Writ,

and it is curious that another great scholar, Bishop Colenso, fifty years earlier, used almost the same expression about the whole tenor of the statements in the Old Testament, saying that on attempting to translate Bible statements which he had hitherto accepted as clear he found, on examination, that " they had no clearness in them."

In my younger days I found this want of clearness and actual contradiction so cunningly cloaked, as I thought, that I called it " infernal cunning," until I found the key, and saw that the whole story was only a frame on which to hang a symbolical statement of some phallic or solar truth, and the priest was thinking of this side of the narrative and had to handle his materials accordingly.   Dr. Benzinger, for instance (and nearly all other critics), point out that the inside of the great tabernacle had no windows or openings of any kind, and was " intensely pitch dark," quite impossible for the priests to discharge their priestly duties they were supposed to exercise in it, but as I will show it represented Sheol or the grave when the sun lay dead 40 hours, and hence *must* be intensely dark. As the complicated ceremonial was probably only written, never acted, the writer disregarded the inconvenience of the darkness where priests were supposed to officiate, and made the tabernacle quite dark, so that his little drama might be correctly staged with its pitch dark Sheol.

I must say, and wish to say it plainly, that very much of the Bible produced the same effect on my mind, not that the writer is stupid in stating such curious and uselessly incorrect assertions, nor yet that it is all due to corruption of the text, but I felt that I was in the presence of a really cunning writer whose purpose is far other than that which appears on the surface. To one given to scientific pursuits, where all statements are direct and mean truly what they say, these parts of the Hebrew Scriptures produce a sense of mental fatigue and irritation, which, however, instantly disappear when the true meaning of the symbolism is found. Religions can only be enforced by some such means, as the priest knows that all the instructions, which he says were given to him by some thundering, flaming, eye-blinding god, are simply the " Ordinances and laws " composed by himself, or acquired from other priests, by which he hopes to control the tribe, just as Jethro, the priest of Midian, instructed Moses to do in Exodus 18.

We must never forget that the Bible was

written a thousand years after the death or the supposed rule of Moses, and the words, " And the Lord spake unto Moses and said," were not written by Moses but by a scribe creating history and writing from tradition. Even if Moses had actually written them, it would be no proof in law that Jové actually spoke these words as there were no other witnesses, but another hearsay witness telling us a thousand years after the death of Moses what Jové said to Moses has no weight as evidence. Its only importance for us is to study it with the view of trying to understand why the priests took the trouble to compose these writings.

I have already said that the Israelites were expelled out of the land of Arks, where the phallus of Osiris was the supreme object of worship. The first word of symbolism in the history of Israel (leaving out for the moment Genesis, the patriarchal period), as the tribe arose out of Egypt, is this same phallus, the Rod of God, which Moses found in " Midian;" and which when he threw it down became a " serpent," the universal symbol of the phallus, and he had an ark built, so he adopted the two principal Egyptian objects of worship. And let us not forget that the earliest phallus of which we read was the tree

of life in the " midst " of the garden, so here
Moses gets another Rod of God, Jové's nissi,
or " tree of life," in the " Midian " or
" midst."

Even Jethro's name is telling a tale. He is
first of all called the priest or prince of the
" midst " or middle part, Midian, and we are
immediately given the sacred sign of seven :
he had " seven daughters." Moses, the man
out of the waters in the Ark, sat down by a
well—moses, a male; and the well, a female—
making a double-sexed combination still much
used in the East. Then this ruler of the
" middle part " is at first called Reuel (verse
18), then Jethro in chapter iii., and later, in
Numbers x., 29, again Raguel; and in these
two verses there is no mention of his name as
Jethro. Now, Rael is the name of the Sun
god of Egypt, in whose worship Moses had
been brought up, so we see he simply para-
phrases the cult of Egypt in worshipping the
rod of the Sun god. The name Jethro, or as
it should be Yetro, because J is Y in oriental
tongues, and " th " is " t " or " d," and as
vowels are absolutely guesswork, was possibly Yadra, the Yad of Ra, or Rod of Ra (our
English yard was a rod), repeating again the
phallus of Osiris or Rod of God, which Moses

found in the " middle." But Jethro is also in Hebrew Ithra or Ithar, a name for the sun in India, so Jethro was named Sun God in two great nations' languages.

Then Moses went up unto the Jové with Aaron, Nadab, and Abihu, and 70 elders, but they worshipped afar off, and " Moses alone shall come near the Jové." After this interview Moses makes the first church, or circle, or kirkle, or kirk, or chirchle (Chauser calls it chirche) of 12 stones. Here is sun worship, as all twelves from the twelve round circles of shewbread to the twelve labours of Hercules or Arthur's twelve knights of the " round " table, are the sun circle, the twelve months of the year; and he then preached obedience to all that he had written in a book, not on two stones, and read it over to them (Exodus xxiv., 4-7), doing exactly what Ra El of Midian had advised him. This sun god whose " glory was like devouring fire on the top of the mount in the eyes " (mid-day sun *is* like a fire in Midian), and Moses were there the period most holy of all, forty days and forty nights. It should be hours instead of days, but the longer period is more miraculous. Then we have the commencement of the wonderful tabernacle, which was to introduce the Queen of Heaven, now rendered local, as all Queens of Heaven are, by being called the Virgin of Israel. The whole materials were to be freewill offerings, and out of these were made the impossible golden tabernacle we have been considering.

It was really a temple like any Egyptian one, but covered with portable roofing of cloth, skins, and hair, to make it portable and fit it for the wandering life of these supposed nomads, fed miraculously from Heaven. But there was wanting one thing absolutely essential to imitate the paraphernalia of the priesthood of Egypt. So Jové tells Moses to tell the children of Israel to make an Ark, and thou shalt put into the Ark the " testimony " " which I shall give thee." This word testimony, we have shown before, was equivalent to Jové himself, but it has a much greater significance, which we will consider later. The ark is then called the Ark of the Testimony, or Eduth, or the Ark of the Witness, or the Ark of Jové; and is the dwelling place of Yové, the Eduth or testimony, the witness or covenant, the Fetish which shone forth between the Cherubim; so these four were different names for the same thing. Then Moses went up the mountain and received a long list

of intricate instructions amounting to about
ten thousand words, which Jové is said to have
written on two stones, which Moses broke.
Moses seems to have written them down as he
read them out of a book (Exodus xxiv., 7). He
tells Moses to make two new stones exactly like
the first, and they must have been quite light,
as Moses carried them up in his one hand, and
I read it that Moses this time wrote upon them
the words of the Covenant and the Ten Commandments, although the "He" who wrote
has a capital "H." How he got 10,000 words
on two small stones is another "miracle." We
are not told at that time where he put the two
stones, but in Deuteronomy x., 5, we are told
he put them in the ark. No doubt there has
been much editing and a wide application of
the Rabbis' rule of deleting all coarse references to the parts of the god, and the account
abruptly ends without telling what the two
stones really represented.

We are not told till later that the two stones
were put in the Ark not till Moses is supposed
to tell his own story in Deuteronomy x., 1-3.
As Moses carried the Rod of God about in his
hand, it only required the two stones, in the
Ark, quite properly called the "Testimony,"
to make the triple male emblem or the Trinity.

In Numbers xvii. the Rod of God was taken out of the tabernacle of " witness," which is identical with " Testimony," and found to have produced almonds; so the " witness " receptacle had contained the Rod of God and his two stones, and the rod was laid up for good with the two stones before the Testimony, which we have seen was the equivalent of Jové in Exodus xvi., 33-34, and is there given divine honours by being spelled with a capital T, whereas afterwards it is reduced to common clay by having a small " t." This is what King James's translators dishonestly did with the word Alé-im, which means gods, and is frankly plural; but when the translators found it applied to Israel's band of gods they made it singular, and gave it the divine capital G, while, when it was applied to " other gods," it was degraded to the livery of a small " g," and translated in the plural as " gods."

Thus we see the mother of god in the old shape of the Ark or Ruach, being built of shittim wood to form the dwelling place of the phallic creative Jové, or triple male reproductive organ.

In the *Romance of the Hebrew Tabernacle* I have given a fairly full account of the sym-

bolism of the Tabernacle as the womb of Ked
or of that of the Virgin of Israel; and I must
summarise it here to show that the mother of
the gods or Ruach was intended. The ark was
deposited in the tabernacle as a very complete
double-sex combination, with Ruach or Ark as
the female member or unity, and with the
complete triple male symbol in the Rod of
God and the two stones as the Trinity; for, as
I have said, the Hebrews were extremely literal
in all their symbolism, and constructed for us
an absolutely literal model complete in all
details of our " incomprehensible mystery,"
the Three in One, Trinity in Unity. This has
remained the Arcanum (see how "Arc" comes
into all " high " words) of Christians ever
since, though its real meaning is never taught
by the Church; it is simply a meaningless
" ghostly " shibboleth.

Then came this scribe with his tabernacle
scheme, to write his miracle play, to set the
Queen of Heaven in her true place as mother
of all, even of the Sun, of whom Iové was a
badly-drawn representative, as we will remember his blinding light on the top of the mountain and " under his feet a paved work of a
" sapphire stone, and as it were the body of

" heaven in its clearness "—a good picture of the sun in the blue sky (Exodus xxiv., 10-17).

But the Queen of Heaven which these literal scribes wished to draw, was in the rôle of a mother giving birth to her child, and we already know their shameless realism in that other female ceremony of birth, the pouring out of the waters, during the feast of the nymphs of Venus; so here they created a real womb, out of which the high priest in his character as a sun god could be born. The materials used are most minutely described and accurately repeated four times, a thing only done with symbolical creations, where every word had a hidden meaning for the priest. Of course, symbolism, emblematic descriptions, or esoteric texts only mean saying one thing and meaning another, an accomplishment in which all ecclesiastics are adepts.

But here the symbolism was painfully direct. In the first place, dolphins' skins hold the chief place. This was rendered "badgers'" skins in the authorised version of King James's translators, who evidently thought that the word dolphin, or delphin in other European languages—but here used symbolically as delphys, the womb—might lead people to inquire further. The authors of the revised

version are more honest, and give dolphins'
skins, although they dishonestly translate
Ale-im as "God" when applied to the
Hebrew band of gods, well knowing that
honest translation in this particular word
would shatter the foundation on which the
Church is built, viz. : the purely fictitious idea
of the monotheism of the Hebrews. But that
foundation is fast crumbling, as it is built on
the sands of fraud.

The scribe built a womb of Ked out
of his materials, which I have minutely
described in my *Christianity* and in my
Romance of the Hebrew Tabernacle, and
will only repeat here that the idea was founded
on four coverings of the impossible tabernacle
looped up into a cleft (peor), out of which the
high priest issued. These fabrics were goats'
hair, long and silky; rams' skins dyed red,
dolphins' skins, and an interior covering of
fine linen or silk, with blue, purple, and scarlet
cherubim on it.

The fine linen or silk formed the inner
ceiling, and, with its cherubim, represented
the Zodiac with its belt of living things,
through which the sun travelled during the
year. Then the products of two animals much

used in phallic symbolism were used—goats'
hair and rams' skins dyed red.

The word goat is used in all languages to
give an idea of excess of sensual desire, is, in
fact, the animal symbol of passion, otherwise
symbolised by pouring wine over a phallus in
actual worship, as we see in Holy Writ. Then
the ram is absolutely the god, as its name is
Al or Ail, identical with that of the Elohim
or Alé-im of the Bible, and translators must
often depend on the context to know whether
to write Ram or God when the word occurs.
Ram actually means coition in Sanscrit, and is
the root of words like Rama, the Saviour, of
the Hindus. Rama was beautiful, but more
frequently delightful. These rams' skins were
dyed red, which is the colour of passion, and
has high phallic significance. Over all was
placed dolphins' skins (delphys womb), so
here we have the womb of Ked charged with
every symbol of passion and fertility.

These curtains with their gold clasps were
left hanging by a large over-plus, at what the
scribe calls the back side or end of the Tabernacle, the end which contained the Holy of
Holies, entered by the high priest only once
a year under pain of death. We are never
told what was done with this great piece hang-

ing down to the ground, all further details
having been cut out from the original description as being too phallic, under the Rabbis'
rule. Even Josephus does not tell us,
although we get some useful information from
him. It is extremely probable that these curtains were looped up by a cord into a " peor "
or cleft, out of which the high priest forced
himself and was born as the sun out of the
Ruach, the Virgin of Israel. We can recon-
struct this from the description of his various
vestments used in the ceremony. In the
description in the Bible and in Josephus we
are told much detail of the symbolical
materials used in the construction of the
Tabernacle and in the dress and ornaments of
the priest, but there is scarcely any information
about what the high priest did when arrayed
in his symbolic robes. The whole religion
seems to have been founded in paying abject
devotion to Jové, which is the same as paying
abject devotion to the priests or temple hierarchy, and in a sort of permissive criminal
system by which a man might escape the
punishment for his crimes by paying the
priests a fine in money or beasts, or what is
called atonement. The great doctrine in all
these old religions is the brutally selfish one

of the innocent suffering for the guilty, and this absolutely immoral doctrine of savage cowardice is still promulgated by our parsons and priests. We see King Mesha when hard pressed in his fortress city, and of course thinking—as the priests from motives of personal gain everywhere and always have taught, that all disasters were a punishment for some " transgression "—taking his innocent child and burning him alive to his god, in the sight of the Hebrews. And this must have been the supreme fetish of the Hebrews, as it is of Christianity, because they thought further effort useless, and at once raised the siege and returned home, foregoing the fruits of all their fighting.

Of course, there is little to record of the practices in any religion, except muttering of fixed prayers, swinging of censers with perfume, eating of cakes, and drinking of wine, and a great display of riches in gold and fine vestments, accompanied by music, and of injunctions of humility and absolute obedience to the system the priests have created, because we see in the case of the Midianite women that whatever was given to the god was really given to the priests, and god's injunctions were only the personal desires of the priests.

But here was a very great preparation of a great special construction and special vestments, and suddenly all is silence, no whisper is allowed out as to what was done. Two explanations are possible : either the priest never finished the writing of the action of his miracle play, for which he had prepared so elaborate a stage and " properties;" or that this description being too phallic, and based on astronomical ideas not capable of being understood by such a rude people, and, lastly, as it dispensed with the personal Jové, except as representing the Sun, and made him secondary to Ruach, the priests suppressed it. They probably left all the curious description to add to the glory of the history of their supposed ancient great wealth even when starving in the desert.

As I have described this symbolical plan very fully in other books, I will summarise this attempt to re-establish the Queen of Heaven and her annual giving birth to the sun. The Temple was, as I have shown, the womb of Ked, or of the dolphin, or Ruach; and the high priest played the part of the Sun. His clothes were gorgeous in gold and precious stones, and loaded with two great phallic symbols—the pomegranate and golden bells.

All over the East, and even in Western Churches, the pomegranate is the symbol of the gravid uterus or fruitful womb, and, as its name indicates, it was the apple or " pome," the erotic symbol par excellence, which held many grains or seeds, " grana," and hence was very fruitful; and we know the chief command was, " Be fruitful." Then, when ripe, it has a veined system of red veins, extremely suggestive of human flesh, and which is so striking that many people of my own acquaintance cannot eat pomegranates from the disgust this appearance produces. When ripe, the thick skin opens and allows of the seeds with the human-like red veins being seen, and the opening is of the Luz shape, almond-like, or lenticular, or Gothic, or like the Vesica piscis so much beloved of the Roman Catholic Church, and shown in their stained glass as the cleft of the pomegranate (Fig. 26); but in every case representing the Yoni, female organ, the fountain of life.

The ecclesiastical pomegranate is generally shown in stained glass as enclosed in a six-leaved decoration (as in Fig. 26), but this I have shown by dotted lines to be the " double triangle "—that with the point upwards being the male, and that with the base upward being

Fig. 26.

the female, derived from the lotus seed-pod.
(See my *Christianity* and *Gods of the Hebrew
Bible*.) Thus the whole design represents the
male and female producing " seed," and the

combined reproductive organs, the " Three-
in-One," are indicated by the four-leaved
crown on the pomegranate, a tetrad used by
all nations to symbolise the triple male and
single female organs combined, often called
the Tetracht or square of Pythagoras, the complete creative symbol.

The whole subject of the Tetrad or " incomprehensible mystery " of all nations is treated
at length in Part II. of my *Gods of the Hebrew
Bible*.

Fig. 27.

Fig. 28.

Fig. 29.

We see the true significance of the Vesica
piscis or cleft pomegranate in this Catholic
representation of the Virgin's conception
(Fig. 27).

The other symbol was the golden bell (Fig.
28). The bell is simply the Lingam-yoni
altar of India turned upside down (Fig. 29),
with the lingam loose, so that it can produce
a sound when shaken. It is the only phallic
symbol which has a voice, and hence is extremely potent in driving away evil spirits.
Exorcising with bell, book, and candle is still

Fig. 30.

common, the bell being the most potent; and
it is used very extensively in the Roman
Catholic service, as the idea is that evil spirits,
as shown here from Didron (Fig. 30), are present in Church, whispering in the ears of everyone, but that the voice of god expressed by the
tinkle of a silver or golden bell (the bell being
the combined symbol of eternal life or god)
will drive the evil spirits away.

Fig. 31.

The mortar and pestle, so much used in
Hindoo and Egyptian symbolism, as in Fig.
31, is another double-sex creative symbol. So
the high priest, representing the sun, giver
of all life, in his scintilating robes goes
into the Tabernacle on the 20th of
December (originally—as New Year perambulated all round the year owing to the Jews
having a moon-governed calendar). He then
re-appeared in an elaborate suit of the Jewish
burial clothes, bound up or swathed like the
dead Osiris with the face cloth and a special
binding used by the Jews by which the
private parts of the dead were specially

bound, and so he exhibited himself to the
multitude as the dead sun, and was supposed
to lie in the tomb over the lying still (Solstice)
of the sun. He went in at the west end of the
Tabernacle when the sun set in Aries in the
Autumn Jewish New Year, and they sacrificed
lambs (aries) in the celebration. As the constellation of the Lamb of God was in conjunction with the sun, or, as astrologers say, the
sun dwelt in the house of Aries, it was swallowed up or burnt up in the sun's rays in the
Spring equinox by which the Zodiac was regulated, so they held services of " burnt " offerings.

But when the sacred 40 hours of Jonah or
Jesus were over and the sun began his northward journey to bring summer again to the
salvation of mankind, the high priest assumed
his gorgeous robes of life again, and at
eight o'clock on the morning of the 22nd
December (by our reckoning) pushed himself
out of the womb of Ked or Ruach,
made of dolphins' skins, rams' skins dyed
red, and ringed round with goats' hair.   It
may have been this terribly realistic symbolism which led to the suppression of this
great effort of some priest to write up the
death and resurrection of the sun and intro-

duce the worship of a solar saviour. The Feast of Tabernacles with their Nymphs of Venus in tents and the breaking of the waters was bad enough, but this was the climax, and so may have been suppressed. Besides, as I have shown, syphilis and all other sexual diseases were rampant owing to the Kadesha, Nymph of Venus, or temple women, and religious prostitution, so the idea of woman being the cause of all evil gained ground (we see a trace of it in the Greek Pandora), and the account of the Fall in Eden degrading Ruach, Heva, or the Queen of Heaven to the position of introducer of evil, and so for ages the Queen of Heaven was dethroned, and her representative on earth, woman, was described as the " door of Hell " by our puritans.

But a study of words clearly shows that the Hebrews thought that syphilis was a male disease. Pestilence was the disease of the pestle or pessel, as Pesselim was the Hebrew word for phalli, shown at Fig. 22, and we see the meaning of " Pestle " in Figs. 28, 29, and 31. The introduction of " t " in Pestle is quite common. We put " t " for " s " in many Saxon words, as Wasser, Kessel in old Teutonic is Water, Kettle in modern English.

CHAPTER XI

" FALL " STORY OF WOMAN

The garden of Eden story, however, does not at all prove that man lost eternal life through eating of forbidden fruit there. How that idea got into the New Testament one can never know, but in the account in Genesis it is stated most explicitly that only by eating of the Tree of Life (another tree in Eden which they did *not* eat) could they " live for ever "; and as this was never consummated they remained mortal and subject to death. Why the Hebrews put two trees of sacred import into their "garden of delight" (a fable common to all nations) can only be guessed, but all other nations had only one tree, the Tree of Life, the phallus. And that the Tree of Life was *the* tree even in the Eden story is shown by its being planted in the " midst " of the garden, while we are not told where the tree of knowledge of good and evil was planted. But that tree planted in the " midst " of the garden was certainly the phallic tree of life. Moses found the creative Rod of God in Midian (in the midst). The tree of knowledge may have been introduced for several reasons. First, I think that the ignorant Hebrews' hatred of Greek knowledge or philosophy may have been one cause, as the Talmud says " Cursed " be he who teaches his son the wisdom of the " Greeks," or as the Hebrews used " know " invariably as a neutral expression for sexual intercourse, as " And Adam knew his wife " Eve, and she conceived and bore Cain," they may have called the phallus the Tree of " Knowing " or knowledge. The woman saw that the *tree* was good for food and that it was a " desire," a *tree* to be desired to make one wise. Note the word " desire " twice repeated, and it is the tree (stem) not its fruit which is now desired, and as this is repeated it is no error but a symbolic statement.

I will summarise the Biblical account :—

(1) In Genesis i., 28, at the moment of creation " the gods " blessed them, " and the gods said unto them, Be fruitful and multiply," so sexual intercourse and child-birth were commanded at the first moment of man's existence.

(2) They are given *every fruit* for food, no restriction.

(3) In Genesis ii., 5, Jové of the Al gods is

creating plants and herbs, when he reflects
that " there is no man to till the ground," so
he makes a man apparently for this purpose.
In any case Jové makes a garden, which contained " every tree that is pleasant to the sight
and good for food " (verse 9), " and Jové of
" the Ale-im took the man and put him into
" the garden of Eden *to dress it and to keep*
" *it.*" If he dressed and kept such a garden
he well " ate his bread in the sweat of his
face." So he was commanded to labour from
the very first. Child-birth and labour for
woman and man were the first conditions imposed on mankind.

(4) In Genesis ii. man is made alone first,
and he is made because Jové in the middle of
his creation reflects that " there was not a man
to till the ground " (Genesis ii., 5).

(5) Jové also plants in the garden " the tree
" of life also in the midst of the garden, and
" the tree of the knowledge of good and evil."

(6) Then he tells man not to eat of the
" tree of knowledge of good and evil " under
penalty of instant death; not a loss of immortality in the world to come, as falsely represented in the New Testament, but physical
death in the same day as he ate " of the tree

of knowledge." This restriction directly contradicts Genesis i., 29.

(7) The woman was not yet made, and we have no proof that Jové repeated the injunction to her, although she discusses it with the serpent.

(8) The only knowledge gained by eating of the tree of the knowledge of good and evil is that they were naked and ashamed, showing that sexual intercourse was the " Fall," a Fallic or Phallic act.

(9) Jové finds out the eating " of the tree " (not fruit), and apparently curses man with the very labour of " tilling," for which he was especially created in chapter ii., and the woman with child-birth, a function she was specially commanded to exercise in chapter i.

(10) To emphasise the fact that the " desire " which caused them to eat of the " tree " was sexual desire, and that the " eating " was sexual intercourse, it is stated that it made Eve " the mother of all living." But the tree of knowledge had nothing to do with life, or living for ever; the power to confer that lay in the tree of life, which was not only never forbidden, but freely allowed (Genesis ii., 16-17), and never eaten (Genesis iii., 11 and 24).

(11) Jové of the Al gods blunders along, and exclaims " the man is become as one of " us, to know good and evil; and now *lest he* " *put forth his hand and take also of the tree* " *of life and eat and live for ever:* Therefore " Jové of the Al gods sent him forth from the " garden of Eden." But they were already Gods, having eaten of the " fruit of the tree in the midst of the garden " (Genesis iii., 3-6), distinctly stated to be the tree of life—not the tree of knowledge (Genesis ii., 9).

(12) To emphasise that he had not yet eaten of the tree of life, and that he was at liberty to do so if he were allowed to re-enter the garden, that tree never having been prohibited, he thinks Adam might turn back and yet eat it; so he " placed at the East of the " garden of Eden cherubim " (winged animals with four heads) " and a flaming sword, which " turned every way, *to keep the way of the* " *tree of life.*" So man was not only made mortal, proved by Jové's plain statement that his expulsion from Eden was to prevent him eating of the tree of life " and live for ever," but Jové took elaborate precautions that he never would get the chance to live for ever.

So the New Testament statement in Romans and Corinthians that death came through

Adam's sin has no support in Genesis, as death was always man's lot, and he got no chance to alter that saddening fact.

This elaborate story was evidently written to show that the crime was really Eve's, and as the whole story is phallic, it was aimed at woman as being the cause of the most deadly thing the Hebrews knew of, namely, syphilis. Then Eve is Heva, the Persian Queen of Heaven; so the Queen of Heaven is degraded into a woman giving bad advice to man and tempting him to break Jové's injunction.

But it failed for a very curious reason. If Eve and Adam had been warned against the tree of life and then eaten it, it would certainly have been a transgression; but it would be too late to remedy it or punish them, as they would at once have become gods; so the writer made two trees, but really both the same, and so transgression could be made, but they had not gained eternal life, never having eaten of the actual " tree of life." This juggling with the two Trees has long blinded people to the falsity of the story.

We have seen that " knowledge " is sexual intercourse, and the Hebrews have a proverb, " Wisdom is the Tree of Life to them that lay hold on her;" so the scribe may have con-

sidered the two trees only two names for one
thing, and thought he had thus subtly overcome his difficulty, but only fell into the error
that by his rendering of the story man never
" fell " at all, *i.e.*, he never lost eternal life,
as he never attained to it.

The Book of Job, which is also a creation
story and a story of the Sun's year, has a
woman in it—Job's wife—who also " tempts "
Job to sin by advising him to " curse God
and die " (see my *Seven Stories of Creation*).

Now, there is one verse in the Genesis story
of Eden which allows the sun myth to peep
out, and that is verse 21 of chapter iii.—
" Unto Adam also and to his wife did the
" Jové of the Ale-im make coats of skins and
" clothed them." So it must have become
colder, and the fig leaves were no longer
warm enough.

Eden is here summer, and the " fall " is the
autumn, as Americans call it ; and when Jové
withdrew his countenance—meaning the en-
feeblement of the sun's rays by winter—and
the expulsion is the man going out of the
garden of summer and his entry into the cold
outer world of winter. But although man
never " fell " from eternal life through the
temptation of Eve, the story was accepted by

Christendom as the basis of their religion; as
it required sin and a " fall " to support the
necessity of an " atonement." It does not
seem to have been generally accepted till about
the middle ages, as many able writers have
pointed out (such as Lecky, and discussed
pretty fully in the Rev. F. R. Tennant's
Original Sin), but it served as a dogmatic
excuse to debase woman and degrade the
Queen of Heaven, Heva, Juno, and all the
others. Mr. Tennant remarks :—" The con-
" sequences of the Fall are, however, gener-
" ally represented as being of the physical
" kind. . . . Here we have, in a very
" coarse and materialistic form, an idea which
" resembles the doctrine of hereditary
" ' moral ' taint acquired by our first parents
" and transmitted to their posterity " (to the
third and fourth generations). (See p. 386.)

This " coarse and materialistic form of
" hereditary taint acquired by our first parents
" and transmitted to their posterity," referred
to in such unmistakable terms by Mr. Tennant, is doubtless the deadly Ophalim called
" Emerods in their secret parts," in 1st
Samuel v., 9, clearly syphilis (see pp. 134
and 138) ; and it was evidently their one
great deadly affliction, as it takes such a pro-

minent part in their principal commandment.
It was referred to in all countries as the
" pestilence," the disease of the Pestle,
Hebrew Pessel, the Phallus (Figs. 12 and 13,
pp. 220-221) ; and, curious to state, the Sun,
Ra, Apollo, in fact all sun gods, were gods of
pestilence ; no doubt because syphilis is more
deadly in hot climates or seasons.

We find that the Ophalim was always in-
flicted as a punishment when there was any
trafficking with strange women and worshipping their gods, or even when merely " looking into " the female ark, although that may
mean the same thing, stated symbolically.
When Korah and his associates revolted (see
Numbers xvi. and my *Gods of the Hebrew
Bible*), and demanded that they were as much
entitled to take part in the temple services as
were Moses, Aaron, and the Levites (these
alluring " services " included the keeping of
the Temple Kadeshah or sacred prostitutes
and the revenue derived from their prostitution), the punishment for this rebellion was
told in several forms, but the chief was that
fourteen thousand seven hundred of the congregation died of the plague, or more correctly
pestilence. The word pestilence is used in
two genders, masculine and feminine, in verses

46 and 48 of Numbers xvi., probably to indicate that the disease was Ophalim, " two sex
disease." Now, in Eden there were three
actors in the great drama, man, woman, and
the serpent. The serpent is used to represent
the phallus, but perhaps quite as frequently to
symbolise sexual passion in either sex. For
instance, the Lingam-yoni altar has nearly
always serpents associated with it, sometimes
in the yoni part, sometimes coiled round the
pedestal, but very rarely round the phallus
(see Figs. 17 and 18 in my *Christianity*), but
on the whole the serpent is associated with the
female. Woman is sometimes represented as
a serpent, and Cleopatra was called the serpent
of Old Nile.

In Genesis, Iové of the Elohim curses the
serpent or makes sexual passion a sin, and
institutes syphilis as a punishment, coupling
the serpent with the woman alone, and thus
blaming woman and not man as the active
source of transgression. The serpent speaks
to and tempts the woman alone, the
superiority of man is proclaimed by his having
no dealings with the serpent—sexual passion.
But the reverse is the truth, man is the pursuer
in sexual matters, but both Adam and Iové
blame the woman. Adam says " the woman

" whom thou gavest to be with me, she gave
" me of the tree and I did eat;" and Jehovah
or Iové said, " because thou hast harkened
" unto the voice of thy wife," both putting
the blame on the woman. In Egyptian stone
pictures the woman and the serpent are one,
and she is shown as a serpent " going erect "
giving the apple to Adam in Fig. 32. This
also occurs in Hindoo sculpture.

Fig. 32.

The degradation of the female is marked by
linking her up in the curse of syphilis with
sexual passion, as personified by the serpent,
which also represents the phallus, and hence
man; but the Hebrew, following an intensely

masculine cult, forebore to blame the man
directly. The words head and heel are well-
known synonyms for the phallus and muliebre
pudendum, and the curse which was pronounced reads :—" And I shall put enmity
" between thee and the woman, between thy
" [male] progeny and her [female] progeny ;
" she shall bruise [or injure] thy secret parts
" and thou shalt bruise [or injure] her secret
" parts." The word bruise is probably employed because the phallus was often called
the Bruiser or Pestle—Pesel in Hebrew (Fig.
31). Pestilence is the disease of the Pestle
(p. 477).

This curse was pronounced against sexual
intercourse even of man and wife, " thou hast
" harkened unto the voice of thy *wife*," yet in
chapter i. they were specially commanded to
be fruitful and multiply. Thus was Heva,
Queen of Heaven, debased. The degradation
of the female has been elaborately constructed
by the Hebrew " Root " system. The female
Eve is called Isha or Eseth, as in Ishethika,
thy wife, or Isheto, his wife, and Isha might
be a feminine form of Ish, man. But these
words are all referred to the root Anash, which
means " incurable," " mortal," " grievous,"
" sorrowful," malignant," adjectives which

well describe syphilis, but sound strange when
applied to woman. The root also means
" woman," " concubine," " wife," " widow,"
and " one another," a very full symbolism
teaching that woman, whether wife, widow,
or concubine is connected with something
incurable, mortal, and malignant, and when
man and woman act together or with " one
another," an incurable state of things may
arise. As in all other religions, it is the female
who urges the male to the creative act,
whether among gods or mortals. The scriptures thus declare that woman—not man—is
the cause of the disease of the " head " and
" heel," and which visits the sins of the fathers
upon the children to the third and fourth
generation. Man's name, Ish, has no association with Anash, so the reference of the female
Isha to Anash is done to debase women.
Nothing could better illustrate the artificial
language or literary composition evolved by
the Masoretes in the service of Rome for
several centuries, collecting materials for,
shaping and constructing a text on which to
found a universal religion.

I therefore think the debasement of the
Queen of Heaven, and the idea that all sin was
introduced by woman, arose from the terrible

results of religious prostitution, as I have
shown in pp. 384-388.   It was universal, and
all the great temples where the natives assem-
bled on holy days to consult the Oracles or
to hold the great feasts had enormous numbers of these Kadeshah, of Pallaki, Nuns,
temple women, or nymphs of Venus.   I have
dealt with this more fully in my larger book,
and only quote sufficient here to prove what
historians tell us, namely, that syphilis was
common amongst the Hebrews, and was one
of the causes of their expulsion from Egypt.
To enable them to " keep their face," their
historians turned this ignominious expulsion
into a great victory, and a proof of the power
of their tribal god or his " Rod."   This boasting is the great feature of their early records.

But we have seen that they did not know
about Jové then, but worshipped other gods
in Egypt, and beyond the river Jordan (Joshua
xxiv., 2 and 14).   Their whole tribal philosophy became directed against woman as the
cause of all evil, and the Queen of Heaven,
woman's prototype in the sky, was totally
expelled from their ideas.

CHAPTER XII

TWO QUEENS OF HEAVEN. RE-INSTATEMENT OF IMMACULATE QUEEN.

But other nations also felt that the Queen of Heaven should be blameless and of pure character and dignified, so they split the female representative of Ruach into two—in the case of the Romans into Juno, the dignified wife of Jové and mother of the gods, and Venus, the goddess of love, whether lawful or illicit was of no consequence. We know from the Greek story of Paris which was the more attractive.

Now, the New Testament was a third and, under the Romans, a successful attempt to introduce the solar " Saviour " idea, as I have shown in my *Christianity*. Every incident in the life of Christ is copied verbatim from that of Christna, the Hindu Sun god, or it might indeed be said from the lives of any of the twenty-six Sun Saviours I have detailed in my larger book.

In the New Testament the Christians for the

first time split their Queen of Heaven into
two persons—Mary or Maya, the mother of
the sun god Jesus, perfectly good and immaculate, and that other Mary, she of Magdala
(Luz, the Almond), equal to Prakriti of the
Hindus, the love goddess. She is given the
special name Magdala, which means Almond,
a word used for the Yoni or Queen of Heaven
all through the Bible (pp. 399-400).

Mary, the mother of Jesus, is called the wife
of Joseph, and Joseph is a name which has
baffled scholars as to its true meaning. The
name is Ioseph, our J being entirely wrong.
" IO " are the Ring and Piercer of Persia or
the Rod and Almond of Jeremiah—the male
and female organs; while " Seph " is the
Serpent, sexual passion, so the name is an
epitome of the Bible doctrine—man and
woman with sexual passion, in the Fall or
Phallic story of Eden. In Egyptian the order
of male and female is reversed, as Ioseph is
O-sar-seph—O, female; sar, " the Rock that
begat thee " (male); and Seph, serpent—a
world-wide sexual method of symbolically
naming Gods or Creators of Life. We
find in Genesis xxx., 24, and the Hebrew
Lexicons, that the name means " add,"
" added," or " additional," from the root

Isp; so Ioseph means the additional god, both in the Old and in the New Testament: in the Old Testament because with Abraham, Isaac, and Jacob the patriarchal " god age " was supposed to be past when an additional one appears; and in the New Testament Joseph is the additional god as the second father of Jesus. The *Encyclopædia Biblica* tells us that Abraham, Isaac, and Jacob, called Iacob-El, the God Jacob, were early Hebrew gods. (See my *Gods of the Hebrew Bible.*)

That Joseph is a god is shown not only by the IO of his name, but when Israel (whose name is also a god name, El of the Asher, or Isra, phallus) is dying, he says that Joseph is a " fruitful Bough by a Well." " Tree and Well " is a symbolic phrase widely used through the East for life, double sex, or the creative power of a god.

Then Pharaoh, who is a god, as all Pharaohs were, makes Joseph equal to himself, investing him with full powers, so by these and five other symbolisms he is declared to be an " additional god " seven times, showing the statement to be one of momentous importance (see my *Gods of the Hebrew Bible* pp. 152-158).

In the New Testament Joseph (whose father

is again Jacob) is again the additional god, because the real father of Jesus was the God Iové or "Kurios," the sun, while he was given an "additional" or god-father on earth—Io Seph, or Joseph—to stand sponsor for him in his youth. In the Christian mythology Joseph is Saint Joseph, now a god in heaven standing near the throne, and in truth the additional father or "god-father," Io, necessary to the double life and parentage of Jesus. This is dealt with fully in my *Gods of the Hebrew Bible.*

In Egypt the name is, as Dr. Sayce has shown, Osar-seph, and Osar is the true name of the Egyptian god, which the Greeks corrupted to Osiris. The Pharoah was always the god of Egypt, the Osar, so Joseph was the additional god, as Pharoah says that "the spirit of God was in Joseph," and he made him ruler over his house, " according to thy " word shall all my people be ruled; only in " the throne will I be greater than thou." " See I have set thee over all the land of " Egypt. And Pharoah took off his ring from " his hand and put it on Joseph's hand;" and we know that invested him with full power, so he became an additional Osar. But in Hebrew he was called Jo seph, so Jo or Io and

Osar must have the same meaning, and we find
that they have. O is the universal female
symbol, and Sar is Tsur or Zur, " the Rock
that begat thee;" so here we have the most
sacred double-sexed symbol. In Jo, or really
Io, we have the same thing, the upright pillar
and the female ring; the dagger and ring
through which all creation was made in Persia.
This, coupled with Seph (serpent), gives Man,
Woman, and Serpent, an epitome of the Eden
story. Now, as I have shown in my larger
book, the Hebrew Jah or Iah or Ia was often
written Io, so the god of Egypt, Osar, and that
of the Hebrews Ia or Io were identical in
meaning; they were the complete " life
creators." The Egyptians had a god entirely
masculine, like Jesus, a sun god also, called
Serapis, and his supposed portraits formed the
models of all portraits of the Christ.

The name Serapis is composed of this same
Tsur, Zur, Sar, or Ser, the pillar or phallus,
and Apis, the Bull of the Zodiac, in which the
Sun " dwelt," when Serapis was made the god
—masculine twice expressed. So the Joseph
of the Old Testament became the vice-god of
Egypt, or the additional father of the country,
or god-father, and the same symbolism was
used to make the other Joseph the vice-father

of Jesus or his god-father, his true father being
in heaven.

In the New Testament Jové entirely disappears, and we find the Christians worshipping Kurios, the sun, misleadingly translated
Lord in the English translation; and Jesus was
thus the Son of the Sun, as are all Emperors,
Kaisers, or even Roman generals, as witness
Japan, India, and China; and even our own
rulers had divine titles and rights at one time.
We may write IO or IAH both as symbols and
as to the vowel, as O and A are female and
interchangeable; so Io Seph or Iah Seph was
the additional or vice-god, Iah of the Old
Testament embodied in hundreds of Iahs,
such as Jeremiah, Ahaziah, Isaiah, Zechariah,
etc. This IAH is double sexed, and is formed
of the first and last syllables of Jehovah
(I(ov)ah).

For the first time the Christians now separated the two rôles played by the Queen of
Heaven—the first, the mother of the god; and
the second, the Queen of Love—as " love "
had brought such terrible diseases in its train.
So we have two Maries or Mayas: one the
true Maya, the lovely rosy dawn, immaculate
virgin, or, in the Roman theocracy, Juno, the
stately matron, dignified Queen of Heaven,

absolutely correct in her behaviour; and that
other Mary, she of Magdala (*of the Almond,*
see p. 340), corresponding to Prakriti or
Venus, goddess of love, illicit or other, who
had " much loved," and who played the part
of Venus to the Adonis or Tammuz of Jesus.

We have seen the " almond " as the symbol
of Luz, the loose one, or the Yoni, or the
female, or love, used all over the East, and
the principal sign used by the Hebrews in this
sense. When they put the masculine Rod of
God before the Ark in the Tabernacle it
brought forth the female almonds to make the
complete god-head, the " incomprehensible
mystery " of the prayer book; and their holy
seven candlestick had on it lotus buds as Rods
of God and bowls with almond-shaped openings, which we have seen all over the world as
symbols of the womb (see my *Christianity*).

Jeremiah, when he begins to prophesy, is
asked by Iové, " What seest thou?" and he
answers to show that he knows the secret
code, " I see rod and almond "—not " rod of
an almond tree," as dishonestly translated in
Jeremiah i., 11, but always *rods and almonds.*
Then the Christians adopted it in the most
holy " vesica piscis (Fig. 27, p. 473), the
almond-shaped vessel of the Virgin Mary, out

of which came Jesus, and in their almond-shaped monstrance; and so at last they purged their Queen of Heaven of all sin, making " the other Mary " a sort of scapegoat sent to Azazel with all " original sin," and leaving the " Mother of God " pure and fit to reign in Heaven; and we have seen Cardinal New-man's attempt to reinstate her (pp. 364-365).

We can form some idea of the church's views as to the two Maries by examining the details of the artists' rendering of their rôles in pictures.

At the Nicene Council in 787 A.D. it was decreed that the Holy Fathers were to invent the details of the Church pictures, and that the artists chosen have but to execute their behests, and it was specially forbidden to the artists to invent anything or to paint aught but that which they were bidden, so the priests were the true authors of religious pictures and symbolism.

Now, we know that the Virgin Mary was the mother of god, and called the Tabernacle or House of God in whom dwells the God-head bodily, and that the monstrance is the vessel or house to contain the pyx, and the pyx represents the god. This can be proved in many ways, but one may suffice here. As late as 400 A.D. the Christian fathers were quite uncertain of the exact date of the birth of the Christ. Saint Crysostom, writing at the beginning of the fifth century, says (Hom. 31) :—" On this day also the birth day of " Christ was *lately* fixed at Rome, in order " that while the heathens were busy with their " profane ceremonies, the Christians might " perform their sacred rites undisturbed. " They [the pagans] call it December 25 (or " VIII. Kal. Jan., as the Romans wrote it)— " the birthday of the ' invincible one,' " Mithras the sun; but who so invincible as " the Lord?" The Christians called it the " birthday of the Solar Pyx "—sun and phallus.

Here we see Jesus as the Pyx, and we know that Mary is the Monstrance, as the dove is her symbol (see pp. 370 and 505), and Pyx and Monstrance were the most holy and sacred " mystery " of the Church—and anyone touching them was hanged, drawn, and quartered— the death penalty being common to all countries for touching or even looking into the " Incomprehensible Mystery." The original form of the Pyx and Monstrance is still in use in India. The Monstrance, or mother of god, is represented by her universal symbol, the

dove, which is made of silver and hung by a
chain round the priest's neck. One wing, or
a lid, can be raised, and so the dove forms a
box, in which lies a realistically modelled complete or triple male organ in silver, which is
used, like the Pyx in Christianity, to drop oil
on the dying to give life to the soul about to
be born into another world, just as the real
pyx or phallus gives life to the child. We
have seen this form being used by Christians
as late as the sixteenth century (p. 369).

In the fifth century the Christ was called the
Sun of Righteousness, and we still recognise
his solar character by putting a round wafer,
called the host, representing the disc of the
sun (but marked with a cross, representing the
phallus), into a yoni, or almond-shaped monstrance, calling it the body of Christ, thus
building up a double-sexed creative emblem.

That is why both Maries have, in many
Ecclesiastical pictures, a flask or vase of an
" almond " shape, as in Figs. 35, 36, 37, and 44,
to indicate femininity in two directions—first,
the yoni, or " almond " shape; and, second, it
contains water, which is the female element
and essential to life. The monstrance is identical in form (Fig. 33), but has the disc of the sun
and the phallic cross on it combining the two

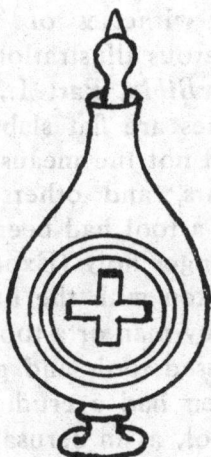

Fig. 33.

creators and saviours of life with the female
symbol and indicating its solo-phallic significance. This combination of cross and circle
is to indicate that there are two creators and
upholders of life, one heavenly and the other
earthly, sun and phallus, or sun and serpent.
These were separated, and each given its rôle
in the New Testament (see my *Gods of the
Hebrew Bible*, Part II.), but were unified in
this symbol.

I have shown that the triple male god or
trinity was represented by a large lingah,
upright stone or pillar, flanked by two smaller

stones (Eduth, witnesses or Testimony), as shown by numerous illustrations in my *Gods of the Hebrew Bible*, Part I., and in many cases these stones are flat slabs, as the early worshippers had not the means of cutting out cylindrical pillars, and others considered a stone on which a tool had been used was unclean and no longer holy (Exodus xx., 25; or xxxi., 18, " written with the finger of God," *i.e.*, untouched by man or a tool). Thus even nations which used tools and produced great architecture often had a crude rock as their most holy symbol, as in Jerusalem to-day, or

Fig. 34.

Fig. 35.

in Spain (see drawing of the Hermitage of
St. Michael, Fig. 14, and others in the *Gods
of the Hebrew Bible*, Part I.).

So we have combinations such as those in
Cumberland, Stirlingshire, and Isle of Man
(Fig. 34), a flat slab with a smaller slab on
either side—the rod of God or El, as Moses
and Jacob called it, and the two stones, the
Eduth or Testimony, as in the Ark.   The
smaller slabs are often absent, having been of
a useful size for building.   The great resemblance between these slabs and that pictured by Pedrini in Fig. 35—amounting to
identity—illustrates clearly that the Church
was again constructing the Three-and-One,
and that their religion was identical in this
particular with the worship of Lingam-yoni
by the Hindoos.

To return to the female emblem (Figs. 33
and 40), it had another form equal to the
almond, inverted, large end uppermost (here
we have a clash of big Endians and little
Endians in Iconography), as shown in Fig. 36
or in pictures (Figs. 35 and 44), and this is
doubtless an image of the symbol of the Queen
of Heaven, the dove, as shown in Fig. 37, as
the Monstrance and Mary as Queen of Heaven
were both the " dwelling place of the Trinity "

Fig. 36.

Fig. 37.

or godhead. We find even the Holy Virgin associated with the " Rock that begat thee " in the Virgin with the Rocks, Fig. 38, in our National Gallery. The very phallic pillar of rock, just over the right of the Virgin, is too obvious to mean anything else.

The picture portrays what is told in Italian architecture in such churches as Milan Cathedral, Pisa Church and Leaning Tower, or St. Mark's at Venice, where the church which is always female and represents the Queen of Heaven, has her husband to the right on looking East in the form of a Bell Tower, just as in Fig. 38.

Fig. 38.

The two Maries are, however, differentiated in that the one has a babe, and is thus associated with Life; while the other has a skull, and is associated with Death; and the one is crowned with seven stars, and the other possessed with seven devils.

There is a curious piece of symbolism secretly telling of the result of the " liberty " of Temple women (Mary Magdalene was a temple harlot or Kadeshah), which is very often, in fact nearly always, misunderstood. Mary is seen with a book as well as a skull, and this is always understood to be the Bible, and to indicate that Mary is repentant. But it will be seen that Rubens in Fig. 40 and many others show no book, yet the gaze is repentant or sorrowful. The Latin word, " liber," free, is used for book also, and as libra, it meant " balance;" but the original libra in the Zodiac was no balance (or scales), but the complete triple male organ, as it is still represented in many dictionaries as shown in Fig. 39; and the real meaning is a purely phallic one. The balance is called in Hebrew Palas, the Phallus, or " Wisdom." To "know" or to be " wise " was always phallic, as, "And Adam ' knew ' his wife Eve," or David did not " know " the young woman put beside him to

Fig. 39.

revive him, or when the sons of Belial (Judges xix.) "knew" the Levite's concubine or wished to "know" the Levite himself, it is the same word in Hebrew—Ada—and was applied to the Tree of "Knowledge," which we know brought shame and made Eve "the mother of all living," while Solomon was the "wisest" man with 700 wives and 300 concubines. So the Liber, something to make one wise, is the symbol of sexual freedom. The Book is Liber, "free," and the book and skull signify that any woman phallically free is the cause of death in others, as syphilis was incurable in early times. The martyred man in Figs. 40 and 41 tells the story of Eden—"It is all the woman's fault, and the poor innocent male is a martyr."

Even the Hindoo Maya (Fig. 42) has a skull " in the midst of the garden."

The same idea was expressed by symbolising sexual passion by the deadly cobra. The

Fig. 40.

Fig. 41.

Fig. 42.   Fig. 43.

serpent was "wise"—a purely phallic aphorism.

Freedom in the Queen of Love or Temple woman, who, we have seen, was a Benoth or Venus, is indelibly imprinted on the Saxon languages. Friday, in German Freitag; Free day was Freia's day, the day of the Free One; and here, in Fig. 43, from Montfaucon—a picture which unites even the female sexual organs with the serpent in the most unmistakable manner—is the goddess worshipped by our ancestors, the Saxons and Gauls. The same idea rules throughout the world—Asia,

Africa, Europe, and America were all serpent
(or phallic) worshippers at one time. Rubens's
picture, Fig. 40, tells us the story with his usual
vigour and wealth of colour and symbolism.
Mary's foot is on a skull (death), but the serpent, sexual passion, is free to play with death,
and an angel is holding up the figure of a martyred man as the result of her " freedom."
The symbolism is repeated in Fig. 41, a graphic
Magdalene, not repentant, by Allori. According to Christianity, woman is the cause of
death, the bane of mankind, and Iové coupled
Eve (not Adam) with the deadly serpent when
he pronounced the curse of syphilis on the
human race. This dogma is repeated in hundreds of Church pictures and sculpture, thus
blaming woman alone for the introduction of
the disease and death into the world of men.

Iové seemed to pronounce secondary curses
on both man and woman—work for the man,
and child-bearing for the woman. These
were no curses, but simply a repetition of
natural conditions enunciated at their creation
—the man made especially to till the ground
in Eden, and the pair to be fruitful and
multiply, in Genesis i., 28, and ii., 5.

A last point may be touched upon while
looking at the Church's pictures.

Fig. 44.

Fig. 45.

Fig. 46.

QUEEN OF HEAVEN 511

In nearly all Church symbolism the solar and the phallic symbols occur together, as they did in nearly all religions. Jesus was a Sun god copied from the Hindoo Sun god Christna (see my *Christianity*). The Church tells us this in Fig. 44, a picture by Pierre Mignard. We see the infant Jesus touching grapes. All Sun gods are gods of the Vine or Wine, because only when there is sunny year does the vine yield good wine.

Jesus was the " True Vine," and his first miracle was to turn water into wine, which, says John ii., 4-11, " Manifested forth his glory," a phrase most significant of the sun's " glory," and applied to no other miracle. John's gospel was the learned priestly expression of the Christian Creed, and highly symbolic, hence his first miracle was a declaration of his solar character, and manifested his glory by making him a true deus Vini, Divine, or God of Wine. In Mignard's picture we see in the background the female monstrance and also the erotic apple by which Eve became a mother, like Mary.

In a beautiful virgin by Luini (Fig. 45) we see the infant Jesus showing his mother the erotic apple, while we find Bellini (Fig. 46) making the infant Jesus hold the pomegranate

—symbol of fruitful woman—as Mary is always the mother, and has carried out the first and most frequently repeated commandment, " Be fruitful and multiply." So we see the Church represented all its religious dogma, as well as its humanised story of the gods, by artistic symbolism founded on the idea of eternal life, or eternal succession of life, expressed in phallic symbolism, understood, however, only by the initiated priesthood. The laity go on repeating texts, prayers, and responses, and adoring images, without the faintest conception of their origin and ultimate meaning, and the clergy are too wise to let them have any glimpse of their very human origin.

With those who cling to the old miraculous religion, whose earliest miracles were made with the " rod of god," where the " sons of god " still saw that the " daughters of men were fair to look upon," it may still be possible to place their perfect ideal of pure womanhood on the highest pinnacle, and seat her on the throne of Isis, on the vault of heaven, with seven stars round her head; but I fear that for many that day is past, and man must be content with the lovely ideal of the divinity of woman, which in the spring-time of his life irradiated all his thoughts and painted for him

a picture of perfection which no Raphael or
Tintoretto can ever equal, when his awakening nature gave him his first glimpse of the
enchanting Prakriti, rosy dawn of the mountains, whose perfection must remain ever
enshrined in the heaven of memory.

Consult also Index of Vol. II.

INDEX

A

522 INDEX

JO should be IO, 108.
Job's Creation, 15.
Joel should be Io El, 108.
Jonah, 79, 166.
Jonah, phallic name, 183.
Jonah and Jesus, 80, 184.
Jonah and Bacchus, 183.
Jonah, Son of Amitai, 183.
Jonah's salvation like that of Jesus, 183-184.
Joseph, additional God, 155-156.
Joseph, a God of sevenfold symbolism, 152.
Joseph, a symbolical name, 494.
Joseph in Old and New Testaments, 494-496.
Joseph, Old Testament, and Joseph, Father of Jesus, compared, 158-159.
Joseph, Old Testament, and Joseph, New Testament, both Gods, 155.
Josephus, 189.
Josiah stamped phalli to powder, 392.
Joshua at phallic pillar, 252, 253.
Jove or Jehovah, 59.
Jove's sons identical with Sons of God (Genesis vi.), 111.
Jove's sons died annually as redeemers, 111.
Jove and Iove identical, 24.

K

Ka Kan, 16-17.
Kaba in Mecca (Makkah), 43.
Kadesh, male prostitute, 389.
Kadeshoth, female prostitutes, 389-394.
Kadesh and Kadeshah were Sodomites and religious harlots, 389.
Ked, mother of all, 451.
King's Gnostics, 52.
"Knowledge" is phallic, 161, 507.
Knowledge, meaning of, 484.
Knowledge is sexual intercourse, 379.
Korah epithet applied to Elisha, 143.

Korah, Phalakra, bald head, phallus point or head, 143.
Korah, 136.
Korah, bald head, 143.
Kubele or Cybele is the Yoni, 63.
Kurios, Father of Jesus, the Sun, 173.
Kubl is Arabic for the muliebre pudendum, 278.

L

Lad, from Lat or Lath, 269.
Lads of God, 269.
Lads are "stones" or Eduth, 269.
Laish, slaughter of gentle people, 120.
Land of the Phallus, many countries so called, Palestina, Philistra, Syria, Suria, Assyria, Ashuria, 443-444.
Lat, Phallic Column of one piece, 12, 244.
Lath, Harlequin's creative piercer, 373.
Latona, Lat and O or On, double sex, 16.
Latona's Isle called Pur and Kunthos, so she was double sexed, 16.
Lecky on Priestly Morals, 254, 288.
Lecky on History of Morals, 305.
Leonardi da Vinci, 371.
Levi had no portion in Israel, 384.
Levites, 72.
Levites invented terrible gods to get money by fear, 112.
Levites' bad influence, 325.
Levites condemned all worship save that which brought them wealth, 384.
Levites starved by serious defaction from Iové, 384.
Levites had no inheritance, 420.
Levites kept concubines, 382.
Levites had no security for their livelihood except fear, 424, 425.
Levites had no portion in Israel, 384.

530 INDEX

Omega or Horseshoe, 87.

Omega, female sign, or horseshoe, 404, 405.

Omega much used as female emblem in India, 405, 406.

Omphalé, 437, 438.

Omphalé same as Phara-Oh or Phala-Oh, double sex Lingam-yoni, 154, 444.

Old Testament God-names abandoned in the New Testament, 172.

Old Testament IhOh replaced by Kurios the Sun in New Testament, 173.

Old Testament written round IhOh, 173.

Old Testament and New Testament tied together by names of Patriarchs; Jacob and Joseph repeated as grandfather and father of Jesus, 224.

Old and New Testaments coupled up by names of Jacob and Joseph, 155, 158.

Old and New Testaments coupled by two Josephs, both "additional Gods," 155, 156.

Old Savage God abandoned in New Testament, 173.

Only great dispute in New Testament was about the Phallus, 290.

Orchis Masculi, 148.

Orchis Testicle, 258.

Orkos Oath (on Testicles), 258.

Orchard, place of "fruits," 258.

Only tree of life could make man live for ever, and it was never eaten, 483.

Ophalim or Ofalim, 438, 487.

Ophalim, meaning of, 437, 438.

Ophalim reversed is same as Phara-oh, which is Phala-O, double-sex god, 444.

Ophalim same as Omphalé, twin-sexed disease and twin-sexed Queen, 438.

O is the female ring of Persia, and phallim, plural of phallus; so

Emerods was woman-man disease, 438.

Ophalim was pestilence, the disease of the Pestle (Hebrew, Pessel), Figs. 12 and 13, 487.

Ophalim is same as Phara-Oh, which is Phala-O, Lingam-yoni, double sev, 444.

Ophalim, "a great slaughter," 438.

Ophalim, "deadly destruction," 438.

Ophalim, two-sexed disease, 487, 488.

Ophalim, a bar to female in heaven, 441.

Ophelim, 437.

Ooma, Uma, Om, or Omph, 344.

Ooma, Yogis of female, 438.

Oracles were always female, 355.

Orchis testicle gives Orkos, oath, orchard, place of fruits; Oath sworn on testicles and called Testimony, 258, 445.

Organs of reproduction symbolise the Creator, 335.

Organs of reproduction symbolise eternal life, 335.

Osar, Greek Osiris, meaning of, 496.

Osiris in an Ark, 442.

Organs of reproduction symbolism, female, 81-82.

Organs of reproduction symbolism, male, 81, 82-84.

P

Palaki and Kadeshoth, Temple prostitutes, 389-394.

Pagans and Christians, 238.

Pahad of Isaac, 170.

Pahad and Alleh (God) identical, 170.

Pahad translated Thigh, but also (Job xl., 17) "stones," "testicles," 170.

Pahad, Creative God, and creative organs the same, 170.

Pairing universal property of matter, 377.

Pala, root word of Phallus, phallism, etc., 346.